WITHDRAWN
UTSA LIBRARIES

FIXED INCOME
FINANCE
A QUANTITATIVE APPROACH

MARK B. WISE
AND
VINEER BHANSALI

New York   Chicago   San Francisco   Lisbon   London
Madrid   Mexico City   Milan   New Delhi   San Jaun
Seoul   Singapore   Sydney   Toronto

The **McGraw·Hill** Companies

Copyright © 2010 by McGraw-Hill, Inc. All rights reserved. Printed in the United States of
America. Except as permitted under the United States Copyright Act of 1976, no part of this
publication may be reproduced or distributed in any form or by any means, or stored in a
data base or retrieval system, without prior written permission of the publisher.

1 2 3 4 5 6 7 8 9 0 WFR/WFR 0 1 0 9

ISBN: 978-0-07-162120-5
MHID: 0-07-162120-2

This publication is designed to provide accurate and authoritative information in regard to
the subject matter covered. It is sold with the understanding that the publisher is not engaged
in rendering legal, accounting, or other professional service. If legal advice or other expert
assistance is required, the services of a competent professional person should be sought.

—*From a Declaration of Principles Jointly Adopted by a Committee of the American Bar
Association and a Committee of Publishers and Associations*

McGraw-Hill books are available at special quantity discounts to use as premiums and sales
promotions, or for use in corporate training programs. To contact a representative, please visit
the Contact Us pages at www.mhprofessional.com.

This book is printed on acid-free paper.

Library
University of Texas
at San Antonio

Contents

Preface

Our primary objective when we started thinking of writing this book was to write a book that we would have liked to have had in our hands when we both started to learn about fixed income. Our paths to fixed income were very different: One of us has been a practitioner for about twenty years, as a bond trader, modeler, risk manager, and portfolio manager; the other as a professor of physics who got interested by the problems faced by bond investors. But there have been common elements in our approach that are reflected in the three features we tried to include in this book. First, the fundamentals should be introduced in the clearest, most direct, and transparent way. We explicitly attempt to show every step; nothing is more frustrating to a reader than a text that "hides the ball" and uses that dangerous phrase, 'it can be shown easily …,'' too often. Second, we wanted the book to be compact so the reader would have a ready toolkit that comes with all the essentials and a minimal amount of the extraneous "stuff" that would only distract and confuse if present in abundance. This required a lot of discipline on our part to stay away from gratuitous discussion of esoteric instruments and methods. We believe that we have collected those fixed income topics, both old and modern, that are likely to be robust to current and future financial crises. Third, we wanted the book to be brave enough to do things differently when doing so would make the most sense. For example, the chapter on term structure models introduces a model that makes explicit the link between term structure factors and the economic underpinnings of asset pricing. Many of the methods described in this book will not be found in typical finance books that one picks off the shelf.

Financial markets have undergone a perfect storm over the last two years. Many new instruments and areas of investments that were invented to take advantage of easy money and regulation have ceased to exist. However, the frenzy of activity has left us with techniques and methods that make the solution of investment problems more efficient. While our discussion of the instruments themselves is cursory, our discussion of techniques is more elaborate.

We assume that any advanced undergraduate with a working knowledge of calculus (and facility with the type of quantitative thinking that is taught in undergraduate physical science and engineering courses) should be able to read and understand all the derivations in this book. Further, and for the book to be a success, they should be able to extend and use the methods to attempt to solve further problems that are not solved in this book. We have a chapter (and some discussions in other chapters) on numerical implementation; the ability to get numbers out of an algorithm adds much to the understanding of problems, and such methods should be an indispensable tool in the reader's toolkit.

Here is an outline of the book. In the first chapter, we discuss the basics of a variety of fixed income instruments and describe their risk characteristics. This chapter gives the reader a background in which the methods of the rest of the book can be applied. The second chapter discusses the fundamental calculus of finance. We stay away from formal proofs—the interested reader can look these up in many excellent books on financial mathematics. In Chapter 3 we shift gears and discuss the pricing of stock options and structural models of stocks and bonds. The understanding of stock options is critical to the understanding of fixed income because of the deep relationship between different levels of the capital structure of the firm (the equity part being the lowest and the senior bonds being the highest). In Chapter 4, we discuss portfolio allocation. We start with the basics of preferences and utility functions, discuss mean-variance allocation, and then go on to introduce examples on how to approach more complex problems where fat-tail risk can be important. We conclude this chapter with a discussion of risk management using the factor approach. Chapter 5 is dedicated to term structure modeling. We first introduce simple and exactly solvable 'àffine" models. However, the main focus of this chapter is to discuss a macro term-structure model that in our view provides a critical link between the factors of the affine model and the underlying macroeconomics that drives the yield curve. Most of this work is original. Chapter 6 is a discussion of the pricing of core interest-rate derivative instruments. Chapter 7 shows the numerical implementation of term structure and option pricing models on binomial trees. This chapter should give the reader who wants to start practicing a ready collection of transparent code to modify and apply to their own modeling problems.

The authors have known each other for 25 years. One (VB) was an undergraduate of the other (MBW) at Caltech in 1984. Over the years, we have discovered great excitement in collaborating with each other in problems of physics and finance, but also have seen frustration in research with false starts that fell by the wayside. What has remained with us is the approach to attack interesting problems in clear ways; it leaves us with the ability and the desire to seek out new problems to solve. Neither one of us thinks that sophisticated mathematics is what makes the work interesting. The relevance of the problem is the interesting part, and a good toolkit, like the one we hope to have provided here, should make the path from conception of the problem to its solution fun and interesting for readers.

None of this research and certainly not this book would be possible without the help of many. We would like to thank first those whose shoulders we have stood on, both in the sciences and finance, and whose methods we have adopted without full acknowledgment. Doing so would use up more pages than we have allowed ourselves. We also want to thank colleagues, past and present, for their questions and ideas that generate thoughts and new things to explore. For one of us, the interaction with our clients provides the fuel for the inquisitive fire; for the other, it's his students who provide the questions. We wish to thank our editor, Jennifer Ashkenazy at McGraw-Hill, for her confidence that got this book approved and finished with only slight delay. We also thank Thomas Tombrello, who encouraged our collaborative research in fixed income finance.

Above all, we want to thank readers Tim Dulaney, Moira Gresham, Yonathan Schwarzkopf, Carol Silberstein, and Roxanne Springer of the preliminary drafts of all or part of this book, who have been able to keep us close to our three intended objectives. We are particularly grateful to Tim Dulaney and Moira Gresham, who carefully worked through the whole manuscript, corrected many errors in the equations and text, and gave us important suggestions for how to make improvements. They also prepared almost all of the figures. Of course we take full responsibility for errors that still remain in the book.

---

[1]Explicit references to the literature are only given for the cases where there is a "named quantity," e.g., the Vasicek model.

1

Bond Basics

1.1   Treasury Bonds and the Yield Curve

A zero coupon bond pays its holder an amount P at some time T years in the future. P is called the principal of the bond, and T is the time of maturity. The bonds can be issued, for example, by corporations or by the U.S. Federal Reserve. Suppose an investor purchases a zero coupon bond today; how much should the investor pay? This depends on a number of factors. For example, how sure is the investor that the institution that issued the bond will be able to make the principal payment at the time of maturity T? If the institution is a corporation, it might go bankrupt before that date and not be able to make the full principal payment P. This possibility is a source of risk for the investor; it is called *credit risk*. If the institution is the U.S. Treasury, the credit risk is nonexistent. Yet even for a Treasury bond, we would not pay $100 today to get $100 at some time in the future because the present value is degraded by inflation and the amount of future inflation is uncertain. The present value, i.e., the amount an investor would pay today for a zero coupon Treasury bond that matures in T years and has principal

P, can be written as

$$\text{Price} = \frac{1}{(1 + Y_1)^T} P \tag{1.1.1}$$

We can think of Y_1 in Equation 1.1.1 as a yearly interest rate by which we are discounting the value of the payment P that occurs at time T. After all, if you had invested that amount today and received yearly interest at a rate Y_1 that was compounded annually, then the value of your investment at maturity T would equal the principal P. Y_1 is called the *yield to maturity T*.

The yield is often quoted in units of percent or basis points (bp). One hundred basis points equals 1 percent. If $T = 10$ years and the (annual) yield to this maturity is equal to 5 percent or 500 bp, the price of a zero coupon Treasury bond with principal $100 is $61.39.

Equation 1.1.1 is written in a way that suggests that the principal is discounted annually. However, there is nothing special about discounting annually. Suppose we discount every $1/n$ years by an amount Y_n/n, where n is a natural number greater than 1. Then Equation 1.1.1 becomes

$$\text{Price} = \frac{1}{(1 + Y_n/n)^{nT}} P \tag{1.1.2}$$

Equating the prices in Equations 1.1.1 and 1.1.2 gives

$$Y_n = n \left[(1 + Y_1)^{1/n} - 1 \right] \tag{1.1.3}$$

Taking the limit of Equation 1.1.2, keeping Y_n fixed at Y, as $n \to \infty$ gives the formula

$$\text{Price} = e^{-YT} P \tag{1.1.4}$$

which corresponds to discounting continuously in time by the fixed yield Y. In this limit, the discount factor for each infinitesimal time interval $dt = 1/n$ is $1/(1 + Y\,dt) \simeq 1 - Y\,dt \simeq e^{-Y\,dt}$, where we have neglected quadratic terms in the infinitesimal time interval dt. Repeating this infinitesimal discounting for each successive time interval of length dt gives the price in Equation 1.1.4 written as the exponential of an integral,

$$\text{Price} = \prod_{k=1}^{nT} e^{-Y\,dt} P = \exp\left[-\sum_{k=1}^{nT} Y\,dt\right] P \to \exp\left[-\int_0^T Y\,dt\right] P$$

(1.1.5)

as $n \to \infty$. The yield for discounting continuously in time Y is related to the yield for yearly discounting Y_1 by

$$Y = \log(1 + Y_1)$$ (1.1.6)

In other words, annual discounting and continuous discounting are equivalent. They are just different ways of writing the same price.

There is no reason that all maturities should be discounted by the same factor. Suppose that the discounting rate for the time interval $[t, t + dt]$ (i.e., the "short rate" at time t) is $y(t)$; the price then becomes

$$\text{Price} = e^{-Y(T)T} P = \exp\left[-\int_0^T y(t)dt\right] P$$ (1.1.7)

and the yield to maturity T can be written as

$$Y(T) = \frac{1}{T} \int_0^T y(t)\,dt$$ (1.1.8)

Multiplying the above by T and differentiating with respect to the maturity, the "short rate" at any time T is given by

$$y(T) = \frac{d[TY(T)]}{dT} \tag{1.1.9}$$

$Y(T)$ is also called the *spot rate*. It is a function of the maturity T, and this function is known as the *yield curve*. Under typical circumstances, we can expect that the spot rate will be an increasing function of T. We may be confident that inflation will be contained over the near term, but as the period of time increases, that confidence diminishes, and the investor who purchases a zero coupon bond should demand compensation for that source of risk. Of course, if investors feel that the economy is about to go into recession, then we might expect that inflationary pressures and interest rates will fall in the future, and in that case $Y(T)$ could, for some range of T, be a decreasing function of T. This is called an *inverted yield curve*.

The value of a zero coupon Treasury bond increases with time until maturity, when it is equal to its principal. Let $V_{rf}(t)$ denote the value of a zero coupon Treasury bond at some time t in the future. The subscript rf emphasizes that the cash flows of Treasury bond investments are risk-free, i.e., the investor is certain to get the full principal returned at the time of maturity. The value of a zero coupon bond at some time t in the future is related to its value today, $V_{rf}(0)$, by

$$\frac{V_{rf}(t)}{V_{rf}(0)} = \exp\left[\int_0^t y(\tau)\, d\tau\right] \tag{1.1.10}$$

This exponential growth is just undoing the effect of the discounting. The instantaneous rate of return for investments in Treasury bonds is equal to the short rate, $y(t)$, since

$$\frac{1}{V_{rf}(t)}\left(\frac{dV_{rf}(t)}{dt}\right) = y(t) \qquad (1.1.11)$$

So far we have only discussed zero coupon bonds. There are more complicated bonds that can be made by putting together zero coupon bonds of varying maturities. For example, suppose you purchase a coupon-paying bond that pays a fixed "coupon" cP every year until it matures at a time T years in the future. At maturity, the principal P is also paid along with the final coupon payment. Each of the coupon payments can be thought of as a zero coupon bond with principal cP and a maturity that corresponds to the date on which that coupon payment is made. Hence if you understand everything about zero coupon bonds, you understand coupon-paying bonds as well. Consider a Treasury bond with principal P and maturity T years that pays a coupon cP annually. Assuming that the yield curve is flat, $Y(T) = Y$, independent of T, it has the price

$$\text{Price} = \left(c\sum_{n=1}^{T} e^{-Yn} + e^{-YT} \right) P = \left[c\left(\frac{1 - e^{-YT}}{e^{Y} - 1}\right) + e^{-YT} \right] P \qquad (1.1.12)$$

where we have used the familiar expression for the sum of a geometric series,

$$\sum_{n=1}^{T} x^n = \frac{x^{T+1} - x}{x - 1} \qquad (1.1.13)$$

The price in Equation 1.1.12 is equal to the principal P for a coupon, cP, when

$$c = e^{Y} - 1 = Y_1 \qquad (1.1.14)$$

A coupon-paying bond that has a price equal to its principal is said to trade at par. If c is greater than Y_1, its price is greater than its principal and the bond is said to trade at a premium, and if c is less than Y_1, the bond is said to trade at a discount. A similar analysis holds for coupon payments made at other intervals. For example, if the bond pays a coupon cP quarterly, then it trades at par if $c = Y_4/4$. Coupon payments provide a fixed income stream that many investors find attractive. They are the origin of the phrase *fixed-income finance*, which is used to describe the part of finance involving bonds.

1.2 Duration and Convexity

As an investor in a zero coupon bond, you might be interested in selling it to another investor sometime in the future. At that future time, the yield curve might be different from what it is today. Hence it is interesting to understand the risk associated with changes in the yield curve. Consider the change in bond price ΔPrice associated with an overall shift in the yield curve $Y(T) \to Y(T) + \Delta Y$. Expanding in a power series in ΔY,

$$\frac{\Delta \text{Price}}{\text{Price}} = -D\Delta Y + \frac{1}{2}C\Delta Y^2 + \cdots \qquad (1.2.15)$$

where we have included only the first two terms in the power series. The duration D and convexity C depend on the bond's maturity and are related to the first and second derivatives of the price with respect to changes in overall yield level:

$$D(T) = -\left(\frac{1}{\text{Price}}\right)\frac{\partial \text{Price}}{\partial Y(T)} \qquad C(T) = \left(\frac{1}{\text{Price}}\right)\frac{\partial^2 \text{Price}}{\partial Y(T)^2}$$

$$(1.2.16)$$

Using the price formula for a zero coupon bond in Equation 1.1.4, we find that the duration and convexity of a zero coupon bond are

$$D = T \qquad C = T^2 \qquad (1.2.17)$$

A duration of 10 years means that for a change in the annualized yield of ± 1 percent or equivalently ± 100 bp, the first-order fractional shift in the bond price is $\mp 10^{-2} \times 10 = \mp 0.1 = \mp 10$ percent. A convexity of $(10 \text{ years})^2$ means that for a change in the annualized yield of ± 1 percent, the second-order fractional shift in the bond price is $0.5 \times 100 \times 10^{-4} = 0.5$ percent. The convexity term increases the bond price no matter what sign the change in yield is. Hence bondholders gain more from a yield decrease than they lose from a yield increase of the same size.

Next consider a bond of principal P that pays an annual coupon cP and matures in T years. We can define an average payment time by weighting the time at which the payment is made with the present value of the payment. This average payment time is the same as the duration D,

$$D = \left(c \sum_{n=1}^{T} n e^{-Y(n)n} + T e^{-Y(T)T} \right) P/\text{Price} \qquad (1.2.18)$$

The duration depends on the definition of the yield used. For example, if we used the annual discounting yield Y_1 to define duration, then, since

$$\Delta Y = \Delta \log(1 + Y_1) = \Delta Y_1/(1 + Y_1) + \mathcal{O}(\Delta Y_1^2) \quad (1.2.19)$$

the duration, defined as the bond price sensitivity with respect to changes of Y_1, is, for a flat yield curve, $D_1 = D/(1 + Y_1)$. The duration D, defined with respect to the continuous discounting yield, is usually referred to as the Macaulay duration.[1]

---

[1] F. Macaulay, *Some Theoretical Problems Suggested by the Movements of Interest Rates, Bond Yields and Stock Prices in the United States since 1865* (New York: National Bureau of Economic Research, 1938).

Duration, which characterizes the impact of small overall changes in the yield curve on bond prices, is the most important risk variable for most Treasury bond investors. As an example, consider a 10-year bond with principal $100 that pays a coupon cP that is 7 percent of the principal. Suppose the yield curve is flat (i.e., independent of maturity T) at a level of 5 percent. This bond trades at a premium and, using Equation 1.1.12, its price is $114.37. Differentiating the price with respect to the yield (and multiplying by minus one divided by the price) gives a Macaulay duration of 7.6935 years, and taking the second derivative, the convexity is 69.02 years^2. For an increase in the (continuously compounding) yield of 1 percent, the duration results in a change in the bond price of $-7.69 \times 0.01 \times \$114.37 = -\$8.80$. The convexity term increases the bond price by $0.5 \times 69.02 \times 10^{-4} \times \$114.37 = \$0.39$. The total change in the bond price is -$8.41. On the other hand, if the yield decreased by 1 percent, the total change in the bond price is $\$8.80 + \$0.39 = \$9.19$.

1.3   Corporate Bonds and Credit Risk

For Treasury bond investors, the instantaneous (i.e., short) risk-free rate of return is $y(t)$. Since the corporate bond investor is exposed to default risk, the short corporate bond rate of return $y_c(t)$ is greater than the Treasury short rate. We write $y_c(t) = y(t) + \lambda(t)$ for an infinitesimal time dt in which the company does not default. Note that $y_c(t)$ is the correct rate of return only in time intervals in which the company does not default. It is sometimes called the *promised corporate rate of return*. The difference between the promised corporate short rate of return and the risk-free short rate is the excess promised short rate of return $\lambda(t)$. It is needed in order to compensate the corporate bond investor for the credit risk. To give a formula for how, on average, the value of an investment in a zero coupon corporate bond increases with time, we assume that if the company defaults, the investor immediately gets a recovery fraction R times the promised value of the bond at the time of default returned to him and reinvests it at the risk-free rate. More explicitly, if the time of default is t_d, the value amount returned to the investor at that time is

$$V_{\text{rec}}(t_d) = RV_c(0) \exp \left[\int_0^{t_d} d\tau\, y_c(\tau) \right] \tag{1.3.20}$$

where $V_c(0)$ is the initial value of the zero coupon corporate bond, i.e., the price paid for it. Before default, investors do not know what the recovery fraction will be. We will treat R as a fixed quantity that the investor estimates using historical recovery fractions from a wide range of corporations and from information specific to the company that issued the bond.

It is useful to introduce the function $P_S(t)$, the probability of the company's surviving to time t without defaulting. Since $-(dP_S(t)/dt)dt$ is the probability of the company's defaulting in the time interval between t and $t + dt$, the formula for how, on average, the value of an investment in a zero coupon corporate bond increases with time is

$$\frac{V_c(t)}{V_c(0)} = \exp\left\{ \int_0^t [y(\tau) + \lambda(\tau)]d\tau \right\} P_S(t) + R \int_0^t ds \left(-\frac{dP_S(s)}{ds} \right)$$

$$\times \exp\left\{ \int_0^s d\tau[\lambda(\tau) + y(\tau)] + \int_s^t d\tau\, y(\tau) \right\}$$

$$= e^{Y(t)t} \left\{ P_S(t) \exp\left[\int_0^t d\tau\, \lambda(\tau) \right] + R \int_0^t ds \left(-\frac{dP_S(s)}{ds} \right) \right.$$

$$\left. \times \exp\left[\int_0^s d\tau\lambda(\tau) \right] \right\} \tag{1.3.21}$$

The term in Equation 1.3.21 without the factor of R takes into account the case in which the corporation does not default between time zero and t, and this happens with probability $P_S(t)$. The term proportional to R takes into account the case in which the corporation does default. It is more complicated than the first term because the default can occur at any time s before t and the compounding factor changes to the risk-free Treasury rate after the default, since we have assumed that the amount recovered is reinvested in a Treasury bond.

It is important to know the additional promised short rate of return $\lambda^*(t)$ that, on average, makes an investment in a corporate bond increase in value by the same amount in the time t as an investment in a risk-free Treasury bond. It can be expressed in terms of the recovery fraction and survival probabilities by solving the equation

$$\frac{V_c(t)}{V_c(0)} = \frac{V_{rf}(t)}{V_{rf}(0)} \tag{1.3.22}$$

Using Equations 1.3.21 and 1.1.10, this implies that

$$1 = \exp\left[\int_0^t d\tau\, \lambda^*(\tau)\right] P_S(t) + R \int_0^t ds \left(-\frac{dP_S(s)}{ds}\right) \exp\left[\int_0^s d\tau\, \lambda^*(\tau)\right] \tag{1.3.23}$$

Differentiating Equation 1.3.23 with respect to the time t, we find that

$$0 = \frac{dP_S(t)}{dt} \exp\left[\int_0^t d\tau\, \lambda^*(\tau)\right] + \lambda^*(t) \exp\left[\int_0^t d\tau\, \lambda^*(\tau)\right] P_S(t)$$
$$+ R\left(-\frac{dP_S(t)}{dt}\right) \exp\left[\int_0^t d\tau\, \lambda^*(\tau)\right] \tag{1.3.24}$$

which after rearranging becomes

$$\lambda^*(t) = (1 - R)\frac{1}{P_S(t)} \left(-\frac{dP_S(t)}{dt}\right) = -(1 - R)\frac{d\log[P_S(t)]}{dt} \tag{1.3.25}$$

Note that if $P_S(t) = 1$, which corresponds to the probability of default being zero, then $\lambda^* = 0$, since there is no credit risk in this case. Similarly, if $R = 1$, there is also no credit risk, since even if the company defaults, the investor gets the full value of her investment returned, and so in that case $\lambda^* = 0$ as well. Corporate bond investors usually demand an average rate of return that is greater than that of a risk-free Treasury bond. So we write

$$\lambda(t) = \lambda^*(t) + \mu(t) \tag{1.3.26}$$

where $\mu(t)$ is called the *risk premium*. A positive risk premium makes the average corporate bond return greater than that of a risk-free zero coupon Treasury bond.

Suppose that if the company survives to time t, there is a probability $h(t)\,dt$ of default occurring between t and $t + dt$.[2] The survival probability decreases in the time interval dt because the company may default in that time interval:

$$\left(-\frac{dP_S(t)}{dt}\right) = h(t)P_S(t) \tag{1.3.27}$$

Integrating this differential equation using the initial condition $P_S(0) = 1$ gives

$$P_S(t) = \exp\left[-\int_0^t d\tau\, h(\tau)\right] \tag{1.3.28}$$

The function $h(t)$ is called the *hazard rate*, and the excess promised short rate of return that makes an investment in a corporate bond return the same amount as in a Treasury bond is given in terms of it by

$$\lambda^*(t) = (1 - R)h(t) \tag{1.3.29}$$

---

[2]This is similar to radioactive decay.

For a constant hazard rate h, the excess promised short rate of return λ^* is also constant.

On average, the value of an investment made at time $t = 0$ in a zero coupon corporate bond with principal P is, at maturity T,

$$V_c(T) = P_S(T)P + R \int_0^T ds \left(-\frac{dP_S(s)}{ds} \right)$$

$$\times \exp \left[\int_0^s d\tau \, y_c(\tau) + \int_s^T d\tau \, y(\tau) \right] V_c(0) \quad (1.3.30)$$

Dividing this by $V_c(0)$ and then using Equation 1.3.21, we find that

$$\text{Price} = V_c(0) = \exp \left[- \int_0^T d\tau \, y_c(\tau) \right] P$$

$$= \exp \left[-Y(T)T \right] \exp \left[- \int_0^T d\tau \, \lambda(\tau) \right] P \quad (1.3.31)$$

It is convenient to introduce the analog of the spot Treasury yield for corporate bonds. We call this quantity $Y_c(T)$, and it is defined by

$$\exp \left[-Y_c(T)T \right] = \exp \left[- \int_0^T d\tau \, y_c(\tau) \right] \quad (1.3.32)$$

In terms of the corporate spot yield, the formula for the price of a zero coupon corporate bond of principal P and maturity T is

$$\text{Price} = \exp \left[-Y_c(T)T \right] P \quad (1.3.33)$$

When $R = 0$, it is straightforward to see that Equation 1.3.33 arises from discounting the expected cash flow (i.e., the principal payment at maturity times the probability of the company's surviving to maturity without default) by the risk-free Treasury rate plus the risk premium.

To review, when the risk premium is zero, on average, a zero coupon corporate bond has the same instantaneous rate of return as an investment in a zero coupon risk-free Treasury bond. In that case, the price of a zero coupon corporate bond is given by Equation 1.3.33 with the corporate short rate $y_c = y + \lambda^*$, where λ^* is given by Equation 1.3.25. Note that this value of y_c takes into account the probability of default, so that even though the average return is the same as that on a Treasury bond, the short corporate rate y_c is greater than y.

The hazard rate can implicitly depend on the yield. The partial derivative

$$\beta_{c,T} = \frac{\partial Y_c(T)}{\partial Y(T)} \tag{1.3.34}$$

is usually less than 1. Recall that Y_c is equal to Y plus an additional term that takes into account the default probability and the risk premium. It is this additional term that causes $\beta_{c,T}$ to differ from unity. If the economy deteriorates, Y usually decreases; however, default risk increases, resulting in a value for $\beta_{c,T}$ that is less than unity.

The duration of a zero coupon corporate bond with respect to the corporate yield Y_c is

$$D_c(T) = -\frac{1}{\text{Price}} \left(\frac{\partial \text{Price}}{\partial Y_c(T)} \right) = T \tag{1.3.35}$$

Applying the chain rule, the familiar duration of a zero coupon corporate bond, defined with respect to the Treasury yield, is

$$D(T) = -\frac{1}{\text{Price}} \left(\frac{\partial \text{Price}}{\partial Y(T)} \right) = \beta_{c,T} D_c(T) \tag{1.3.36}$$

Investors in corporate bonds look to ratings agencies to assign them grades that indicate the probability of default. Corporate bonds that are investment-grade have a low probability of default. For poorer-quality non-investment-grade corporate bonds, $\beta_{c,T}$ can be negative, since the Treasury spot yield forms a smaller part of the total discount factor Y_c.

Consider a zero coupon corporate bond with maturity of 10 years issued by a company that has a constant annualized hazard rate of $h = 2$ percent, and suppose the recovery rate on that bond is $R = 30$ percent. Then λ^* is 1.4 percent and the price of such a bond that makes its return the same as that on a zero coupon Treasury bond of the same maturity is 87 percent of the price of the Treasury bond. If the risk premium is a constant $\mu = 1$ percent, then the price drops to 79 percent of the cost of a zero coupon Treasury bond with the same maturity.

So far we have discussed only zero coupon corporate bonds, but a coupon-paying bond is just a collection of zero coupon bonds, and so the results presented here apply for those as well. A corporate bond with principal P that pays a coupon cP at times t_n and matures at time T has price

$$\text{Price} = c \sum_n \exp\left[-Y_c(t_n)t_n\right] P + \exp\left[-Y_c(T)\right] P \qquad (1.3.37)$$

If we use the same parameters as in the previous example, $h = 2$ percent, $\mu = 1$ percent, $R = 30$ percent, and $T = 10$ years, and take the annualized Treasury spot yield to be a constant $Y = 5$ percent, the price of a corporate bond with principal P and maturity T that pays a semiannual coupon of cP is $(13.87c + 0.4771) P$. Taking $P = \$100$ and $c = 3.5$ percent, the price is $\$96.26$. On the other hand, if $c = 4$ percent, the price is $\$103.20$.

1.4   Stocks

Public companies raise capital not only through the debt market but also by issuing equity. The total firm value V is the sum of a company's debt plus its equity. It is the amount of capital with which the firm can build and operate its business. Hence we write

$$V = D + E \qquad (1.4.38)$$

where D is the total value of the firm's debt and E is the total value of its equity, i.e., the stock it has issued. The total value of a company's equity E divided by the number of shares issued[3] gives the stock price S. The debt may consist of several types, e.g., bank loans and/or corporate bonds of various maturities. It can be seen from this equation that the value of corporate debt and that of stock are related. If the firm is near bankruptcy, then its debt is close to the firm's value, and so the value of its stock is small. Models that price corporate bonds by taking the firm value V as evolving in time according to some stochastic process and have the firm enter bankruptcy if V falls below a threshold are called *structural models*. Usually historical information on the company's stock price is used to determine the parameters in the model used for stochastic time evolution of the firm value. We will discuss such models in more detail in a later chapter.

For public companies, their corporate debt and stock are the fundamental quantities that are traded and have a market value. Investors can purchase stocks, and they can short them. Shorting a stock means that the investor borrows the stock and immediately sells it at its current market value. Since the stock was borrowed, it must be returned at a later time; the investor repurchases it and returns it to the party from which it was borrowed. An investor might short a stock if there is a good reason to believe that its price will drop, since it will then be repurchased at a lower price than that at which it was sold.

1.5   Arbitrage Opportunities

One of the basic principles of finance is that no investment can maintain a guaranteed rate of return that is greater than the risk-free rate of return. An investment with a guaranteed rate of return that is greater than the risk-free rate of return is called an *arbitrage opportunity*.

---

[3]This is a simplification. There can be different classes of shares issued.

Suppose an arbitrage opportunity existed. Then a large investment firm could borrow money at very near the risk-free rate and invest it in a portfolio of assets that provided the arbitrage opportunity. It would be guaranteed to make money and hence would continue making this investment until the price of the portfolio of assets that provided the arbitrage opportunity rose enough that it no longer provided a certain return that was greater than the risk-free rate. Hence, in practice, such opportunities may exist for periods of time but not indefinitely. Assuming that arbitrage opportunities cannot exist, even for short periods of time, is a method that is used to price some investments. Similarly, assuming that any investment can be shorted, then no investment can maintain a guaranteed return that is less than the risk-free rate. In this case, a large investment firm would be guaranteed to make money by shorting the investment and using the funds received from selling it to buy Treasury bonds.

Suppose two parties enter into what is called a *forward contract* on a stock (that doesn't pay a dividend) today, i.e., $t = 0$. In a forward contract, one party (the buyer) agrees to pay a price F for the stock at some time $t = T$ in the future. No money changes hands until the time $t = T$, when the buyer gets the stock and the seller gets paid F for it. We will see that if there is no arbitrage opportunity, the price F to be paid at the future time $t = T$ is

$$F = S(0) \exp\left[Y(T)T\right] \qquad (1.5.39)$$

where $S(0)$ is the stock value at $t = 0$. This is a surprisingly low price. After all, on average, stocks grow in value by more than the risk-free rate. Shouldn't the buyer of the forward contract pay more than the present price of the stock, increased by the amount that the value of a zero coupon risk-free Treasury bond grows? The answer is no, because if the price F were greater or less than this, it would create an arbitrage opportunity. To see this, imagine that at time $t = 0$, we have $S(0)$ of cash. We sell the forward contract at price F and use the cash to actually buy the stock. Note that in the forward contract, no money changes hands at time $t = 0$. At time $t = T$, the stock has market value $S(T)$ and the sale of the forward contract nets us $F - S(T)$. Even though at time $t = 0$ we don't know what the price $S(T)$ of the stock will be at time T, we are certain that our initial investment of $S(0)$ at time $t = 0$ will have the value $F - S(T) + S(T) = F$ at time $t = T$. So if the price paid for the forward contract is greater than Equation 1.5.39, our return on our initial investment of $S(0)$ is guaranteed to be greater than the risk-free rate.

Similarly, if F is less than Equation 1.5.39, there is also an arbitrage opportunity. To see this, imagine that at time $t = 0$ we buy the forward contract at price F, short the corresponding stock, and use the money we got from the sale of the shorted stock to buy a risk-free zero coupon Treasury bond. At time $t = 0$, the total amount invested is zero. We invested $S(0)$ in a zero coupon Treasury bond; however, this is compensated by shorting the stock, and furthermore no money changes hands in the forward contract until time $t = T$. What is the value of our investments at time $t = T$? The Treasury bonds are worth $S(0) \exp[Y(T)T]$. The shorted stock is returned at this time, so its purchase in the market at time T costs us $S(T)$. The forward contract is worth $S(T) - F$ at time T when it is settled. Hence at time T our zero investment has the value $S(0) \exp[Y(T)T] - S(T) + S(T) - F = S(0) \exp[Y(T)T] - F$. So we are sure to have a positive return if $F < S(0) \exp[Y(T)T]$, no matter what value the stock has at time T. Since we invested nothing to get this positive return, we are clearly beating the risk-free rate of return, and there is an arbitrage opportunity.

1.6   Derivatives

From stocks and bonds, we can form other derived quantities that can be invested in, and these go under the general name *derivatives*. A forward contract is a derivative. There are many different types of derivatives, and we will discuss some of them in more detail later in the book. The previous argument implies that the price of a forward contract on a stock is the expected future value of the stock provided that, on average, the stock price grows at the risk-free rate. Of course, stocks typically grow at rates greater than the risk-free rate of return. A "risk-neutral" price of a derivative on an underlying asset (e.g., a stock in the case of a forward contract on a stock) is the price that would be derived from taking the expected value of the cash flows under the assumption that, on average, the underlying asset grows in value at the risk-free rate of return.

We discuss now a derivative that is of particular importance to corporate bond investors. If such investors do not wish to take the risk of loss of principal from a corporate default, they can buy insurance from another party on the principal of the bond to protect against this loss. In such an arrangement, they pay the party providing the insurance a certain amount at fixed intervals, and if the company defaults on the bond, the insurer pays the principal that is not recovered to the bondholder at the time of default. Such an arrangement is called a *credit default swap*. We want to determine what the payments to the insurer should be if neither party has, on average, a net gain from this arrangement, i.e., the fair value for the payments. To simplify this problem, let us imagine that the payments to the insurer are made continuously in time. If the company has not defaulted, then in the time interval dt, the payment is $c_{ds} P dt$. The probability of the company's surviving to t without default is the survival probability $P_S(t)$. So in a time interval dt, the expected present value of the payment made to the insurer on an amount of principal P is

$$c_{ds} P P_S(t) \exp\left[-Y(t)t\right] dt \qquad (1.6.40)$$

and it is the fair value of the credit default swap spread c_{ds} that we would like to find. On the other hand, in this time interval, the payment to the holder of the bond is made only if the company defaults. The probability of this is $-dP_S(t)$. Then to compensate for this loss, on average the present value of this payment would be

$$(1 - R)P\left(-\frac{dP_S(t)}{dt}\right) \exp\left[-Y(t)t\right] dt \qquad (1.6.41)$$

Here it is assumed that RP of the principal is recovered. Equating Equations 1.6.40 and 1.6.41 and then integrating both of them over the time period for which the insurance is bought, we arrive at a value for c_{ds} that is called the *credit default par spread*,

$$c_{ds} = (1 - R)\frac{\int_0^T dt \left(-\frac{dP_S(t)}{dt}\right) \exp\left[-Y(t)t\right]}{\int_0^T dt\, P_S(t)\, \exp\left[-Y(t)t\right]} \qquad (1.6.42)$$

Equation 1.6.42 can be evaluated analytically when the hazard rate h is a constant independent of time. This gives

$$c_{ds} = (1 - R)h \qquad (1.6.43)$$

For an annualized hazard rate $h = 2$ percent and recovery fraction $R = 30$ percent, the par spread is $c_{ds} = 1.4$ percent.

In this book we will learn about many types of derivatives, including futures contracts on stocks and bonds, options on stocks and bonds, interest-rate swaps, and interest-rate caps. Some of the most common options that individual investors encounter are call and put options on a stock. The purchaser of an American call option on a stock has the right to purchase the stock at a particular strike price at any time before the option matures. The purchaser of this type of option hopes that the stock price rises above the strike price during this time period. The purchaser of an American put option on a stock has the right to sell the stock at a particular strike price at any time before the option matures. European options are defined in a similar fashion, except that the purchase (call) or sale (put) can be made only when the option matures. We will have more to say about the pricing of options in Chapters 3, 6, and 7.

1.7   Mortgages

A bondholder receives fixed payments, and then the principal is returned at maturity. With a mortgage (or an annuity), the monthly payments are fixed and there is no final principal payment. Hence, in a mortgage, part of the principal is paid off each month. If the monthly interest rate is fixed at i, the present value of the total payments (i.e., the original mortgage balance M_0) is given by

$$M_0 = C \sum_{n=1}^{N} \frac{1}{(1+i)^n} = C \left(\frac{1}{i}\right) \left(1 - \frac{1}{(1+i)^N}\right) \quad (1.7.44)$$

where N is the total number of months in the mortgage (e.g., for a 30-year mortgage, $N = 360$) and C is the monthly payment made by the borrower. Note that in terms of our previous notation, $i = Y_{12}/12$, and M_0 in Equation 1.7.44 is the present value of the sum of all the monthly payments C under the assumption that the yield curve is flat and that the mortgage interest rate is the monthly yield. We can rearrange this expression to get a formula for the monthly payment in terms of the original mortgage balance M_0 and the monthly interest rate i. Explicitly,

$$C = M_0 \left(\frac{i(1+i)^N}{(1+i)^N - 1}\right) \quad (1.7.45)$$

At the end of month 1, an amount of interest iM_0 has been paid and the remaining balance on the mortgage (i.e., the principal remaining) M_1 is the original balance minus the difference between the monthly payment C and the interest payment,

$$M_1 = M_0 - (C - M_0 i) = M_0(1 + i) - C \qquad (1.7.46)$$

Similarly, the interest paid in the second month on the balance after the first month is iM_1, and so at the end of the second month, the remaining principal on the mortgage M_2 is given by

$$M_2 = M_1(1 + i) - C = M_0(1 + i)^2 - C(1 + i) - C \qquad (1.7.47)$$

Clearly we have the following recursion relation that relates the monthly balance at the end of month n to the monthly balance at the end of the previous month:

$$M_n = M_{n-1}(1 + i) - C \qquad (1.7.48)$$

Equations 1.7.46 and 1.7.47 suggest that the solution to this recursion relation takes the form

$$M_n = \alpha(1 + i)^n + \beta \qquad (1.7.49)$$

Plugging this into the recursion relation gives

$$\beta = \frac{C}{i} \qquad (1.7.50)$$

Using Equation 1.7.49 for the case $n = 0$ implies that

$$\alpha = M_0 - \frac{C}{i} \qquad (1.7.51)$$

Combining these results,

$$M_n = \left(M_0 - \frac{C}{i}\right)(1 + i)^n + \frac{C}{i} \qquad (1.7.52)$$

Using Equation 1.7.45 to eliminate the monthly payment C gives the following expression for the balance left on the mortgage after month n in terms of the original balance and the monthly interest rate:

$$M_n = M_0 \left(\frac{(1+i)^N - (1+i)^n}{(1+i)^N - 1} \right) \qquad (1.7.53)$$

Consequently, the principal payment in each month, P_n, is

$$P_n = M_{n-1} - M_n = M_0 \left(\frac{i(1+i)^{n-1}}{(1+i)^N - 1} \right) \qquad (1.7.54)$$

and the interest payment each month is

$$I_n = C - P_n = M_0 \left(\frac{i\left[(1+i)^N - (1+i)^{n-1}\right]}{(1+i)^N - 1} \right) \qquad (1.7.55)$$

Investors in mortgages face risks that Treasury bond holders do not. For example, borrowers may default on their payments. While a default is a loss of principal, investors in mortgages also face the risk that the timing and amount of the cash flows might not be what they expected. For example, the borrower may move, and then the remaining principal is usually paid off at the time of the sale of the residence. This reason for the reduction in the number of borrowers in a collection of mortgages is called *turnover*. Furthermore, if mortgage rates drop, the borrower can refinance into a loan with a more favorable interest rate. It is possible to model average borrower prepayments resulting from turnover and refinancings and also model default rates using historical data.

The price an investor should pay for a mortgage is calculated by discounting the stream of cash flows by the risk-free rate plus an additional risk premium term. To simplify the discussion, we neglect defaults and the risk premium. However, we do include the possibility of complete prepayment of the loan balance in any month (the possibility of partial prepayments is also neglected in this analysis). With these (and some other) simplifying assumptions, the price of a new mortgage (i.e., the average present value of the borrower's payments) is

$$
\text{Price} = M_0 \sum_{n=1}^{N} \left\{ \left(\frac{i(1+i)^N}{(1+i)^N - 1} \right) P_S^{(M)}(n) \right.
$$
$$
\left. + \left(\frac{(1+i)^N - (1+i)^n}{(1+i)^N - 1} \right) \left[P_S^{(M)}(n-1) - P_S^{(M)}(n) \right] \right\}
$$
$$
\times \exp[-Y(t_n)t_n] \tag{1.7.56}
$$

where $P_S^{(M)}(n)$ is the probability that the borrower has not prepaid up to the end of month n. By definition, $P_S^{(M)}(0) = 1$.

Let us model the prepayment probability using the same hazard-rate approach as in the corporate case. Discretizing the integral over time to a sum over months, the survival probability at the end of month n is

$$
P_S^{(M)}(n) = \exp\left(-\sum_{k=1}^{n} \lambda_k \right) \tag{1.7.57}
$$

where λ_n is the monthly hazard rate in month n. As was mentioned before, there are two sources of prepayments. The owners of the house may move, and then their mortgage is paid off. Another possibility is that the interest rates drop in the future and it is economically advantageous for the homeowner to pay off the existing mortgage by refinancing the mortgage into one with a lower mortgage rate. Hence we write $\lambda_n = \lambda_n^{(t)} + \lambda_n^{(r)}$, where the superscript t denotes the turnover piece and the superscript r denotes the refinancing contribution. We take for the monthly dependence of the turnover hazard rate

$$
\lambda_n^{(t)} = \lambda^{(t)} \left[\theta(30 - n)\frac{n}{30} + \theta(n - 30) \right] \tag{1.7.58}
$$

where $\theta(x)$ is the step function[4] defined to be 1 for $x > 0$ and 0 for $x < 0$. The form for $\lambda_n^{(t)}$ in Equation 1.7.58 takes into account the fact that homeowners are unlikely to move shortly after purchasing their home. A typical value for $\lambda^{(t)}$ is 6 percent on an annual basis or, with the monthly convention we have adopted, $0.06/12 = 0.005$, which we shall use currently. To start, we take the Treasury spot yield to be a constant annualized 5 percent and the mortgage rate to be an annualized 6 percent (i.e., $i = 0.06/12 = 0.005$), and we set the refinancing part of the prepayment hazard rate to zero. With these assumptions, the price of a 30-year mortgage with an original balance of \$100,000 is \$107,541. Note that if we had also set the turnover rate to zero, $\lambda^{(t)} = 0$, the price would have been \$111,553. If the mortgage were held for the full 30 years, the homeowner would have paid a total of \$215,838.

Next, for the same mortgage, i.e., $i = \lambda^{(t)} = 0.005$, $M_0 = \$100,000$, and $T = 30$ years, we consider a case where the Treasury short rate is not constant. To make the analysis as simple as possible, we assume that the annualized Treasury short rate is constant until month n^*, when it drops abruptly from the value y_i to the value y_f and then stays constant at this lower value for the remainder of the mortgage. More explicitly, the spot yield is taken to be

$$Y(t_n) = y_i - (y_i - y_f)\theta(n - n^*)\left(\frac{t_n - t_{n^*}}{t_n}\right) \qquad (1.7.59)$$

We take $y_i = 5$ percent, $y_f = 3$ percent, and $n^* = 60$. If there were no prepayments at all (i.e., $\lambda_n = 0$), the price of this mortgage would be \$130,187. It is more expensive than in the previous case where the short rate was a constant 5 percent because after five years the spot yield is smaller, and hence the discounting factor is larger. With the same assumptions as previously adopted, turnover prepayments alone

---

[4]We adopt the convention that $\theta(0) = 1/2$.

reduce the price to \$117,014. However, the value $y_f = 3$ percent is small enough that starting in month n^*, the homeowner has an economic incentive to refinance his mortgage. The economic incentive is the difference between the homeowner's monthly mortgage rate i and the new monthly mortgage rate, $y_f/12 + i^*$, available to him after the annualized Treasury short rate drops to y_f. Here i^* takes into account the fact that the new mortgage rate will be somewhat higher than $y_f/12$. We have absorbed refinancing costs into i^*. We will use $i^* = 0.01/12$, i.e., 1 percent on an annualized basis. Linearizing the prepayment hazard rate in the homeowner's economic incentive to prepay, $i - i^* - y_f/12$, gives

$$\lambda_n^{(r)} = a \left[\theta(n - n^*) + \frac{\delta_{n,n^*}}{2} \right] \left(i - i^* - \frac{y_f}{12} \right) \qquad (1.7.60)$$

where the Kronecker delta δ_{n,n^*} is 1 if $n = n^*$ and 0 otherwise. We take $a = 15$, so the annualized refinance hazard rate is 30 percent after the fifth year. Including both turnover and refinancing prepayments, this mortgage has a price of \$107,624. The prepayments due to refinancing have reduced the value of the mortgage to the investor by \$117,014 − \$107,624 = \$9,390.

Since prepayments depend on the yield, they have an impact on the duration and convexity of the mortgage. Recall that if the yield curve shifts by a very small constant amount $Y(t_n) \to Y(t_n) + \Delta Y$, then the price changes by, $\Delta \text{Price} = (-D\Delta Y + C\Delta Y^2/2)\text{Price}$. For the mortgage discussed here, we compute the duration and convexity by shifting the yield curve by small finite amounts and recalculating the price. This gives that $D = 3.94$ years and $C = 17.8$ years^2. In Figures 1.1 and 1.2, we plot the duration and convexity of this mortgage as a function of the parameter a that determines the size of the prepayment hazard rate. The striking feature of mortgages is that the convexity can be negative. Convexity effects increase

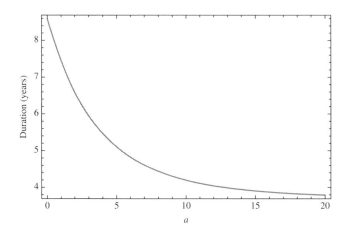

Figure 1.1 Duration in years as a function of a.

prices for Treasury bonds, but they can decrease prices for mortgages.

Prepayments rise as yields decrease and fall as yields increase. Furthermore, homeowner refinancings reduce the value of a mortgage to an investor. Convexity is a second-derivative effect, and the negative contribution to convexity comes from the product of one derivative acting on the prepayment probability and the other acting on the discounting factor. When a is very small or very large, the convexity is positive, since

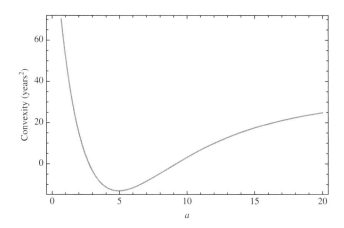

Figure 1.2 Convexity in years^2 as a function of a.

it is dominated, respectively, by the second derivative of the discount factor or the second derivative of the prepayent factor. The convexity and duration are defined with respect to infinitesimal changes in the level of the yield curve. For mortgages, it is also useful to study the impact of finite changes in the level of the yield curve, since they can take you from a regime in which there is no incentive for the homeowner to refinance to one in which the homeowner has an incentive to refinance.

Mortgages are combined into large pools and sold off to institutional investors as mortgage-backed securities. As we have already seen, pricing mortgage-backed securities requires modeling default rates and prepayment rates. Two of the largest issuers and securitizers of mortgages are the government-sponsored agencies Freddie Mac and Fannie Mae.

The prepayment rate on home mortgages is influenced by psychological factors. For example, some homeowners will not refinance their mortgage even long after it has become economically advantageous to do so, while others will refinance almost as soon as the economic incentive exists. Homeowners come with different propensities to prepay their mortgage for a fixed economic incentive. If mortgage rates drop below the rate paid by a large pool of homeowners, then those with the greatest propensity to prepay their mortgages will prepay first. Hence, if the economic incentive to prepay remains constant, the prepayment rate associated with the pool of homeowners decreases with time. This phenomenon is called *burnout*. Over the period of a 30-year mortgage, several periods in which the economy slows and interest rates drop can be expected. Hence, it is likely that homeowners who took out mortgages when interest rates were not depressed will have an economic incentive to refinance several times over that period. Burnout implies that the fastest prepayment rates will occur the first time this happens. Pools that contain seasoned mortgages that have already experienced a period in which the homeowners had an economic incentive to refinance should experience less refinancing the next time mortgage rates drop below the rate that the homeowners in that pool are paying than pools that have a similar mortgage rate but have not experienced a previous period of refinancing.

1.8   Municipal Bonds

Some of the largest issuers of bonds in the United States are municipalities. The states of the union, counties and cities, and (in many cases) special private entities can issue bonds whose coupons are exempt from federal, state, and local taxes. For instance, if a California bond investor who is a California resident buys a California state-issued bond then the income from that bond is exempt from both federal and California taxes. In general, states can tax the bonds issued in other states, but municipal bonds (munis) always remain exempt from federal taxes.

Suppose we purchase a zero coupon municipal bond with a maturity of T years and yield $Y_M(T)$. Assume that the credit quality of the municipal authority is exactly the same as that of the federal government, so there is no additional credit risk from purchasing the municipal bond. Assume further that the spot Treasury yield is $Y(T)$ for a zero coupon Treasury bond of the same maturity. Then, since the municipal bond is tax-exempt, we should expect that the price of a municipal zero coupon bond should be obtainable by discounting either on the municipal yield curve or, equivalently, on a tax-adjusted Treasury yield curve. So,

$$\text{Price} = e^{-Y_M(T)T} P = e^{-Y(T)T[1-\tau(T)]} P \qquad (1.8.61)$$

where τ is the (continuously compounded) income tax rate expected to prevail at maturity T, and P is the principal. This implies that

$$Y_M(T) = Y(T)[1 - \tau(T)] \qquad (1.8.62)$$

If we plot $\tau(T)$ as a function of T, we should expect to see $\tau(T)$ to be close to the current income tax rate applicable to muni buyers. This should be true because if Treasury bonds yielded a higher after-tax return than munis, then no one would want to buy the munis, and if munis yielded a higher pretax equivalent return—obtained by $Y_M(T)/[1 - \tau(T)]$—then one could get a higher return than on Treasury bonds by buying munis.

In practice, if we observe $Y_M(T)$ and $Y(T)$ and deduce the market implied tax rate $\tau(T)$, we find that $\tau(T)$ is a strictly decreasing function of T, i.e., the implied tax rate falls. For example, for very short maturities (such as $T = 1$ year), we find that the implied tax rate is close to the actual income tax rate (today the marginal income tax rate for the highest earners is 38.6 percent), but as the maturity extends, the implied tax rate falls. For very long term municipal bonds, the implied tax rate computed by comparing Treasuries and municipal bond yields has frequently been in single digits, and sometimes even 0 percent or negative! For an investor in long-term munis, unless the actual tax rate falls below the implied tax rate, the municipal bond will outperform an equivalent maturity Treasury with complete certainty.

Of course, municipal bonds are not Treasuries, so perhaps the explanation has to do with their worse credit quality and lower liquidity, but even after making various adjustments for credit and liquidity, implied tax rates fall with maturity to extremely low values. When we compare municipal bonds with the corporate credit yield curve (it is safe to assume that the highest-rated municipal bonds are no worse than the highest-rated corporate bonds in aggregate, since the realized default rate for municipal bonds over almost the last 100 years is very small), we find that long-term implied tax rates are still in the 15 to 20 percent range, which is much lower than the marginal tax rates applicable today. One additional explanation could be that tax rates are uncertain, so the long-term muni investor requires a higher premium to buy muni bonds because of this uncertainty. However, even with the most conservative estimates for tax rates as inputs, we are not able to justify the low implied tax rates for long-maturity munis. This so-called muni puzzle has persisted for many years, and as of this writing there are no convincing explanations other than the hypothesis of market segmentation and preferred habitat, which basically states that long-term munis are attractive only to certain types of investors, and their demand is not enough to push the municipal implied tax rates higher.

The duration of a municipal bond can be determined by taking the first derivative with respect to the municipal yield. However, when a municipal bond is included in a portfolio with taxable (nonmunicipal) bonds, we need to decide on the proper yield (taxable or tax-exempt) relative to which durations are being computed. In other words,

$$D_M(T) = -\frac{1}{\text{Price}}\left(\frac{\partial \text{Price}}{\partial Y_M(T)}\right) = T \qquad (1.8.63)$$

but the usual duration of a municipal bond, which is defined with respect to the taxable Treasury yield, is

$$D(T) = -\frac{1}{\text{Price}}\left(\frac{\partial \text{Price}}{\partial Y(T)}\right) = -\frac{1}{\text{Price}}\left(\frac{\partial \text{Price}}{\partial Y_M(T)}\right)\left(\frac{\partial Y_M(T)}{\partial Y(T)}\right)$$

$$(1.8.64)$$

If we define

$$\beta_{M,T} \equiv \frac{\partial Y_M(T)}{\partial Y(T)} \qquad (1.8.65)$$

then we can mix municipal bonds with Treasury bonds in a portfolio and state the portfolio duration relative to the same underlying yield curve. In other words, the beta-adjusted municipal duration is now a taxable duration of the municipal bond:

$$D(T) = \beta_{M,T} D_M(T) \qquad (1.8.66)$$

For the zero coupon case, from Equation 1.8.62,

$$\beta_{M,T} = [1 - \tau(T)] \qquad (1.8.67)$$

A bond is callable if the issuer has the right to return the buyer's principal before the maturity date. In practice, most long-term municipal bonds are callable and there are numerous liquidity and credit adjustments, so for coupon-bearing muni bonds, it is usually easier to compute the adjustment $\beta_{M,T}$ by running a linear regression of $Y_M(T)$ on the Treasury yield $Y(T)$, using the time series of municipal and Treasury yields. The typical range for $\beta_{M,T}(T)$ is in the 0.25 to 0.6 range, although it depends a lot on the absolute level of yields and the shape of the Treasury yield curve, along with other things such as the demand for Treasuries in periods of crisis and increasing risk aversion.

1.9   Real Bonds

So far, we have been dealing with what are called *nominal bonds*. For nominal Treasury bonds, the yield $Y(T)$ for maturity T is not adjusted for inflation. If inflation is a problem, investors care more about the real yield (i.e., the yield minus the inflation rate) that their investment gives them, since inflation will wipe out a large portion of the nominal yield. We can think of inflation as a different type of tax. Imitating Equation 1.8.61, we can write the yield $Y_R(T)$ of a "real" or inflation-linked bond as

$$Y_R(T) + I(T) = Y(T) \qquad (1.9.68)$$

where $I(T)$ is the inflation rate we expect to prevail for time T. For the last 20 or so years, real bonds have been traded in many developed markets, such as the United Kingdom, the United States (the last 10 years), and Australia. When we observe the actual yields of nominal and real bonds in these markets, the value of $I(T)$ extracted by using Equation 1.9.68 results in a rough estimate of the market's inflation expectations. The estimate is rough, since inflation-linked bonds are still much smaller than nominal bonds as a fraction of outstanding bonds, and hence some component of their extra yield is due to a liquidity risk premium. Nonetheless, by observing the time dependence of implied inflation, we can create what is called the *breakeven* inflation curve. If inflation turns out to be higher (lower) than the breakeven inflation over the holding period, then inflation-linked bonds are a better (worse) investment than the comparable nominal bonds.

For computation of duration, we can again state either the real duration, i.e., the sensitivity relative to the real curve only, or, when mixing real and nominal bonds, the usual duration, which is defined relative to nominal yields. The usual duration of a real return bond is

$$D(T) = -\frac{1}{\text{Price}}\frac{\partial \text{Price}}{\partial Y(T)} = -\frac{1}{\text{Price}}\left(\frac{\partial \text{Price}}{\partial Y_R(T)}\right)\left(\frac{\partial Y_R(T)}{\partial Y(T)}\right) \quad (1.9.69)$$

We write

$$D(T) = \beta_{R,T} D_R(T) \quad\quad\quad (1.9.70)$$

where the duration with respect to changes in the real spot yield $Y_R(T)$ is

$$D_R(T) = -\frac{1}{\text{Price}}\frac{\partial \text{Price}}{\partial Y_R(T)} \quad\quad\quad (1.9.71)$$

Empirically $\beta_{R,T}$ is in the 0.6 to 0.8 range, although over short periods of time, if there are inflation shocks or other issues related to liquidity, the realized $\beta_{R,T}$ can temporarily be greater than 1 or even negative.

1.10   Convertible Bonds

Convertible bonds are the simplest type of hybrid securities—ones that carry exposure to different asset classes. Convertible bonds have both equity and bond elements. A convertible bond is a fixed-income instrument issued by a corporation that may be converted into a predefined number of shares of stock at a given share price called the *conversion price*. As long as the price of the stock is low, the convertible bond pays a coupon like any other coupon-paying bond. On the other hand, if the stock price rises, the holder of the convertible bond can exercise the conversion option and convert the bond to shares. If the market price of the shares is higher than the conversion price, then there is potential gain from converting the bond into shares and selling them at a profit. Since we can think of a convertible bond as the sum of a nonconvertible bond and a long-term stock call option with some value, the yield on the convertible bond is lower than the yield on a nonconvertible bond. This allows the issuer of the convertible bond to borrow funds at a lower market rate than would be charged on the nonconvertible bond. The holder of the convertible bond gives up some yield but participates in the potential increase in the value of the investment if the stock of the firm goes up. Pricing of stock options will be discussed later in the book. We will also discuss the valuation of credit risk. Since a falling stock price has an adverse impact on the credit rating of the issuing corporation, even when the stock price is below the conversion price, the bond's price can fall in response to the falling stock price.

1.11   CDOs and Tranches

In a later chapter of this book, we discuss the evaluation of correlated default probabilities. The most direct application of correlated defaults is in the area of a relatively new type of credit derivative called a collateralized debt obligation (CDO) tranche. A CDO is a collection of corporate bonds or credit default swaps. (Recall that credit default swaps are an instrument that is simply an insurance contract against corporate defaults.) Since there is the possibility of none, one, or more defaults happening, different slices or tranches from this collection of bonds can be created that are exposed to different amounts of losses. The lowest or most exposed tranche is called the junior or equity tranche, and it suffers the first few losses. For example, the tranche that suffers the first 3 percent of all losses is a standard equity tranche. Once the losses wipe out the principal of this tranche, then the next safest tranche (called the *mezzanine tranche*) starts to suffer losses. For example, a typical mezzanine tranche starts to suffer losses exceeding 3 percent but below 7 percent. After the mezzanine tranches suffer complete loss, the senior tranches are exposed. A senior tranche could be one that does not suffer any losses until the aggregate amount of losses has exceeded 15 percent. One can easily see that if defaults become highly correlated, there is an increased likelihood of the senior tranches suffering losses. Since losses are most likely to hit the junior tranches first, they compensate the holder with a higher yield than the senior tranches. Thus knowing the probability of losses of each of the tranches, as well as the timing of such losses and the amount lost if the defaults happen, is critical to the valuation of CDOs and their tranches.

2

The Mathematics of Financial Modeling

2.1   Normal Random Variables

Suppose a real variable x has probability $\mathcal{P}(x)\,dx$ of being between x and $x + dx$. Since the probability of x being somewhere on the real line is unity, the probability distribution $\mathcal{P}(x)$ satisfies the normalization condition

$$\int_{-\infty}^{\infty} dx\ \mathcal{P}(x) = 1 \qquad (2.1.1)$$

The average or expected value of any function of x is

$$E[f(x)] = \int_{-\infty}^{\infty} dx\ f(x)\mathcal{P}(x) \qquad (2.1.2)$$

The probability distribution $\mathcal{P}(x)$ is positive, and so it is convenient to write it as the exponential of a function that can have either sign,

$$\mathcal{P}(x) = \exp\left[-U(x)\right] \qquad (2.1.3)$$

Now we assume that U has a minimum at $x = \bar{x}$, which is where the probability distribution is concentrated. We expand U in a power series about $\bar{x}$, neglecting terms higher than second order in the expansion. This should be a good approximation for the integral in Equation 2.1.2 if U is strongly peaked at $\bar{x}$ and $f(x)$ is not too small in the region around $x = \bar{x}$. Then we have

$$E[f(x)] = \int_{-\infty}^{\infty} dx \, f(x) \exp\left[-U(\bar{x}) - \frac{U''(\bar{x})}{2}(x - \bar{x})^2\right] \quad (2.1.4)$$

where U'' denotes the second derivative of U. There is no first-derivative term, and $U'' > 0$ because we are expanding about the minimum of U. We can write this as

$$E[f(x)] = \int_{-\infty}^{\infty} dx \, f(x) \frac{1}{\sqrt{2\pi\sigma^2}} \exp\left(-\frac{(x - \bar{x})^2}{2\sigma^2}\right) \quad (2.1.5)$$

where

$$\sigma^2 = \frac{1}{U''(\bar{x})} \quad (2.1.6)$$

and we have adjusted the normalization so that the approximate probability distribution is still normalized (see Appendix 1 to this chapter). The probability distribution

$$P_{\text{norm}}(x) = \frac{1}{\sqrt{2\pi\sigma^2}} \exp\left(-\frac{(x - \bar{x})^2}{2\sigma^2}\right) \quad (2.1.7)$$

is called a *normal distribution*, and random variables that are governed by it are called *normal random variables*. Our derivation shows that many random variables will be approximately normal for fluctuations that are not too far from the mean. However, for very large fluctuations, this reasoning cannot be used to justify using a normal distribution. The importance of normal distributions in probability theory is similar to the importance of the harmonic oscillator in physics. In Equation 2.1.7, $\bar{x} = E[x]$ is the expected value of x, and σ is its volatility or standard deviation. The square of the volatility $\sigma^2 = E[(x - \bar{x})^2]$ is called the variance.

There are probability distributions that for very large $|x - \bar{x}|$ fall like a power law, i.e., $\mathcal{P}(x) \sim c/|x - \bar{x}|^\alpha$, where c is a constant. For such distributions, we require $\alpha > 1$ for them to be normalizable. However, for normalizable probability distributions that have $1 < \alpha \leq 2$, the volatility is infinite. This can be the case even if for small $|x - \bar{x}|$, the probability distribution $\mathcal{P}(x)$ is approximately normal.

A particularly important choice for the function $f(x)$ in fixed-income finance is the exponential. For a normal random variable x (see Appendix 1),

$$
\begin{aligned}
E[\exp(-ax)] &= \frac{1}{\sqrt{2\pi\sigma^2}} \int_{-\infty}^{\infty} dx \exp\left(-\frac{(x - \bar{x})^2}{2\sigma^2} - ax\right) \\
&= \exp(-a\bar{x}) \exp\left(\frac{a^2 E[(x - \bar{x})^2]}{2}\right) \quad (2.1.8)
\end{aligned}
$$

A linear combination of independent (i.e., uncorrelated) normal variables is also a normal variable. To see this, take n normal variables x_i with zero mean,[1] where $i = 1, \ldots, n$. We are interested in knowing the probability distribution for the following linear combination:

$$
z = \sum_{i=1}^{n} \alpha_i x_i \quad (2.1.9)
$$

where the α_i are real constants. The average value of any function of z, $f(z)$, is

$$
E[f(z)] = \frac{1}{\sqrt{(2\pi)^n \sigma_1^2 \cdots \sigma_n^2}} \int_{-\infty}^{\infty} dx_1 \cdots \int_{-\infty}^{\infty} dx_n\, f(z) \exp\left(-\sum_{i=1}^{n} \frac{x_i^2}{2\sigma_i^2}\right)
$$

$$(2.1.10)$$

---

[1] The assumption of zero mean does not give rise to any loss of generality and can be relaxed.

It is convenient to rescale the variables to $y_i = x_i/\sigma_i$. Then

$$E[f(z)] = \frac{1}{\sqrt{(2\pi)^n}} \int_{-\infty}^{\infty} dy_1 \cdots \int_{-\infty}^{\infty} dy_n \; f(z) \exp\left(-\sum_{i=1}^{n} \frac{y_i^2}{2}\right)$$

$$(2.1.11)$$

with

$$z = \sum_{i=n}^{n} \alpha_i y_i \sigma_i \qquad (2.1.12)$$

Considering the y_i's as coordinates in a Cartesian coordinate system, we can rotate to new ones

$$z_k = \sum_{l=1}^{n} O_{kl} y_l \qquad (2.1.13)$$

where

$$O_{1l} = \frac{\alpha_l \sigma_l}{\sigma} \qquad (2.1.14)$$

Here

$$\sigma^2 = \sum_{l=1}^{n} \alpha_l^2 \sigma_l^2 \qquad (2.1.15)$$

Note that $z_1 = z/\sigma$. The rest of the matrix O can be found using the Gram-Schmidt procedure for constructing orthonormal coordinate systems. Since O is orthogonal, its determinant is 1. Changing our integration from over the y_i's to over the z_i's, the expression for the expected value of $f(z)$ becomes

$$E[f(z)] = \frac{1}{\sqrt{(2\pi)^n}} \int_{-\infty}^{\infty} dz_1 \cdots \int_{-\infty}^{\infty} dz_n \; f(z_1 \sigma) \exp\left(-\sum_{i=1}^{n} \frac{z_i^2}{2}\right)$$

$$(2.1.16)$$

where we have used the fact that orthogonal transformations preserve lengths so that $\sum_{i=1}^{n} z_i^2 = \sum_{i=1}^{n} y_i^2$. Performing the integrations over $z_2, \ldots, z_n$, we arrive at

$$E[f(z)] = \frac{1}{\sqrt{2\pi}} \int_{-\infty}^{\infty} dz_1 \, f(z_1\sigma) \exp\left(-\frac{z_1^2}{2}\right)$$

$$= \frac{1}{\sqrt{2\pi\sigma^2}} \int_{-\infty}^{\infty} dz \, f(z) \exp\left(-\frac{z^2}{2\sigma^2}\right) \quad (2.1.17)$$

Hence the linear combination $z = \sum_{i=n}^{n} \alpha_i x_i$ of independent normal random variables is also a normal variable, and its variance is $\sigma^2 = \sum_{l=1}^{n} \alpha_l^2 \sigma_l^2$.

2.2 The Central Limit Theorem

Next consider N random variables $x_i, i = 1, \ldots, N$, that have the joint probability distribution $P(x_1, \ldots, x_N)$. Functions of these variables have an average or expected value given by

$$E[f(x_1, \ldots, x_N)] = \int_{-\infty}^{\infty} dx_1 \cdots \int_{-\infty}^{\infty} dx_N f(x_1, \ldots, x_N) P(x_1, \ldots, x_N)$$

$$(2.2.18)$$

The variables are independent or uncorrelated if their joint probability distribution can be factored into the product of the individual probability distributions for the variables, i.e.,

$$P(x_1, \ldots, x_N) = P_1(x_1) \cdots P_N(x_N) \quad (2.2.19)$$

where

$$E[f(x_j)] = \int_{-\infty}^{\infty} dx_j \, f(x_j) P_j(x_j) \quad (2.2.20)$$

Now consider a random variable z that is the sum of N uncorrelated random variables x_i of zero mean and variance σ_i^2,

$$z = \frac{1}{\sqrt{N}} \sum_i \alpha_i x_i \tag{2.2.21}$$

Since the random variables x_i are uncorrelated and have zero mean, $E[x_{i_1} \cdots x_{i_n}] = 0$ for $i_1 \neq i_2 \neq \cdots \neq i_n$. We have inserted the factor of $1/\sqrt{N}$ so that the variance of z,

$$\sigma^2 = E[z^2] = \frac{1}{N} \sum_i \alpha_i^2 \sigma_i^2 \tag{2.2.22}$$

does not grow with N if the α_i are order unity. We want to consider the properties of the variable z for very large N. We have already shown that its variance is order unity.

Next, consider the skewness of the probability distribution for z. It is defined as $s = E[z^3]/\sigma^3$ and is zero for a normal distribution. (Recall that we are assuming $E[z] = 0$.) Since the underlying variables x_i are independent,

$$s = \left(\frac{1}{\sqrt{N}\sigma}\right)^3 \sum_i \alpha_i^3 E[x_i^3] \tag{2.2.23}$$

The sum has only N terms, and so $s \to 0$ as $N \to \infty$. Next we consider the excess kurtosis k. It is defined by

$$k = \frac{E[z^4]}{\sigma^4} - 3\frac{E[z^2]E[z^2]}{\sigma^4} = \frac{E[z^4]}{\sigma^4} - 3 \tag{2.2.24}$$

For a normal random variable, the excess kurtosis is equal to zero. In our case,

$$\frac{E[z^4]}{\sigma^4} = \left(\frac{1}{\sqrt{N}\sigma}\right)^4 \sum_i \alpha_i^4 E[x_i^4] + 3\left(\frac{1}{\sqrt{N}\sigma}\right)^4 \sum_{i \neq j} \alpha_i^2 \alpha_j^2 \sigma_i^2 \sigma_j^2 \tag{2.2.25}$$

And so the excess kurtosis k is equal to

$$k = \left(\frac{1}{\sqrt{N}\sigma}\right)^4 \left(\sum_i \alpha_i^4 E[x_i^4] - 3\sum_i \alpha_i^4 \sigma_i^4\right) \qquad (2.2.26)$$

which is order $1/N$ and hence vanishes as $N \to \infty$. So the third and fourth moments of the probability distribution for z approach those of a normal distribution as $N \to \infty$. It is possible to show that this pattern persists and all the moments of the probability distribution for z approach those of a normal distribution. This result is the celebrated central limit theorem. The sum of a large number of independent random variables approaches a normal random variable even when the individual variables in this sum are not normally distributed. This is another reason why normal distributions play such a crucial role in probability theory. However, it is very important to remember that the central limit theorem holds only for uncorrelated random variables. The central limit theorem cannot be used to argue that the sum of a large number of correlated random variables is normally distributed.

2.3   The Probability Distribution for Corporate Bond Returns

For the statistical properties of corporate bond returns, it is convenient to introduce a random variable $\hat{n}(t)$ that takes the value 1 if the firm defaults in the time horizon t and 0 otherwise. $P_D(t) = E[\hat{n}(t)]$ is the probability that the firm defaults sometime in the time period t. The random variable $\hat{n}'(t) = [1 - \hat{n}(t)]$ takes the value 1 if the company does not default sometime in the time horizon t, and is 0 otherwise. $P_S(t) = E[\hat{n}'(t)]$ is the probability that the company does not default in the time period t.

As in Chapter 1, we assume that a zero coupon bond grows in value (if it doesn't default) at the (short) corporate promised rate $y_c(t)$. To simplify the analysis in this section, we take the recovery fraction R to be zero. Then

$$\frac{\hat{V}_c(t)}{V_c(0)} = \exp\left[\int_0^t d\tau \ y_c(\tau)\right] \hat{n}'(t) \tag{2.3.27}$$

where $V_c(0)$ is the initial value or the price of the zero coupon bond and $\hat{V}_c(t)$ is a random variable that represents the value of the zero coupon bond at time t. In Equation 2.3.27 we have continuously compounded the returns, and we have assumed that t is less than or equal to the maturity date of the bond. Note that the expectation value of this formula corresponds to Equation 1.3.21 of Chapter 1. The random variables $\hat{n}$ and $\hat{n}'$ can take on only the values 0 and 1. Hence, if they are raised to any power, then they are equal to themselves. Therefore, with the recovery fraction equal to zero,

$$E\left[\left(\frac{\hat{V}_c(t)}{V_c(0)}\right)^m\right] = \exp\left[(m-1)\int_0^t d\tau \ y_c(\tau)\right] \frac{V_c(t)}{V_c(0)} \tag{2.3.28}$$

Here we have adopted the notation of Chapter 1 that $E[\hat{V}_c(t)/V_c(0)] = V_c(t)/V_c(0)$. The random variable that corresponds to the return on the investment in the zero coupon bond after the time t is

$$\hat{r}_c = \left(\frac{\hat{V}_c(t)}{V_c(0)}\right) - 1 \tag{2.3.29}$$

Hence the expected or mean return on an investment in a zero coupon corporate bond with zero recovery fraction is

$$E[\hat{r}_c] = \frac{V_c(t)}{V_c(0)} - 1 = \exp\left[\int_0^t d\tau \ y_c(\tau)\right] P_S(t) - 1 \tag{2.3.30}$$

and the variance of the return is

$$\sigma_c^2 = E[(\hat{r}_c - E[\hat{r}_c])^2] = \exp\left[\int_0^t d\tau \, y_c(\tau)\right]\left(\frac{V_c(t)}{V_c(0)}\right) - \left(\frac{V_c(t)}{V_c(0)}\right)^2$$

$$= \exp\left[2\int_0^t d\tau \, y_c(\tau)\right] P_S(t) P_D(t) \quad (2.3.31)$$

The skewness of the probability distribution for corporate returns is

$$s = \frac{1}{\sigma_c^3} E\left[(\hat{r}_c - E[\hat{r}_c])^3\right] = \frac{1}{\sigma_c^3} \exp\left[3\int_0^t d\tau \, y_c(\tau)\right] P_S(t) P_D(t)[2P_D(t) - 1]$$

$$(2.3.32)$$

Using the result in Equation 2.3.31 for the variance, the skewness takes the simple form

$$s = \frac{2P_D(t) - 1}{\sqrt{P_S(t) P_D(t)}} \quad (2.3.33)$$

If the probability of default before the time t is small, then the skewness of the probability distribution is large in magnitude and negative. That is because typically no loss from default occurs, but when it does occur, the loss is catastrophic. In this case one can easily go beyond working with moments, since the whole probability distribution is known. There are only two possible values that the random return $\hat{r}_c$ can take depending on whether the firm defaults or not. So at time t its probability distribution is

$$\mathcal{P}(r_c) = P_S(t)\delta\left\{r_c - \exp\left[\int_0^t d\tau \, y_c(\tau)\right] + 1\right\} + P_D(t)\delta(r_c + 1)$$

$$(2.3.34)$$

where δ denotes the Dirac delta function.[2] The probability that $\hat{r}_c$ takes a value between r_c and $r_c + dr_c$ is $\mathcal{P}(r_c)\, dr_c$. Recall that the Dirac delta function $\delta(\tau)$ is defined to be zero for nonzero τ, but the integral of it over any interval that includes $\tau = 0$ is equal to unity. Obviously the Dirac delta function is not an ordinary function, but it can be defined as the limit of a sequence of ordinary functions. It was first introduced in quantum mechanics, where a probabilistic interpretation of the laws of physics is essential. We derive some of the properties of the Dirac delta function in Appendix 2 to this chapter. The second term in Equation 2.3.34 corresponds to the firm's defaulting, and in this case the return is -1, since the zero coupon corporate bond is worthless.

2.4   Correlated Random Variables

The correlation matrix ξ_{ij} of n random variables x_i, $i = 1, \ldots, n$ with volatilities σ_i and mean values $\bar{x}_i = E[x_i]$ is defined by

$$\xi_{ij} = \frac{E[(x_i - \bar{x}_i)(x_j - \bar{x}_j)]}{\sigma_i \sigma_j} \tag{2.4.35}$$

It is a symmetric matrix with 1s along the diagonal, and it can be diagonalized by an orthogonal transformation. The magnitude of the off-diagonal elements of the correlation matrix is less than or equal to unity. This follows from

$$E\left[\left(\frac{x_i - \bar{x}_i}{\sigma_i} \pm \frac{x_j - \bar{x}_j}{\sigma_i}\right)^2\right] = 1 + 1 \pm 2\xi_{ij} \geq 0 \tag{2.4.36}$$

---

[2] P. Dirac, *The Principles of Quantum Mechanics*, 4th ed. (Oxford: Clarendon Press, 1958).

The covariance matrix c_{ij} of the variables x_i is defined by

$$c_{ij} = E[(x_i - \bar{x}_i)(x_j - \bar{x}_j)] \tag{2.4.37}$$

This is also a symmetric positive definite matrix, but its diagonal elements are the variances of the x_i's, and the magnitude of its off-diagonal elements do not have to be less than unity.

A positive definite $n \times n$ matrix M is one that satisfies

$$\sum_{ij} w_i M_{ij} w_j = w^{\mathrm{T}} M w > 0 \tag{2.4.38}$$

where w is any nonzero n-dimensional vector with components w_i and the superscript T denotes the transpose. A correlation matrix ξ_{ij} is positive definite, since

$$\sum_{ij} w_i \xi_{ij} w_j = E\left[\left(\sum_i (x_i - \bar{x}_i) w_i / \sigma_i\right)^2\right] \tag{2.4.39}$$

Any positive real number can be written as the square of another real number. Similarly, a positive matrix M can be written as $M = vv^{\mathrm{T}}$, where the matrix v is not constrained to be positive. We do this for the correlation matrix, writing for the n^2 elements of ξ,

$$\xi_{ij} = \sum_{k=1}^{n} v_{ik} v_{jk} \tag{2.4.40}$$

It is convenient to view v_{ik} as the components of the n-dimensional vector v_i. The row index of v is labeling the vector, and the column index gives its components. These are unit vectors, since the diagonal components of M are equal to unity. The correlation matrix is invariant if we make an orthogonal transformation on the components of the vectors v_i,

$$v_{ik} \rightarrow \sum_{l=1}^{n} O_{kl} v_{il} \qquad (2.4.41)$$

where O is an orthogonal matrix, $O^{\mathrm{T}} O = 1$. Geometrically, O is a rotation matrix in the n-dimensional vector space. We can use the freedom to make a rotation to set the last $n-1$ components of v_1 equal to zero. After doing this, we can make another orthogonal transformation that leaves the last $n-1$ components of v_1 equal to zero and sets the last $n-2$ components of v_2 equal to zero, and so on. Then we parameterize the nonzero components of the unit vectors v_i in terms of cosines and sines of angles. For example, suppose $n = 2$. We use the freedom to make orthogonal transformations on the v's to write $v_{1k} = (1, 0)$ and $v_{2k} = (c_1, s_1)$, where $c_1 = \cos\theta_1$ and $s_1 = \sin\theta_1$. Performing the matrix multiplication, the correlation matrix has off-diagonal components $\xi_{12} = \xi_{21} = c_1$.

Next consider the case $n = 3$. Aligning the vectors v_i as outlined previously, we now need three angles, θ_1, θ_2, and θ_3, to parameterize their components. Using the notation $c_i = \cos\theta_i$, $s_i = \sin\theta_i$ and performing orthogonal transformations lets us write the components as

$$v_{1k} = (1, 0, 0)$$

$$v_{2k} = (c_1, s_1, 0)$$

$$v_{3k} = (c_2, s_2 c_3, s_2 s_3) \qquad (2.4.42)$$

Hence, we have the following parameterization for any 3×3 correlation matrix:

$$\xi = \begin{pmatrix} 1 & c_1 & c_2 \\ c_1 & 1 & c_1 c_2 + s_1 s_2 c_3 \\ c_2 & c_1 c_2 + s_1 s_2 c_3 & 1 \end{pmatrix} \qquad (2.4.43)$$

Let's do one more case explicitly before generalizing to $n \times n$ correlation matrices. For $n = 4$, we need six angles θ_i, $i = 1, \ldots, 6$, and using orthogonal transformations we write the components of the vectors v_i as

$$v_{1k} = (1, 0, 0, 0)$$

$$v_{2k} = (c_1, s_1, 0, 0)$$

$$v_{3k} = (c_2, s_2c_3, s_2s_3, 0)$$

$$v_{4k} = (c_4, s_4c_5, s_4s_5c_6, s_4s_5s_6) \qquad (2.4.44)$$

Any 4×4 correlation matrix can be written as

$$\xi = \begin{pmatrix} 1 & c_1 & c_2 & c_4 \\ c_1 & 1 & c_1c_2 + s_1s_2c_3 & c_1c_4 + s_1s_4c_5 \\ c_2 & c_1c_2 + s_1s_2c_3 & 1 & c_2c_4 + s_2s_4c_3c_5 + s_2s_3s_4s_5c_6 \\ c_4 & c_1c_4 + s_1s_4c_5 & c_2c_4 + s_2s_4c_3c_5 + s_2s_3s_4s_5c_6 & 1 \end{pmatrix}$$

$$(2.4.45)$$

It should now be clear how to generalize the parameterization of the vectors v_i to cases where $n > 4$. The jth vector has j nonzero components and requires $j - 1$ angles to specify it. So in total we need

$$\sum_{j=1}^{n}(j - 1) = \frac{n(n-1)}{2} \qquad (2.4.46)$$

angles θ_m to specify the vectors v_j and hence the $n \times n$ correlation matrix ξ. To write an explicit parameterization for the components v_{jk}, where $j, k = (1, \ldots, n)$, we introduce the quantity $x_j = (j - 1)$ $(j - 2)/2 + 1$, and the familiar notation $c_m = \cos \theta_m$, $s_m = \sin \theta_m$. For $j = 1$, we have that $v_{11} = 1$ and $v_{1k} = 0$ when $k > 1$. For $j > 1$,

$$v_{j1} = c_{x_j}$$

$$v_{jk} = \left(\prod_{m=0}^{k-2} s_{x_j+m}\right) c_{x_j+k-1} \qquad j > k > 1$$

$$v_{jj} = \prod_{m=0}^{j-2} s_{x_j+m}$$

$$v_{jk} = 0, \qquad k > j \tag{2.4.47}$$

This parameterization for the components v_{jk} can be useful when one is forecasting a correlation matrix, since it is guaranteed that the matrix $\xi = vv^{\mathrm{T}}$ is a consistent positive correlation matrix.

Correlated normal random variables have the joint probability distribution

$$\mathcal{P}(x_1, \cdots, x_n) = \frac{1}{(2\pi)^{\frac{n}{2}}\sqrt{\det c}} \exp\left[-\frac{1}{2}\sum_{ij}(x_i - \bar{x}_i)c_{ij}^{-1}(x_j - \bar{x}_j) \right]$$

$$\tag{2.4.48}$$

The normalization follows from the results in Appendix 1 of this chapter. Any linear combination z of correlated normal random variables is also a normal random variable, since it is always possible, by going to a basis of random variables where the covariance matrix is diagonal, to rewrite z as a sum of uncorrelated normal variables.

It is sometimes useful to introduce the generating function,

$$G(J_1, \ldots, J_n) = E\left[\exp\left(\sum_k J_k(x_k - \bar{x}_k) \right) \right] \tag{2.4.49}$$

Then, for example,

$$\left.\frac{\mathrm{d}^2 G(J_1, \ldots, J_n)}{dJ_i\, dJ_j}\right|_{J=0} = E[(x_i - \bar{x}_i)(x_j - \bar{x}_j)] \tag{2.4.50}$$

More derivatives of the generating function, with respect to the J_i, give expected values of products with more factors of $(x_i - \bar{x}_i)$.

Using the probability distribution in Equation 2.4.48, we can perform the integrations in Equation 2.4.49 by changing variables from x_i

to z_i, where

$$x_i - \bar{x}_i = z_i + \sum_j c_{ij} J_j \tag{2.4.51}$$

since then

$$\exp\left[-\frac{1}{2} \sum_{ij} (x_i - \bar{x}_i) c_{ij}^{-1} (x_j - \bar{x}_j) + \sum_k J_k (x_k - \bar{x}_k) \right]$$

$$= \exp\left(-\frac{1}{2} \sum_{ij} z_i c_{ij}^{-1} z_j \right) \exp\left(\frac{1}{2} \sum_{ij} J_i c_{ij} J_j \right) \tag{2.4.52}$$

Performing the integrations over the variables z_i yields

$$G(J_1, \ldots, J_n) = \exp\left(\frac{1}{2} \sum_{kl} J_k c_{kl} J_l \right) \tag{2.4.53}$$

For corporate bond investors, it is important to know the correlations of the random variables $\hat{n}_i(t)$ that take the value 1 if firm i defaults in the time horizon t and 0 otherwise. The joint default probabilities are expectations of products of these random variables,

$$P_D(i_1, \ldots, i_m; t) = E[\hat{n}_{i_1}(t) \cdots \hat{n}_{i_m}(t)] \quad \text{when } i_1 \neq i_2 \neq \cdots \neq i_m \tag{2.4.54}$$

$P_D(i_1; t)$ is the probability that firm i_1 defaults in the time period t, and $P_D(i_1, \ldots, i_m; t)$ is the joint probability that the m firms $i_1, \ldots, i_m$ default in the time period t.

The default correlation of firms i and j, $d_{ij}(t)$, is the correlation between the random variables $\hat{n}_i$ and $\hat{n}_j$. Since $\hat{n}_i^2 = \hat{n}_i$, it follows that $\sigma_i = \sqrt{E[\hat{n}_i] - E[\hat{n}_i]^2}$ and the default correlation of two different firms (which we choose to label 1 and 2) is

$$
\begin{aligned}
d_{12}(t) &= \frac{E[\hat{n}_1 \hat{n}_2] - E[\hat{n}_1]E[\hat{n}_2]}{\sqrt{(E[\hat{n}_1] - E[\hat{n}_1]^2)(E[\hat{n}_2] - E[n_2]^2)}} \\
&= \frac{P_D(1,2;t) - P_D(1;t)P_D(2;t)}{\sqrt{P_D(1;t)[1 - P_D(1;t)]P_D(2;t)[1 - P_D(2;t)]}}
\end{aligned}
\qquad (2.4.55)
$$

Typically default correlations are small and can be extracted from historical data on a sectorwide basis, for companies that are not investment grade.[3] Table 2.1 shows the one-year default correlations for non-investment-grade bonds during the period 1981–2001 for some of the sectors in the S&P.

Sector Default Correlation Table

	Auto	Cons	Ener	Fin	Chem	HiTec	Trans	Util
Auto	3.8%	1.3%	1.2%	0.4%	1.6%	2.8%	1.3%	0.5%
Cons	1.3%	2.8%	−1.4%	1.2%	1.6%	1.8%	2.7%	1.9%
Ener	1.2%	−1.4%	6.4%	−2.5%	0.4%	−0.1%	−0.1%	0.7%
Fin	0.4%	1.2%	−2.5%	5.2%	0.1%	0.4%	1.5%	4.5%
Chem	1.6%	1.6%	0.4%	0.1%	3.2%	1.4%	1.1%	1.0%
HiTec	2.8%	1.8%	−0.1%	0.4%	1.4%	3.3%	1.9%	1.0%
Trans	1.3%	2.7%	−0.1%	1.5%	1.1%	1.9%	4.3%	−0.2%
Util	0.5%	1.9%	0.7%	4.5%	1.0%	1.0%	−0.2%	9.4%

Table 2.1 One-year default sector correlations for non-investment-grade bonds. The notation used for the S&P sectors considered is: Auto = aerospace/automotive/capital goods; Cons = consumer/service sector; Ener = energy and natural resources; Fin = financial institutions; Chem = health care/chemicals; HiTec = high-technology/computers/office equipment; Trans = transportation; Util = utility. This table is part of a table that appeared in A. de Servigny, "Correlation Evidence," *Risk Magazine*, 90, July 2003.

---

[3]Investment-grade companies default so infrequently that extraction of their default correlations from historical data is not possible.

The auto-auto correlation of 3.8 percent, for example, is the typical correlation between any two different firms in that sector. Some of the signs of the sector correlations are easy to understand. For example, one expects a negative correlation between the energy sector and the consumer sector because high energy prices diminish consumer spending.

A very convenient way to model joint default probabilities is to use what is called a *multivariate normal copula function*. This amounts to setting the joint default probabilities[4]

$$P_D(i_1, \ldots, i_n; t_1, \ldots, t_n) = E[\hat{n}_{i_1}(t_1) \cdots \hat{n}_{i_n}(t_n)] \qquad (2.4.56)$$

to the joint cumulative normal,

$$P_D(1, \ldots, n; t_1, \ldots, t_n) = \frac{1}{(2\pi)^{\frac{n}{2}}\sqrt{\det \xi}} \int_{-\infty}^{\chi_1(t_1)} dx_1 \cdots \int_{-\infty}^{\chi_n(t_n)} dx_n$$

$$\times \exp\left(-\frac{1}{2}\sum_{ij} x_i \xi_{ij}^{(-1)} x_j\right) \qquad (2.4.57)$$

where the sum goes over $i, j = 1, \ldots, n$, and $\xi_{ij}^{(-1)}$ is the inverse of the $n \times n$ correlation matrix ξ_{ij}. The functions $\chi_i(t_i)$ are determined by the single-firm default probabilities. Since default probabilities go to unity as the time interval goes to infinity, we want $\chi_i(t_i) \to \infty$ as $t_i \to \infty$.

The motivation for this approach is to suppose that company i defaults in time t_i if some economic factor x_i fluctuates below a threshold $\chi_i(t_i)$. Assuming that the probability distribution for the factors x_i is given by a multivariate normal distribution results in Equation 2.4.57. Note that we have expressed the joint probability distribution in terms of the correlation matrix instead of the covariance matrix. We can switch back to the covariance matrix expression by changing the factors x_i to $\sigma_i x_i$.

---

[4]Note that we are generalizing the previous definition of joint default probabilities to one where the time intervals in which the corporations must default are different.

Equation 2.4.57 gives, for the case $n = 1$,

$$P_D(i; t_i) = \frac{1}{(2\pi)^{\frac{1}{2}}} \int_{-\infty}^{\chi_i(t_i)} dx_i \, \exp\left(-\frac{1}{2} x_i^2\right) \qquad (2.4.58)$$

Hence for an explicit choice for the time dependence of the single-firm default probabilities, the limits of integration in Equation 2.4.57 are known. A simple and often used model for the default probabilities is the constant-hazard-rate assumption introduced in Chapter 1. Then

$$P_D(i; t_i) = 1 - \exp\left(-h_i t_i\right) \qquad (2.4.59)$$

where the hazard rates h_i are independent of time. Unfortunately, there isn't a very good economic motivation for the constant-hazard-rate model or the use of a multivariate normal copula function to model joint default probabilities. It is an attractive approach partly because it is very easy to use.

2.5   Random Walks

Suppose a particle moves on the real line in discrete steps that occur in time intervals of length Δt. The particle starts at the origin, and at each step it has a 50 percent probability of increasing its position by an amount of magnitude ϵ and a 50 percent probability of decreasing its position by an amount of magnitude ϵ. Such a motion is called a *random walk*. Let x_N denote its position after N steps. If $\hat{\epsilon}$ is a random variable that takes on the values $\pm\epsilon$, each with probability $1/2$, then

$$E[x_N^2] = E[(x_{N-1} + \hat{\epsilon})^2] = E[x_{N-1}^2] + 2E[x_{N-1}]E[\hat{\epsilon}] + E[\hat{\epsilon}^2]$$
$$= E[x_{N-1}^2] + \epsilon^2 \qquad (2.5.60)$$

This recursion relation is satisfied by $E[x_N^2] = N\epsilon^2$. Setting $N\Delta t = t$, and writing $x_N = x(t)$, we get a smooth limit as $\Delta t \to 0$ provided $\epsilon^2 \propto \Delta t$. Hence, for a random walk, $E[x(t)^2] \propto t$. Furthermore, after a large number of steps, the central limit theorem implies that $x(t)$ becomes a normal random variable, since it is the sum of many independent random steps. In finance, random variables, e.g., the logarithm of stock prices, that evolve in time are sometimes taken to undergo a random walk (after a drift term is subtracted).

Let $w(t)$ denote a random variable that has initial value zero and undergoes a random walk in time. For a random walking variable, the net excursion it makes grows not linearly with time but rather as the square root of time. Hence, in an infinitesimal time interval[5] dt, we take the change in the variable w, $dw(t)$, to be normally distributed about zero with a volatility $\sqrt{dt}$. The average (i.e., expectation) value of $dw(t)$ is zero, $E[dw(t)] = 0$; however, $dw(t)^2$ has the nonzero expectation value

$$E[dw(t)^2] = dt \qquad (2.5.61)$$

For a random walk, the changes dw that occur in different time intervals are uncorrelated, and so

$$E[dw(t)dw(t')] = E[dw(t)]E[dw(t')] = 0 \qquad t \neq t' \qquad (2.5.62)$$

We can combine Equations 2.5.61 and 2.5.62 into a single equation using the Dirac delta function:

$$E\left[\frac{dw(t)}{dt}\frac{dw(t')}{dt'}\right] = \delta(t - t') \qquad (2.5.63)$$

where $\delta(\tau)$ is a Dirac delta function of τ. Recall that a linear combination of normal variables is a normal variable. Then, since $w(t)$ is a linear combination of the normal changes dw,

$$w(t) = \int_0^t dw(\tau) = \int_0^t d\tau \left(\frac{dw(\tau)}{d\tau}\right) \qquad (2.5.64)$$

---

[5] Even though dt is infinitesimal, it contains many steps in the random walk.

it is also normally distributed. The expected value $E[w(t)] = 0$, but the values of $w(t)$ at different times are correlated,

$$E[w(t)w(t')] = \int_0^t d\tau \int_0^{t'} d\tau' E\left[\frac{dw(\tau)}{d\tau}\frac{dw(\tau')}{d\tau'}\right]$$

$$= \int_0^t d\tau \int_0^{t'} d\tau' \, \delta(\tau - \tau') \qquad (2.5.65)$$

For $t > t'$, the variable τ' is always in the region of integration for τ, and so performing the τ integration first gives unity and

$$E[w(t)w(t')] = \int_0^{t'} d\tau' = t' \qquad (2.5.66)$$

Using a similar calculation for $t' > t$, we arrive at

$$E[w(t)w(t')] = \theta(t - t')t' + \theta(t' - t)t \qquad (2.5.67)$$

where $\theta(\tau)$ is the step function equal to unity for $\tau > 0$, zero for $\tau < 0$, and $1/2$ for $\tau = 0$.

At any given time there is a probability that $w(t)$ will take a value between w and $w + dw$. We denote that probability by $p_0(w, t)\, dw$. Now consider the probability density p_0 at a later time $t + dt$. The variable $w(t + dt)$ arrived at w by random walking from some other value $w - dw$ in the time dt, and so

$$p_0(w, t + dt) = E[p_0(w - dw, t)] = p_0(w, t) - E[dw]\frac{\partial p_0(w, t)}{\partial w}$$

$$+ \frac{1}{2}E[dw^2]\frac{\partial^2 p_0(w, t)}{\partial w^2} + \cdots \qquad (2.5.68)$$

where we expanded $E[p_0(w - dw, t)]$ in a power series in dw. Expanding the left-hand side of the equation in powers of dt, using $E[dw] = 0$ and $E[dw^2] = dt$, and equating terms linear in dt, we arrive at the differential equation

$$\frac{\partial p_0(w, t)}{\partial t} - \frac{1}{2} \frac{\partial^2 p_0(w, t)}{\partial w^2} = 0 \qquad (2.5.69)$$

The solution to this equation is not unique. For example, $p_0(w, t) = w$ solves it. To get the solution that corresponds to the probability density, we impose an initial condition in time and a boundary condition at $w = \pm\infty$. Since $w(0) = 0$ at time $t = 0$, the probability density must satisfy $p_0(w, 0) = \delta(w)$. At any finite time, w cannot have random walked all the way to $w = \pm\infty$, and hence the boundary conditions $p_0(\pm\infty, t) = 0$ are imposed. We now show that the solution to the differential equation that satisfies these boundary conditions is

$$p_0(w, t) = \frac{1}{\sqrt{2\pi t}} \exp\left(-\frac{w^2}{2t}\right) \qquad (2.5.70)$$

Differentiating this equation with respect to t gives

$$\frac{\partial p_0(w, t)}{\partial t} = \frac{1}{\sqrt{2\pi t}} \exp\left(-\frac{w^2}{2t}\right)\left(-\frac{1}{2t} + \frac{w^2}{2t^2}\right) \qquad (2.5.71)$$

Differentiating with respect to w gives

$$\frac{\partial p_0(w, t)}{\partial w} = \frac{1}{\sqrt{2\pi t}} \exp\left(-\frac{w^2}{2t}\right)\left(-\frac{w}{t}\right) \qquad (2.5.72)$$

and performing one more derivative with respect to w yields

$$\frac{\partial^2 p_0(w, t)}{\partial w^2} = \frac{1}{\sqrt{2\pi t}} \exp\left(-\frac{w^2}{2t}\right)\left(\frac{w^2}{t^2} - \frac{1}{t}\right) \qquad (2.5.73)$$

Comparing Equations 2.5.71 and 2.5.73, we see that $p_0(w, t)$ in Equation 2.5.70 does satisfy the partial differential equation in Equation 2.5.69.

Next consider the evolution

$$dz = \mu \, dt + \sigma \, dw \qquad (2.5.74)$$

where w is the familiar random walk we have just discussed and the volatility σ and drift μ are constants. Denote by $p(z, t) \, dz$ the probability that at time t, $z(t)$ is between z and $z + dz$. Since $w(t) = [z(t) - z(0) - \mu t]/\sigma$, we have that $p(z, t) \, dz = p_0(w, t) \, dw$. Using the fixed time relation $dz = \sigma \, dw$, we arrive at the formula

$$p(z, t) = \frac{1}{\sqrt{2\pi\sigma^2 t}} \exp\left(-\frac{[z - z(0) - \mu t]^2}{2\sigma^2 t}\right) \qquad (2.5.75)$$

In this case, the differential equation that the probability density satisfies can be derived by expanding the condition $p(z, t + dt) = E[p(z - \mu \, dt - \sigma \, dw, t)]$ to linear order in dt, and it yields

$$\frac{\partial p(z, t)}{\partial t} + \mu \frac{\partial p(z, t)}{\partial z} - \frac{1}{2}\sigma^2 \frac{\partial^2 p(z, t)}{\partial z^2} = 0 \qquad (2.5.76)$$

A random variable $z(t)$ is called a *martingale* if $E[dz] = 0$. With the evolution in Equation 2.5.74, the random variable $z(t)$ is a martingale when the drift $\mu = 0$.

So far we have considered a variance σ^2 that is constant in time. In fact, we can generalize this discussion to a time-dependent variance $\sigma^2(t)$. To make things simple, we set the drift to $\mu = 0$. Notice that when the drift is zero, the probability density $p(z, t)$ for the constant-volatility case given in Equation 2.5.75 has the volatility and time always occurring in the combination $\sigma^2 t$. Introduce the quantity

$$\xi(t) = \int_0^t dt \, \sigma^2(\tau) \qquad (2.5.77)$$

and consider the probability density

$$\bar{p}(z, \xi) = p[z, \xi(t)]|_{\sigma=1} \qquad (2.5.78)$$

that has time replaced by this variable and the volatility set to unity. Given Equation 2.5.69, clearly

$$\frac{\partial \bar{p}(z, \xi)}{\partial \xi} - \frac{1}{2} \frac{\partial^2 \bar{p}(z, \xi)}{\partial z^2} = 0 \qquad (2.5.79)$$

But $d\xi/dt = \sigma^2(t)$, and so, using the chain rule, we find that

$$\frac{\partial \bar{p}[z, \xi(t)]}{\partial t} - \frac{\sigma^2(t)}{2} \frac{\partial^2 \bar{p}[z, \xi(t)]}{\partial z^2} = 0 \qquad (2.5.80)$$

Note that this is the differential equation that we want the probability density to satisfy when the variance is time-dependent. It follows that in the case where the volatility is time-dependent, we get the correct probability density by taking the probability density when the volatility is constant and replacing that constant variance with its time-averaged value, $\sigma^2 \to \sigma_{avg}^2(t)$, where

$$\sigma_{avg}^2(t) = \frac{1}{t} \int_0^t d\tau\, \sigma^2(\tau) \qquad (2.5.81)$$

The final generalization we consider in this section has constant σ but allows the drift μ to depend on both z and t. In other words, we consider the evolution

$$dz = \mu(z, t)\, dt + \sigma\, dw \qquad (2.5.82)$$

An easy way to find the differential equation that the probability distribution solves in this case is to consider the limit where $\sigma = 0$, and then afterward add in the effect of the volatility. With $\sigma = 0$, we can integrate the differential equation for z, giving the solution $z = a(t)$. The function $a(t)$ satisfies the initial condition $a(0) = z(0)$ and

$$\frac{da}{dt} = \mu[a(t), t] \qquad (2.5.83)$$

Since the path is fixed, the probability distribution for z is $p(z, t) = \delta[z - a(t)]$. Differentiating with respect to time,

$$\frac{\partial}{\partial t} p(z, t) = -\left(\frac{da(t)}{dt}\right) \frac{\partial}{\partial z} \delta[z - a(t)] = -\mu[a(t), t] \frac{\partial}{\partial z} \delta[z - a(t)]$$

$$(2.5.84)$$

Consider the quantity

$$Q(z) = \frac{\partial p(z, t)}{\partial t} + \frac{\partial[\mu(z, t) p(z, t)]}{\partial z} \qquad (2.5.85)$$

Integrating $Q(z)$ against an arbitrary smooth function $f(z)$,

$$\int dz \ f(z) Q(z) = \int dz \ f(z) \left(-\mu[a(t), t] \frac{\partial}{\partial z} \delta[z - a(t)] + \frac{\partial}{\partial z} \left\{\mu(z, t) \delta[z - a(t)]\right\}\right)$$

$$(2.5.86)$$

Integrating by parts and performing the z integration using the delta function gives

$$\int dz \ f(z) Q(z) = f'[a(t)] \left\{\mu[a(t), t] - \mu[a(t), t]\right\} = 0 \quad (2.5.87)$$

where the prime denotes the derivative of the function f with respect to its argument. Since this equation is zero for arbitrary functions f, we conclude that $Q(z) = 0$. This is the differential equation that the probability distribution solves when $\sigma = 0$. Adding in the effects of the volatility in the standard way gives

$$\frac{\partial p(z, t)}{\partial t} + \frac{\partial[\mu(z, t) p(z, t)]}{\partial z} - \frac{1}{2}\sigma^2 \frac{\partial^2 p(z, t)}{\partial z^2}$$

$$= \frac{\partial p(z, t)}{\partial t} + \mu(z, t)\frac{\partial[p(z, t)]}{\partial z} + \frac{\partial[\mu(z, t)]}{\partial z} p(z, t) - \frac{1}{2}\sigma^2 \frac{\partial^2 p(z, t)}{\partial z^2} = 0$$

$$(2.5.88)$$

Note that Equation 2.5.88 contains not only a term where μ multiplies the derivative with respect to z of the probability distribution p but also a term where the probability distribution multiplies the derivative with respect to z of the drift μ.

2.6 Survival Probabilities

Suppose a random variable $z(t)$ evolves in time according to Equation 2.5.74 and has the initial value $z(0) = z_0$. We have already shown that the probability that it lies in the interval between z and $z + dz$ at the time t is determined by the probability density

$$p(z;t) = \frac{1}{\sqrt{2\pi\sigma^2 t}} \exp\left(-\frac{(z - \mu t - z_0)^2}{2\sigma^2 t}\right) \qquad (2.6.89)$$

In this section we are interested in the probability that z lies in the interval between z and $z + dz$ and has never touched the threshold $z = z^*$ before time t. One can think of the line $z = z^*$ as a barrier. If the random variable $z(t)$ hits the barrier at some time t, it is terminated and does not survive to propagate further in time. Let $p_S(z;t)\,dz$ be the probability that $z(t)$ does not touch the barrier at $z = z^*$ before the time t and lies in the interval $[z, z + dz]$ at the time t. Clearly $p_S(z, t)$ obeys the same differential equation as $p(z, t)$. To be concrete, let's imagine that the initial value z_0 is above the barrier z^*. Then it is only the region $z > z^*$ that is relevant. In addition to the initial condition $p_S(z, 0) = \delta(z - z_0)$, for $z > z^*$, and the boundary condition as $|z| \to \infty$ at finite t, the survival probability density must obey the boundary condition $p_S(z^*, t) = 0$. We can easily solve this problem using the method of images, which is used in physics to solve boundary-value problems in electrodynamics. Suppose the drift was zero and imagine an image random walking variable that has the same time evolution equation as z but starts off at the point $2z^* - z_0$. At any time t, it has the same probability of hitting the barrier as the original random walking variable. Hence, a solution for the survival probability density when $\mu = 0$ is

$$p_S(z;t) = \frac{1}{\sqrt{2\pi\sigma^2 t}}\left[\exp\left(-\frac{(z-z_0)^2}{2\sigma^2 t}\right) - \exp\left(-\frac{(z+z_0-2z^*)^2}{2\sigma^2 t}\right)\right] \quad (2.6.90)$$

We want to be able to solve the problem with a drift. Equation 2.6.90 solves the differential equation by replacing the variable z with $z - \mu t$. The drift breaks the symmetry, and so the cancellation is not perfect. It is easy to see that the cancellation can be restored by multiplying the image term by the factor $\exp\left[2\mu(z^* - z_0)/\sigma^2\right]$. Hence the solution including the drift is

$$p_S(z;t) = \frac{1}{\sqrt{2\pi\sigma^2 t}}\left[\exp\left(-\frac{(z-\mu t-z_0)^2}{2\sigma^2 t}\right) - \exp\left(\frac{2\mu(z^*-z_0)}{\sigma^2}\right)\right.$$

$$\left. \times\ \exp\left(-\frac{(z-\mu t+z_0-2z^*)^2}{2\sigma^2 t}\right)\right] \quad (2.6.91)$$

Notice that $p_S(z;t)$ satisfies the initial condition

$$p_S(z;0) = \delta(z-z_0) - \exp\left(\frac{2\mu(z^*-z_0)}{\sigma^2}\right)\delta(z-2z^*+z_0) \quad (2.6.92)$$

However, the argument of the second delta function is never zero for $z > z^*$, and so in the region of interest, it does not contribute to the initial condition. The probability of the variable z surviving to the time t without hitting the barrier is

$$P_S(t) = \int_{z^*}^{\infty} dz\, p_S(z;t) \quad (2.6.93)$$

The integration over z gives

$$P_S(t) = \Phi\left(\frac{\mu t + (z_0 - z^*)}{\sqrt{\sigma^2 t}}\right) - e^{2\mu(z^*-z_0)/\sigma^2}\Phi\left(\frac{\mu t - (z_0 - z^*)}{\sqrt{\sigma^2 t}}\right)$$

$$(2.6.94)$$

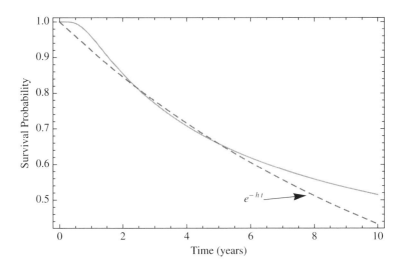

Figure 2.1 Random walk with a barrier survival probability $P_S(t)$ plotted as a function of time t in years using $\mu = 0.01$, $z_0 - z_* = 0.5$, and $\sigma = 0.25$, and hazard-rate survival probability plotted as a function of t in years using $h = 0.0837$.

where the cumulative normal function Φ is defined by

$$\Phi(z) \equiv \frac{1}{\sqrt{2\pi}} \int_{-\infty}^{z} dx\, e^{-x^2/2} \tag{2.6.95}$$

Note that $\Phi(\infty) = 1$, $\Phi(-\infty) = 0$, and $\Phi(z) + \Phi(-z) = 1$.

Equation 2.6.94 can be used to compute the corporate survival probabilities[6] that are used to price corporate bonds. In that case the random walking variable z is the logarithm of the firm value, and the default threshold z_* is set by the amount of corporate debt.

In Figure 2.1 we plot the survival probability $P_S(t)$ as a function of time in years for the case where $\mu = 0.01$, $z_0 - z_* = 0.5$, and $\sigma = 0.25$. For small times, the survival probability is very close to unity, since

---

[6]We will use a model similar to this in the next chapter.

the random walking variable has not had time to fluctuate below the default barrier. With these parameters, the five-year survival probability is 65.81 percent.

In Figure 2.1 we also plot the hazard-rate survival probability $P_S(t) = \exp(-ht)$ with the hazard rate taken to be $h = 0.0837$. With this value, the five-year survival probabilities coincide in the two models. However, in the hazard-rate model, the one-year survival probability is about 92 percent, while Equation 2.6.94 with the same parameters as in Figure 2.1 gives a survival probability of about 96 percent. The hazard-rate and random walk models also give very different survival probabilities at large times. For example, the 20-year survival probability in the hazard-rate model ($h = 0.0837$) is $P_S(20 \text{ years}) \simeq 19$ percent, while the random walk with a barrier model gives (using the same parameters as in Figure 2.1) $P_S(20 \text{ years}) \simeq 40$ percent.

The value of the drift μ has an important impact on the survival probability. In Figure 2.2 we plot the survival probability as a function of time using the same parameters as in Figure 2.1, but with the drift equal

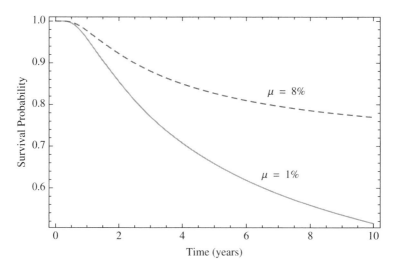

Figure 2.2 Survival probability $P_S(t)$ plotted as a function of time t in years using $z_0 - z_* = 0.5$, $\sigma = 0.25$, and both $\mu = 8$ percent and $\mu = 1$ percent.

to both $\mu = 1$ percent and $\mu = 8$ percent. The survival probability with $\mu = 8$ percent is much larger than with $\mu = 1$ percent because the larger drift helps keep the random walking variable above the threshold.

2.7   Lognormal Variables

Sometimes variables that can take on only positive values are taken to evolve according to the evolution formula

$$\frac{dz}{z} = \mu\, dt + \sigma\, dw \qquad (2.7.96)$$

This differs from the usual random walk formula by the factor of z in the denominator on the left-hand side. Multiplying both sides of the equation by z, we note that if z starts off positive, it will stay positive, since for very small z the changes in z are very small. We can convert this into the usual random walk formula by introducing the variable $z' = \log z$. Working to linear order in dt, we have that

$$dz' = \log\,(z + dz) - \log z = \frac{dz}{z} - \frac{1}{2}\frac{(dz)^2}{z^2} = \mu\, dt + \sigma\, dw - \frac{\sigma^2}{2}dt$$

$$(2.7.97)$$

The variable z' obeys the usual random walk formula, but with a drift $\mu' = \mu - \sigma^2/2$. This change in the drift arises because dw is of order $\sqrt{dt}$. The variable z' is normally distributed, and the variable z is said to have a lognormal probability distribution.

2.8   Mean-Reverting Random Walks

For the simple random walk with a drift $dy = \mu\, dt + \sigma\, dw$ and initial condition $y(0) = y_i$, the variable y has a mean value $E[y(t)] = y_i + \mu t$ and variance $E[\{y(t) - E[y(t)]\}^2] = \sigma^2 t$. Suppose we want to use this simple model for the Treasury short rate $y(t)$. This model has the nice feature that the changes that occur in the short rate $dy(t)$ as one moves forward in time do not depend on the short rate's values at times less than t. However, a number of issues are encountered. First (apart from times of extreme risk aversion), the Treasury short rate should not be less than zero, whereas the random walk allows for negative y. If the probability of fluctuating to negative y is very small, then, in practice, this is not a concern.[7] More important is the fact that the mean value and variance grow with time. This is not a feature that one would want for the short rate. An extension of the random walk plus drift model that cures this problem is the one-factor Vasicek interest-rate model[8]

$$dy = \alpha(\gamma - y)\, dt + \sigma\, dw \qquad (2.8.98)$$

with α a positive number. If y is less than γ, then the coefficient of dt is positive, and so the drift term increases the value of y. On the other hand, if y is greater than γ, then the coefficient of dt is negative and the drift term decreases the value of y. So for long times, y should approach γ in this model. We can convert this evolution equation into a standard drift plus random walk evolution by the change of variables

$$y = e^{-\alpha t} z \qquad (2.8.99)$$

Since

$$dy = -\alpha y + e^{-\alpha t}\, dz \qquad (2.8.100)$$

we have the following evolution for z:

$$dz = e^{\alpha t}\, (\alpha\gamma\, dt + \sigma\, dw) \qquad (2.8.101)$$

---

[7] Another option is to use a lognormal variable for the short rate.
[8] O. Vasicek, "An Equilibrium Characterisation of the Term Structure," *Journal of Financial Economics* 5, (1977): 177.

Integrating this equation gives

$$z(t) = z(0) + \gamma \left(e^{\alpha t} - 1\right) + \sigma \int_0^t e^{\alpha \tau} \, dw(\tau) \qquad (2.8.102)$$

and hence

$$y(t) = e^{-\alpha t} y(0) + \gamma \left(1 - e^{-\alpha t}\right) + \sigma e^{-\alpha t} \int_0^t e^{\alpha \tau} \, dw(\tau) \qquad (2.8.103)$$

where we have used $z(0) = y(0)$. It follows that the mean value of $y(t)$ is

$$E[y(t)] = e^{-\alpha t} y(0) + \gamma \left(1 - e^{-\alpha t}\right) \qquad (2.8.104)$$

Clearly for large times, $E[y(t)]$ approaches γ. The variance of $y(t)$ is

$$E\left[\{y(t) - E[y(t)]\}^2\right] = \sigma^2 e^{-2\alpha t} \int_0^t d\tau \int_0^t d\tau' e^{\alpha \tau} e^{\alpha \tau'} E\left[\frac{dw(\tau)}{d\tau} \frac{dw(\tau')}{d\tau'}\right]$$

$$= \sigma^2 e^{-2\alpha t} \int_0^t d\tau \, e^{2\alpha \tau} = \frac{\sigma^2}{2\alpha} \left(1 - e^{-2\alpha t}\right)$$

$$(2.8.105)$$

where we have made use of Equation 2.5.63 to convert the integrals of τ and τ' to a single integral over τ. Now the variance of $y(t)$ approaches the constant $\sigma^2/(2\alpha)$ for large times.

2.9   Correlated Random Walks

Next we consider a collection of n random walking variables z_i that obey the stochastic evolution equation

$$dz_i = \mu_i \, dt + \sum_{j=1}^{n} \sigma_{ij} \, dw_j \qquad (2.9.106)$$

where w_i are standard independent Brownian motions, i.e.,

$$E[dw_i\, dw_j] = dt\, \delta_{ij} \tag{2.9.107}$$

Define the covariance matrix c_{ij} by

$$E[(dz_i - E[dz_i])(dz_j - E[dz_j])] = c_{ij}\, dt \tag{2.9.108}$$

Equations 2.9.106 and 2.9.107 imply that

$$c_{ij} = \sum_{k=1}^{n} \sigma_{ik}\sigma_{jk} \tag{2.9.109}$$

The associated volatilities are

$$\sigma_i = \sqrt{\sum_{k=1}^{n} \sigma_{ik}\sigma_{ik}} \tag{2.9.110}$$

and the corresponding correlation matrix is

$$\xi_{ij} = \frac{1}{\sigma_i\sigma_j} \sum_{k=1}^{n} \sigma_{ik}\sigma_{jk} \tag{2.9.111}$$

Let $p(z_1, \ldots, z_n; t)\, dz_1 \cdots dz_n$ be the joint probability that at t each z_i is in the interval $[z_i, z_i + dz_i]$. Using the same methods as before, we can show that this probability distribution obeys the differential equation

$$\left(\frac{\partial}{\partial t} + \sum_i \mu_i \frac{\partial}{\partial z_i} - \frac{1}{2} \sum_{i,j} c_{ij} \frac{\partial^2}{\partial z_i \partial z_j} \right) p(z_1, \ldots, z_n; t) = 0 \tag{2.9.112}$$

Given what we have already done, it is not difficult to guess that the solution to this differential equation with the appropriate initial and boundary conditions is

$$p(z_1, \ldots, z_n; t) = \frac{1}{(2\pi t)^{\frac{n}{2}} \sqrt{\det c}}$$

$$\times \exp\left(-\frac{1}{2} \sum_{i,j} \frac{[z_i - \mu_i t - z_i(0)]c_{ij}^{-1}[z_j - \mu_j t - z_j(0)]}{t}\right) \quad (2.9.113)$$

We can define joint survival probabilities as before, assuming that each variable z_i survives to time t if it does not fall below a barrier at z_i^*. For correlated random walks, no analytic solution to this problem is known in general. For two firms, an expression for the joint survival probability $P_S(1, 2; t)$ has been derived. If the off-diagonal elements of the correlation matrix ξ are small, then one can express the joint survival probabilities for several firms in terms of the two-firm joint survival probability.

2.10 Simulation

In many practical situations, it is impossible to value the price of securities in closed form. There might be securities that pay off based on the particular realization of the value of an asset, or on whether one or more of the assets hits trigger or barrier levels, or on some sort of smoothing (such as averaging) of asset returns. Furthermore, for risk management purposes, it is important to know the dependence of security prices on input parameters, and this also may not be available in closed form. A general-purpose numerical approach is to use what is called a Monte Carlo simulation. Basically the algorithm is as follows:

- Write down the stochastic process for the assets.
- Generate random numbers using a random number generator from the distribution.
- Generate many such paths and store them.

- Numerically compute the payoff function on the stored paths.
- Average the discounted present value of the payoff function on the paths to get the price.
- Change the initial parameters, and run the simulations all over again with the same stored paths to compute the sensitivities of the security to the parameters.

Suppose for the stochastic process we take the Vasicek interest-rate model for the short Treasury rate y,

$$dy = \alpha(\gamma - y)\, dt + \sigma\, dw \qquad (2.10.114)$$

Using discrete times separated by the interval Δt, we can write this as

$$y_{t+\Delta t} = y_t + \Delta y = y_t + \alpha(\gamma - y)\Delta t + \sigma \hat{z}\sqrt{\Delta t}$$

$$(2.10.115)$$

where $\hat{z}$ is a normal random variable with mean zero and variance unity. We can simulate this using the following Mathematica codelet.

```
random[mu_, sigma_] := Random[NormalDistribution
  [mu, sigma]];
deltay[alpha_, gamma_, y_, sigma_, deltaT_] :=
alpha*(gamma - y)*deltaT +
sigma*random[0, 1]*Sqrt[deltaT]
shortrate[alpha_, gamma_, y_, sigma_, deltaT_] :=
y + deltay[alpha, gamma,y, sigma, deltaT]
```

To run a single path of 3,000 steps where $\Delta t = 0.01$ year, we seed the random number generator (to be able to replicate the paths), specify the initial conditions and values for the parameters [mean reversion parameter $\alpha = 0.1$, long-term target rate $\gamma = 0.065$, volatility $\sigma = 0.01$, and starting short rate $y(0) = 0.04$], and call the function pathsample to generate one path:

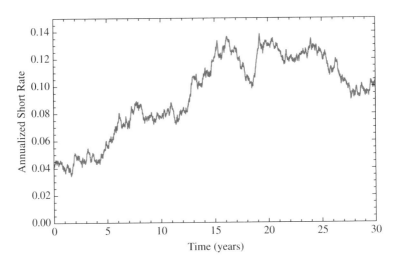

Figure 2.3 Sample short-rate path with mean reversion term giving a long-term target rate of 6.5 percent. The vertical axis is *y*, and the horizontal axis is time.

```
SeedRandom[10]
pathsample = NestList[shortrate[0.1,0.065,#,0.01,
  0.01]&,0.04,3000];
```

A sample path is plotted in Figure 2.3.

The following Mathematica codelet returns a list of points $\{t, E[y(t)]\}$, where $E[y(t)]$ is the average short rate gotten from averaging over nPaths random walk paths and *t* ranges from $t = 0$ to $t = n$ years with time steps of size deltaT years. This codelet requires the definition for shortrate[ ] in the previous codelet.

```
avgShortRate[nPaths_, alpha_, sigma_, y0_, gamma_,
  deltaT_, nYears_] :=
  Module[{n = 1,nMax = nPaths,avg,nSteps =
  Floor[nYears/deltaT]},
SeedRandom[n];
avg = NestList[shortrate[alpha,gamma,#,sigma,
  deltaT] &,y0,nSteps]/nMax;
```

```
n = 2;
 While[n <= nMax,
 SeedRandom[n];
 avg += (NestList[shortrate[alpha,gamma,#,sigma,
  deltaT]&,y0,nSteps]/nMax);
  n = n+1];
 Transpose[{Table[x,{x,0,nYears,deltaT}],avg}]
 ]
```

A similar codelet can be used to calculate $E\left[\{y(t) - E[y(t)]\}^2\right]$.

Using the same parameters as Figure 2.3, Figures 2.4 and 2.5 show $E[y(t)]$ calculated using, respectively, 1,000 and 10,000 paths. The smooth curve is the analytic result in Equation 2.8.104, and the other curve is the result of the simulation. We can clearly see the convergence as the number of paths that are averaged over increases. Similarly, Figures 2.6 and 2.7 show $E\left[\{y(t) - E[y(t)]\}^2\right]$ calculated using, respectively, 1,000 and 10,000 paths.

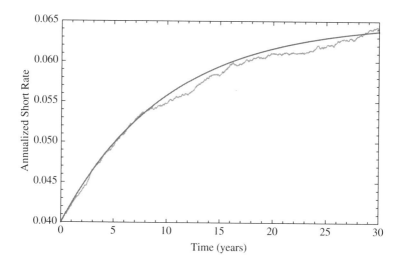

Figure 2.4 Expected short rate $E[y(t)]$ as a function of t using 1,000 interest-rate paths. The smooth curve is the analytic result in Equation 2.8.104.

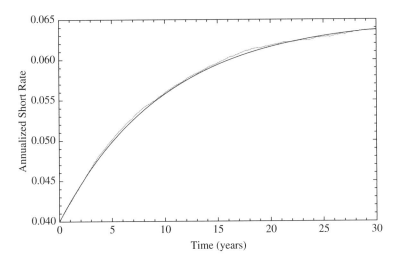

Figure 2.5 Expected short rate $E[y(T)]$ as a function of t using 10,000 interest-rate paths. The smooth curve is the analytic result in Equation 2.8.104.

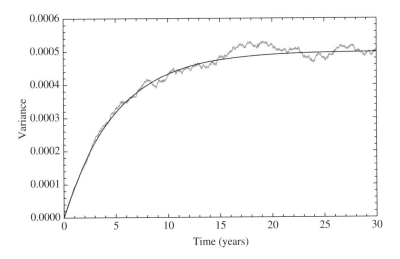

Figure 2.6 Expected variance $E[\{y(t) - E[y(t)]\}^2]$ as a function of t using 1,000 interest-rate paths. The smooth curve is the analytic result in Equation 2.8.105.

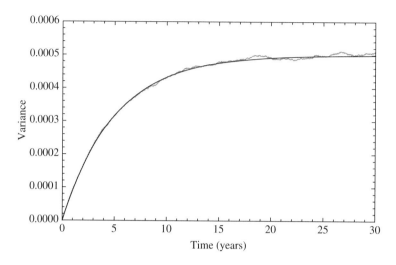

Figure 2.7   Expected variance $E\left[\{y(t) - E[y(t)]\}^2\right]$ as a function of t using 10,000 interest-rate paths. The smooth curve is the analytic result in Equation 2.8.105.

2.11   Appendix 1: Gaussian Integrals

In this appendix, we evaluate some of the definite integrals used in the chapter. First consider

$$I(a) = \int_{-\infty}^{\infty} dx \, \exp\left(-ax^2\right) \qquad (2.11.116)$$

The square of this integral is

$$I(a)^2 = \int_{-\infty}^{\infty} dx_1 \int_{-\infty}^{\infty} dx_2 \, \exp\left[-a(x_1^2 + x_2^2)\right] \qquad (2.11.117)$$

We may view x_1 and x_2 as coordinates in a two-dimensional space and change integration variables to the polar coordinates θ and $r = \sqrt{x_1^2 + x_2^2}$ using $dx_1 \, dx_2 = d\theta \, rdr$. The integrand does not depend on

θ, and integrating over it, we have

$$I(a)^2 = 2\pi \int_0^\infty r\, dr \exp\left(-ar^2\right) = -\frac{\pi}{a} \int_0^\infty dr \frac{d}{dr}\left[\exp\left(-ar^2\right)\right] = \frac{\pi}{a}$$

$$(2.11.118)$$

In particular, this gives $I[1/(2\sigma^2)] = \sqrt{2\pi\sigma^2}$.

In fixed-income finance, a particularly important quantity to know is the expected value for $\exp\left(-ax\right)$. For a normal variable x,

$$\begin{aligned}
E[\exp\left(-ax\right)] &= \frac{1}{\sqrt{2\pi\sigma^2}} \int_{-\infty}^\infty dx \exp\left(-\frac{(x-\bar{x})^2}{2\sigma^2} - ax\right) \\
&= \exp\left(-a\bar{x}\right) \frac{1}{\sqrt{2\pi\sigma^2}} \int_{-\infty}^\infty dx \exp\left[-\frac{(x-\bar{x})^2}{2\sigma^2} - a(x-\bar{x})\right] \\
&= \exp\left(-a\bar{x}\right) \frac{1}{\sqrt{2\pi\sigma^2}} \int_{-\infty}^\infty dz \exp\left(-\frac{z^2}{2\sigma^2} - az\right) \\
&= \exp\left(-a\bar{x}\right) \exp\left(\frac{a^2\sigma^2}{2}\right) \frac{1}{\sqrt{2\pi\sigma^2}} \int_{-\infty}^\infty dz \exp\left(-\frac{(z+a\sigma^2)^2}{2\sigma^2}\right) \\
&= \exp\left(-a\bar{x}\right) \exp\left(\frac{a^2\sigma^2}{2}\right) \qquad (2.11.119)
\end{aligned}$$

Next we consider the n-dimensional integral

$$I_n = \int_{-\infty}^\infty dx_1 \cdots \int_{-\infty}^\infty dx_n \exp\left(-\sum_{i,j} x_i A_{ij} x_j\right) \qquad (2.11.120)$$

where A is an $n \times n$ symmetric matrix with components A_{ij}. Since A is a symmetric matrix, it can be diagonalized by an orthogonal matrix O. We change to coordinates $y_i = \sum_j O_{ij} x_j$, and use the fact that OAO^{T} is a diagonal matrix with diagonal elements a_i and that $\det O = 1$

to write

$$I_n = \int_{-\infty}^{\infty} dy_1 \exp\left(-a_1 y_1^2\right) \cdots \int_{-\infty}^{\infty} dy_n \exp\left(-a_n y_1^2\right) = \sqrt{\frac{\pi}{a_1}} \cdots \sqrt{\frac{\pi}{a_n}}$$

$$(2.11.121)$$

Since $\det A = a_1 \cdots a_n$, we can write

$$I_n = \sqrt{\frac{\pi^n}{\det A}} \qquad (2.11.122)$$

2.12 Appendix 2: Dirac Delta Function

The Dirac delta function $\delta(x - a)$ is zero if $x \neq a$ and is infinite when $x = a$. Although it is infinite when $x = a$, the integral of it exists. For any positive ϵ and any smooth function $f(x)$,

$$\int_{a-\epsilon}^{a+\epsilon} dx\, f(x)\delta(x - a) = f(a) \qquad (2.12.123)$$

Equation 2.12.123 and the fact that $\delta(x - a)$ is zero for $x \neq a$ completely characterize the Dirac delta function. Next consider $\delta[c(x - a)]$ for some constant c. This function of x is also zero for $x \neq a$ and infinite when $x = a$. It is proportional to the Dirac delta function

$$\delta[c(x - a)] = \frac{1}{|c|}\delta(x - a) \qquad (2.12.124)$$

To check this, consider the integral

$$I_1(a) = \int_{a-\epsilon}^{a+\epsilon} dx\, f(x)\delta[c(x - a)] \qquad (2.12.125)$$

Changing the variables to $y = c(x - a)$, this integral becomes

$$I_2(a) = \int_{-|c|\epsilon}^{|c|\epsilon} dy \frac{1}{|c|} f(y/c + a)\delta(y) = \frac{1}{|c|} f(a) \quad (2.12.126)$$

which verifies the constant of proportionality in Equation 2.12.124.

Now consider the function $\delta(g(x))$ where $g(x)$ is differentiable and has a single zero at $x = a$, i.e., $g(a) = 0$. Again we note that $\delta(g(x))$ vanishes for $x \neq a$ and is infinite when $x = a$. This suggests that it is also proportional to $\delta(x - a)$. We can find the constant of proportionality by considering the integral

$$I_3(a) = \int_{a-\epsilon}^{a+\epsilon} dx \; f(x)\delta(g(x)) \quad (2.12.127)$$

Expanding the argument of $g(x)$ of the delta function in a power series[9] about $x = a$,

$$g(x) = 0 + g'(a)(x - a) + \frac{g''(a)}{2}(x - a)^2 + \cdots \quad (2.12.128)$$

The terms of quadratic order and higher in $x - a$ can be neglected, and so, using the previous result with $c = g'(a)$, we arrive at

$$\delta(g(x)) = \frac{1}{|g'(a)|}\delta(x - a) \quad (2.12.129)$$

If the function $g(x)$ has n zeros at $a_1, \ldots, a_n$, this argument can be generalized to give

$$\delta(g(x)) = \sum_{i=1}^{n} \frac{1}{|g'(a_i)|}\delta(x - a_i) \quad (2.12.130)$$

---

[9]Here we are using primes to denote derivatives.

There are other useful relations that the Dirac delta function satisfies, for example, $f(x)\delta(x - a) = f(a)\delta(x - a)$.

The Dirac delta function is the derivative of the theta function,

$$\delta(x - a) = \frac{d\theta(x - a)}{dx} \tag{2.12.131}$$

Since $\theta(x - a)$ is 0 for $x < a$ and 1 for $x > a$, its derivative vanishes unless $x = a$. At that point, its derivative is infinite. To verify Equation 2.12.131, we integrate the right-hand side over a region that contains the point $x = a$,

$$I_4(a) = \int_{a-\epsilon}^{a+\epsilon} dx \frac{d\theta(x - a)}{dx} = \theta(\epsilon) - \theta(-\epsilon) = 1 \tag{2.12.132}$$

The theta function can be written as an integral of the Dirac delta function,

$$\theta(a - b) = \int_{b}^{\infty} dx\, \delta(x - a) \tag{2.12.133}$$

The theory of Fourier transforms implies the following inegral representation of the Dirac delta function:

$$\delta(x - a) = \int_{-\infty}^{\infty} \frac{db}{2\pi} e^{ib(x-a)} \tag{2.12.134}$$

Finally, we consider the integral

$$I_5(a) = \int_{a-\epsilon}^{a+\epsilon} dx\, f(x) \frac{d\delta(x - a)}{dx} \tag{2.12.135}$$

Integrating by parts, we find that

$$I_5(a) = -\left(\frac{df}{dx}\right)(a) \tag{2.12.136}$$

3

Structural Models

3.1   Risk-Neutral Pricing of European Stock Options

Our main interest in this chapter is a structural model for corporate bond (and stock) prices that includes the possibility of corporate default. However, we begin by considering European options on stocks because in the structural model for corporate stock and bond prices that we eventually introduce, stock and bond prices are options on the firm value.

The purchaser of a European call option on a stock is buying the right to purchase a stock at the price S^* at some time T in the future. S^* is called the *strike price*. If at time T the value of the stock $S(T)$ is less than S^*, the investor in the call option will not make the purchase and the payoff for the investor at time T is zero. On the other hand, if the stock price at time T is greater than S^*, the investor will purchase it for the strike price S^*, which gives a payoff of $S(T) - S^*$ after the investor sells the stock at the prevailing market price $S(T)$. We can combine these two results and write the payoff as $\max[S(T) - S^*, 0]$, where $\max[a, b]$ takes the value a if $a > b$, and b if $b > a$. This payoff can also be expressed in terms of the step function introduced earlier, since $\max[S(T) - S^*, 0] = [S(T) - S^*]\theta[S(T) - S^*]$. There are other types of options with different payoff functions.

In this section, we assume that a company's stock price $S(t)$ evolves in time according to

$$\frac{dS}{S} = \mu \, dt + \sigma \, dw \tag{3.1.1}$$

This gives a lognormal probability distribution for the stock price at any time t in the future. Note that with this evolution, the probability that the stock price reaches zero is zero. It is a realistic evolution only for companies with a negligible probability to default in the time horizon under consideration. Later in this chapter, we derive a formula for stock prices that includes the probability of default. Following Chapter 2, we introduce the variable $S'(t) = \log S(t)$, which then evolves according to

$$dS' = \mu' \, dt + \sigma \, dw \tag{3.1.2}$$

where $\mu' = \mu - \sigma^2/2$.

Let $p(S', t) \, dS'$ be the probability that the logarithm of the stock price S' lies between S' and $S' + dS'$ at time t. In Chapter 2 we calculated the probability density $p(S', t)$ and found that it is given by

$$p(S', t) = \frac{1}{\sqrt{2\pi\sigma^2 t}} \exp\left(-\frac{(S' - \mu't - S_0')^2}{2\sigma^2 t}\right) \tag{3.1.3}$$

where $S_0' = S'(0)$ is the logarithm of the stock price today. Then the average value (expected value) of the stock price at time t is

$$E[S(t)] = \int_{-\infty}^{\infty} dS' \, p(S', t) e^{S'} = S_0 e^{\mu t} \tag{3.1.4}$$

This integral was evaluated by completing the square in the argument of the exponential. When[1] $\mu = y$, the expected stock price grows in time at the same rate as risk-free Treasuries, and so, on average, the instantaneous rate of return from investing in the stock is the same as for investing in Treasuries. This choice of the drift μ (i.e., $\mu = y$) is used for risk-neutral pricing of options on stocks. Recall that this is also the choice of drift that gives the correct pricing of a forward contract on a stock because with $\mu = y$, the price of a forward contract on the stock that matures at time T, $e^{yT} S_0$, is the same as the expected value of the stock at time T, $E[S(T)]$.

Risk-neutral pricing of a European call option fixes its price today to be

$$\text{Price} = e^{-yT} E[\max[S(T) - S^*, 0]] \qquad (3.1.5)$$

In this formula, the drift μ is set equal to y. The expected value $E[\ ]$ is taken over all possible random walks for the stock price. The factor of e^{-yT} discounts the value of the expected payoff at time $t = T$ to today, $t = 0$.

When the strike price is greater than the current stock price, $S^* > S$, the option is said to be "out of the money," and when the strike price is less than the stock price, $S^* < S$, the option is said to be "in the money." The seller of a call option is said to be "short the call option," and the buyer is said to be "long the call option."

Using the probability density in Equation 3.1.3, the price of a European call option becomes

$$\text{Price} = e^{-yT} \int_{S^{*\prime}}^{\infty} dS' \, p(S', T) \left(e^{S'} - e^{S^{*\prime}} \right) \qquad (3.1.6)$$

---

[1] Here y is the Treasury short rate, which, throughout this chapter, we are taking to be a constant.

where $S^{*'} = \log S^*$. It is straightforward to perform the integration over S' by completing the square in the argument of the exponential. Setting $\mu' = y - \sigma^2/2$, this gives

$$
\begin{aligned}
\text{Price} = S_0\Phi &\left(\frac{\log(S_0/S^*) + (y + \sigma^2/2)T}{\sqrt{\sigma^2 T}} \right) \\
- S^* e^{-yT}\Phi &\left(\frac{\log(S_0/S^*) + (y - \sigma^2/2)T}{\sqrt{\sigma^2 T}} \right)
\end{aligned}
\tag{3.1.7}
$$

where Φ is the cumulative normal function defined in Equation 2.6.94 of Chapter 2. In the next section we present an arbitrage argument that justifies this risk-neutral price.

To get a feeling for the implications of Equation 3.1.7, consider a European call option that matures in three months on a stock with price today $S_0 = \$100$ and annualized volatility $\sigma = 30$ percent $= 0.30$. Suppose the annualized Treasury yield is $y = 4$ percent $= 0.04$. If the strike price is $S^* = \$125$, then the price of the option is $\$0.58$. In Figure 3.1 we plot the price of a European call option on a stock as a function of the strike price S^* when the stock price today is $S_0 = \$100$, the annualized volatility of the stock price is $\sigma = 30$ percent $= 0.30$, the maturity of the option is three months (i.e., $T = 0.25$ year), and the risk-free rate is $y = 4$ percent $= 0.04$. The price of an out-of-the-money call option increases as the volatility increases, since the larger the volatility, the greater the probability that the stock price has fluctuated to a value above the strike price at maturity. In Figure 3.2 we plot the price of a European call option on a stock as a function of the volatility σ using $S_0 = \$100$, $S^* = \$125$, $y = 4$ percent, and $T = 0.25$.

Finally, we note that the shorter the maturity, the lower the price of an out-of-the-money European call option. For shorter maturities, the stock has less time to fluctuate above the stike price, and hence the probability of this occurring is lower. In Figure 3.3 we plot the

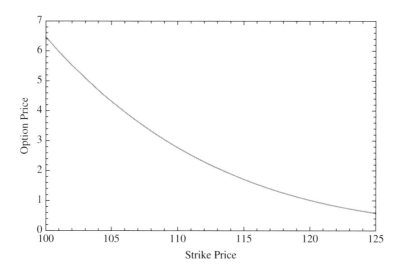

Figure 3.1 Price (in dollars) of a European call option as a function of the strike price S^* (in dollars) using $S_0 = \$100$, $\sigma = 0.3$, $T = 0.25$ year, and $y = 4$ percent.

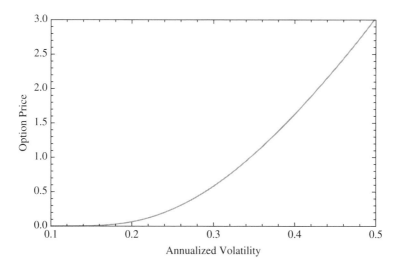

Figure 3.2 Price (in dollars) of a European call option as a function of the volatility σ using $S_0 = \$100$, $S^* = \$125$, $T = 0.25$ year, and $y = 4$ percent.

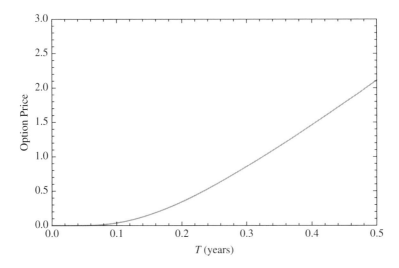

Figure 3.3 Price (in dollars) of a European call option as a function of the date it matures T using $S_0 = \$100$, $\sigma = 0.3$, $S^* = \$125$, and $y = 4$ percent.

option price as a function of the maturity using $S_0 = \$100$, $S^* = \$125$, $y = 4$ percent, and $\sigma = 0.3$.

A European put option with strike price S^* that matures at date T gives the purchaser the right, at time T, to sell the stock to the seller of the option at the strike price S^*. The payoff to the purchaser of the option is $\max[S^* - S(T), 0]$, since if the stock is above the strike price, the option will not be exercised. The purchaser of the put option is said to be taking the "long position," and the seller is taking the "short position." Note that the risk-neutral price of a put option is related to the risk-neutral price of a call option, since

$$
\begin{aligned}
\max[S^* - S(T), 0] &= [S^* - S(T)]\theta[S^* - S(T)] \\
&= [S^* - S(T)]\{1 - \theta[S(T) - S^*]\} \\
&= [S^* - S(T)] + \max[S(T) - S^*, 0] \quad (3.1.8)
\end{aligned}
$$

Hence, the difference between the risk-neutral price of a European put option on a stock and the risk-neutral price of a European call option is

$$\text{Price}_{\text{put}} - \text{Price}_{\text{call}} = e^{-yT} E[S^* - S(T)] = e^{-yT} S^* - S_0 \quad (3.1.9)$$

where the expected value $E[\;]$ is taken by averaging over all possible stock price evolutions with the drift term μ set equal to the risk-free rate y.

European options on a stock can be exercised only at maturity of the option, T. American call and put options are similar to European ones except that they can be exercised at any time before maturity T. For American call options on a stock (that does not pay a dividend), there is no incentive to exercise the option before maturity. If the stock is above the strike price at a time before T, exercising the option and purchasing the stock results, on average, in a return that is the same as the risk-free rate, since, in risk-neutral pricing, the stock price rises at the risk-free rate. The holder of the call option might as well invest the money he would have used to purchase the stock in risk-free Treasury bonds and exercise the option at maturity. The same situation does not occur for put options. The prices of European and American put options are different even for stocks that do not pay a dividend. A stock price cannot go negative, and so if the stock price fluctuates to a very low value before maturity, there isn't much further that it can fall. An investor that is long a put option on that stock is better off exercising the option and investing the proceeds from selling the stock in risk-free Treasury bonds.

3.2   Arbitrage Argument for the Pricing of Stock Options

A company's stock is a risky asset with value $S(t)$ that we take to evolve in time according to Equation 3.1.1. A (European) call option on that stock also has a value $O(t)$ at any time that depends on the stock price at that time, $O(t) = O[S(t), t]$. The value of the option evolves in time according to the formula

$$\frac{dO}{O} = \mu_O \, dt + \sigma_O \, dw \qquad (3.2.10)$$

Working to linear order in dt,

$$
\begin{aligned}
dO &= \frac{\partial O}{\partial S} dS + \frac{1}{2} \frac{\partial^2 O}{\partial S^2} (dS)^2 + \frac{\partial O}{\partial t} dt \\
&= \left(\frac{\partial O}{\partial S} \right) (\mu S \, dt + \sigma S \, dw) + \frac{1}{2} \left(\frac{\partial^2 O}{\partial S^2} \right) S^2 \sigma^2 \, dt + \frac{\partial O}{\partial t} dt
\end{aligned}
$$

$$(3.2.11)$$

and so

$$\mu_O = \frac{1}{O} \left(\frac{1}{2} \frac{\partial^2 O}{\partial S^2} \sigma^2 S^2 + \frac{\partial O}{\partial S} \mu S + \frac{\partial O}{\partial t} \right) \qquad (3.2.12)$$

and

$$\sigma_O = \frac{1}{O} \sigma S \frac{\partial O}{\partial S} \qquad (3.2.13)$$

A portfolio is a collection of assets (e.g., stocks, bonds, and options). Consider a portfolio consisting, at time t, of w_1 dollars of the stock and w_2 dollars of call options. So $w_1 \propto S(t)$ and $w_2 \propto O[S(t), t]$. A negative value of w_j means that the portfolio is short the corresponding investment. The value of the portfolio at time t is $\Pi(t) = w_1 + w_2$. The change in the value of the portfolio in a time dt is

$$d\Pi = \frac{w_1}{S} dS + \frac{w_2}{O} dO = (w_1 \mu + w_2 \mu_O) \, dt + (w_1 \sigma + w_2 \sigma_O) \, dw$$

$$(3.2.14)$$

Suppose we arrange the volatility in the portfolio to be zero by choosing the particular values $w_1 = w_1^*$ and $w_2 = w_2^*$ so that

$$w_1^* \sigma + w_2^* \sigma_O = 0 \qquad (3.2.15)$$

Then the change in the portfolio value is guaranteed to be

$$d\Pi = (w_1^* \mu + w_2^* \mu_O)dt \qquad (3.2.16)$$

We have constructed a portfolio from an option and the underlying asset (in this case, a stock) that has no risk. Such a portfolio is said to be hedged. To keep the portfolio hedged as time evolves, we must adjust the number of stocks held, and we are neglecting the transaction costs associated with this.

Assuming that an arbitrage opportunity cannot exist, for the infinitesimal time interval dt, this change $d\Pi$ must be given by the risk-free rate of return on Treasury bonds, i.e.,

$$w_1^* \mu + w_2^* \mu_O = (w_1^* + w_2^*)y \qquad (3.2.17)$$

Using Equation 3.2.15 and Equations 3.2.12 and 3.2.13, this implies that

$$\frac{\mu - y}{\sigma} = \frac{\mu_O - y}{\sigma_O} = \left(\frac{1}{\sigma S(\partial O/\partial S)}\right)\left[\frac{\partial^2 O}{\partial S^2}\left(\frac{\sigma^2 S^2}{2}\right) + \frac{\partial O}{\partial S}\mu S + \frac{\partial O}{\partial t} - yO\right] \qquad (3.2.18)$$

Multiplying this by $\sigma S(\partial O/\partial S)$ and taking all the terms to one side gives the following partial differential equation for the option price at any time t:

$$\frac{1}{2}\sigma^2 S^2 \frac{\partial^2 O}{\partial S^2} + yS\frac{\partial O}{\partial S} - yO + \frac{\partial O}{\partial t} = 0 \qquad (3.2.19)$$

This partial differential equation is the result of the arbitrage argument we made. It did not depend on the type of option. It only required that the option value at any time t has the functional form $O = O(S, t)$. Note that the drift term μ in the evolution of the stock does not appear in the previous differential equation.

We now proceed to solve Equation 3.2.19. For a European call option, we solve Equation 3.2.19 for $O(S, t)$ at any time $t < T$ by integrating backward in time using the "initial value" $O(S, T) = \max[S - S^*, 0]$. In addition, we have the boundary condition $O(0, t) = 0$, since the stock price is positive, and the boundary condition $O(S, t) \to S$ as $S \to \infty$ with S^* fixed. The price of the call option is equal to $O(S_0, 0)$. It is convenient to change variables from O as a function of S and t to v as a function of x and τ by the following change of variables:

$$S = S^* e^x \qquad t = T - \frac{2\tau}{\sigma^2} \qquad O = S^* v(x, \tau) \qquad (3.2.20)$$

Now the initial condition becomes

$$v(x, 0) = \max[e^x - 1, 0] \qquad (3.2.21)$$

and the price of the European call option is

$$\text{Price} = S^* v \left[\log (S_0 / S^*), \frac{\sigma^2}{2} T \right] \qquad (3.2.22)$$

The chain rule implies that

$$\frac{\partial}{\partial S} = \left(\frac{\partial x}{\partial S} \right) \frac{\partial}{\partial x} = \frac{1}{S} \frac{\partial}{\partial x} \qquad \frac{\partial^2}{\partial S^2} = \frac{1}{S^2} \frac{\partial^2}{\partial x^2} - \frac{1}{S^2} \frac{\partial}{\partial x} \qquad \frac{\partial}{\partial t} = -\frac{\sigma^2}{2} \frac{\partial}{\partial \tau}$$

$$(3.2.23)$$

and so, introducing

$$k = \frac{2y}{\sigma^2} \qquad (3.2.24)$$

Equation 3.2.19 becomes

$$\frac{\partial v}{\partial \tau} = \frac{\partial^2 v}{\partial x^2} + (k-1)\frac{\partial v}{\partial x} - kv \qquad (3.2.25)$$

This would be the diffusion equation if not for the last two terms on the right-hand side. We try to convert this to the diffusion equation by changing from v to the function u defined by

$$v(x, \tau) = e^{\alpha x + \beta \tau} u(x, \tau) \qquad (3.2.26)$$

for some α and β. The needed derivatives are

$$\frac{\partial v}{\partial \tau} = e^{\alpha x + \beta \tau}\left(\beta u + \frac{\partial u}{\partial \tau}\right) \qquad \frac{\partial v}{\partial x} = e^{\alpha x + \beta \tau}\left(\alpha u + \frac{\partial u}{\partial x}\right) \qquad (3.2.27)$$

and

$$\frac{\partial^2 v}{\partial x^2} = e^{\alpha x + \beta \tau}\left(\alpha^2 u + 2\alpha\frac{\partial u}{\partial x} + \frac{\partial^2 u}{\partial x^2}\right) \qquad (3.2.28)$$

Using these derivatives, Equation 3.2.19 becomes

$$\beta u + \frac{\partial u}{\partial \tau} = \alpha^2 u + 2\alpha\frac{\partial u}{\partial x} + \frac{\partial^2 u}{\partial x^2} + (k-1)\left(\alpha u + \frac{\partial u}{\partial x}\right) - ku$$

$$(3.2.29)$$

The term proportional to the partial derivative of u with respect to x is eliminated if

$$\alpha = -\frac{1}{2}(k-1) \qquad (3.2.30)$$

and the term linear in u is eliminated if

$$\beta = \alpha^2 + (k-1)\alpha - k = \frac{1}{4}(k-1)^2 - \frac{1}{2}(k-1)^2 - k = -\frac{1}{4}(k+1)^2$$

$$(3.2.31)$$

In summary, at this point we have that the function $u(x, \tau)$ obeys the diffusion differential equation

$$\frac{\partial u}{\partial \tau} = \frac{\partial^2 u}{\partial x^2} \qquad (3.2.32)$$

where

$$v(x, \tau) = \exp\left[-\frac{1}{2}(k - 1)x - \frac{1}{4}(k + 1)^2\tau\right] u(x, \tau) \qquad (3.2.33)$$

The constant k is given by $k = 2y/\sigma^2$. The variable $\tau = (1/2)\sigma^2 (T - t)$ takes on values that are greater than or equal to zero, and $x = \log(S/S^*)$ ranges from minus infinity to infinity. Furthermore, the value of a European call option on a stock that matures at time T with strike price S^* is given at any time before maturity by

$$O(S, t) = S^* \exp\left[-\frac{1}{2}(k - 1)x - \frac{1}{4}(k + 1)^2\tau\right] u[\log(S/S^*), (1/2)\sigma^2(T - t)] \qquad (3.2.34)$$

Now we have the initial condition that at the time $t = T$ (i.e., $\tau = 0$), $O(S, T) = \max[S - S^*, 0] = S^* \max[e^x - 1, 0]$. Using the relation between O and u given previously, this implies that

$$\max[e^x - 1, 0] = e^{-(k-1)x/2} u(x, 0) \qquad (3.2.35)$$

which gives the intitial condition,

$$u(x, 0) = e^{(k-1)x/2} \max[e^x - 1, 0] = \left(e^{(k+1)x/2} - e^{(k-1)x/2}\right) \theta(x) \qquad (3.2.36)$$

Recall from Chapter 2 that a solution to Equation 3.2.32 is

$$u(x, \tau) = (1/\sqrt{4\pi\tau}) \exp\left[-(x - s)^2/(4\tau)\right] \qquad (3.2.37)$$

This is a solution for any value of the parameter s, and it satisfies the initial condition $u(x, 0) = \delta(x - s)$. In particular, the following expression satisfies Equation 3.2.32 and the initial condition:

$$u(x, \tau) = \frac{1}{\sqrt{4\pi\tau}} \int_{-\infty}^{\infty} ds\, e^{-(x-s)^2/4\tau} u(s, 0) \qquad (3.2.38)$$

where $u(s, 0)$ is given by Equation 3.2.36. Let's try this solution. We will verify later that it satisfies the correct boundary conditions. The θ function in $u(s, 0)$ restricts the integration to be over positive s, and so

$$u(x, \tau) = \frac{1}{\sqrt{4\pi\tau}} \int_0^{\infty} ds \exp\left[\frac{1}{2}(k+1)s - \frac{(x-s)^2}{4\tau}\right]$$
$$- \frac{1}{\sqrt{4\pi\tau}} \int_0^{\infty} ds \exp\left[\frac{1}{2}(k-1)s - \frac{(x-s)^2}{4\tau}\right] \qquad (3.2.39)$$

We want to express the answer in terms of the cumulative normal function. To achieve this, it is convenient to change variables from s to x' using $s = \sqrt{2\tau}x' + x$ and then perform the integrations by completing the square in the exponents. This gives[2]

$$u(x, \tau) = \exp\left[\frac{1}{2}(k+1)x + \frac{1}{4}(k+1)^2\tau\right] \Phi\left[\frac{x}{\sqrt{2\tau}} + \frac{1}{2}(k+1)\sqrt{2\tau}\right]$$
$$- \exp\left[\frac{1}{2}(k-1)x + \frac{1}{4}(k-1)^2\tau\right] \Phi\left[\frac{x}{\sqrt{2\tau}} + \frac{1}{2}(k-1)\sqrt{2\tau}\right]$$
$$(3.2.40)$$

Plugging this into Equation 3.2.34 and using

$$\left[-\frac{1}{2}(k-1)x - \frac{1}{4}(k+1)^2\tau\right] + \left[\frac{1}{2}(k+1)x + \frac{1}{4}(k+1)^2\tau\right] = x$$
$$(3.2.41)$$

---

[2]We will do similar integrations more explicitly in the next section.

and

$$\left[-\frac{1}{2}(k-1)x - \frac{1}{4}(k+1)^2\tau \right] + \left[\frac{1}{2}(k-1)x + \frac{1}{4}(k-1)^2\tau \right] = -k\tau$$

$$(3.2.42)$$

we arrive at the formula for $O(S, t)$:

$$O(S, t) = S^* e^x \Phi \left[\frac{x}{\sqrt{2\tau}} + \frac{1}{2}(k+1)\sqrt{2\tau} \right]$$

$$- S^* e^{-k\tau} \Phi \left[\frac{x}{\sqrt{2\tau}} + \frac{1}{2}(k-1)\sqrt{2\tau} \right] \quad (3.2.43)$$

Using the definitions of x, k, and τ, this becomes

$$O(S, t) = S\Phi[d_1(t)] - S^* e^{-y(T-t)} \Phi[d_2(t)] \qquad (3.2.44)$$

where

$$d_1(t) = \frac{1}{\sigma\sqrt{T-t}} \left[\log\left(\frac{S}{S^*}\right) + \left(y + \frac{1}{2}\sigma^2\right)(T-t) \right] \quad (3.2.45)$$

and

$$d_2(t) = \frac{1}{\sigma\sqrt{T-t}} \left[\log\left(\frac{S}{S^*}\right) + \left(y - \frac{1}{2}\sigma^2\right)(T-t) \right] \quad (3.2.46)$$

Since $\Phi(\infty) = 1$, as $S \to \infty$, we have that $O(S, t) \to S$, and since $\Phi(-\infty) = 0$, as $S \to 0$, we deduce that $O(S, t) \to 0$. Hence our solution satisfies the correct boundary conditions.

The option price is

$$\text{Price} = O(S_0, 0) = S_0 \Phi\left(\frac{\log(S_0/S^*) + (y + \sigma^2/2)T}{\sqrt{\sigma^2 T}} \right)$$

$$- S^* e^{-yT} \Phi\left(\frac{\log(S_0/S^*) + (y - \sigma^2/2)T}{\sqrt{\sigma^2 T}} \right)$$

$$(3.2.47)$$

This agrees with Equation 3.1.7. It is called the Black-Scholes option pricing formula.[3]

If we try to fit European stock option prices to Equation 3.2.47, or the analogous formula for options that are not European, we find that options that are very far out of the money and therefore require a very large fluctuation to pay off are priced with a higher volatility than options where the strike price is closer to the current stock price. This is because large fluctuations are not described by a normal (or lognormal) distribution but rather by a probability distribution with fatter tails.

3.3   A Structural Model Relating Equity and Debt

In this section, we will present a model for corporate bonds that is a generalization of one presented by Merton.[4] We first recall that a corporation's firm value is the sum of its equity plus its debt, $V = E + D$. We take the debt to consist of zero coupon bonds that mature at a time T. The value of the equity $E = E(V, t)$ is the number of shares N_s times the stock price $S(V, t)$, and the value of the debt $D = D(V, t)$ is just the number of bonds N_b times the bond price $B(V, t)$.

We also assume that at any time t before the bonds mature, the company defaults if the firm value V falls below the threshold $V_d(t)$. The default threshold $V_d(t)$ is given by a fraction R of the value of the debt at maturity d discounted back to the time t by the risk-free rate. Explicitly,

$$V_d(t) = Rde^{-y(T-t)} \tag{3.3.48}$$

where R is the recovery fraction for the bondholders. If the firm defaults, the equity is worthless. Consequently, the equity satisfies the boundary

---

[3] F. Black and M. Scholes, "The Pricing of Options and Corporate Liabilities," *Journal of Political Economy* 81(1973), 637.

[4] R. Merton, "On the Pricing of Corporate Debt: The Risk Structure of Interest Rates," *Journal of Finance* 29(1974): 449.

condition

$$E[V_d(t), t] = E(Rde^{-y(T-t)}, t) = 0 \qquad (3.3.49)$$

Furthermore, we have the firm paying the equity (i.e., stock) holders a dividend $qE\,dt$ in the time dt and take q to be constant. The dividend payout to the equity holders induces a negative drift term in the firm value evolution, and so we arrive at the equation

$$dV = \mu V\,dt + \sigma V\,dw - qE\,dt \qquad (3.3.50)$$

An investor in firm value owns both the equity and the debt of the firm and gets the same return whether the firm pays a dividend to the stockholders or not. The positive return from cash dividend payments is compensated for by the negative drift in the firm value. Even though an investor in firm value does not care if the firm pays a dividend, the investors in the debt do care. Dividends are bad for the bondholders. The cash payment goes to the equity holders and the dividend lowers the firm value, increasing the probability that the firm will default before the maturity of the debt.

At $t = T$, the zero coupon bonds mature, and if the firm value is below $V = d$, the firm is in default. Thus the value of the stock at maturity of the bonds is

$$E(V, T) = \max[V - d, 0] = (V - d)\theta(V - d) \quad (3.3.51)$$

There is no default risk to the bondholders if the recovery fraction R is 1, and so, in that case, the value of the debt is $D(V, t) = d \exp[-y(T - t)]$ and the value of the equity is $E(V, t) = V - d \exp[-y(T - t)]$. When the recovery fraction is less than unity, the firm value can fluctuate to a value below d before the debt matures without the firm defaulting. If it fluctuates so low that it hits the default barrier V_d at time $t < T$, then the firm is in default. In a default that occurs before $t = T$, the bondholders receive only a fraction R of the value of the principal, discounted by the risk-free rate from maturity back to time t. So when $R < 1$, the bondholders are exposed to the risk of a partial loss of their principal. One way in which the structural model introduced in this chapter differs from the corporate bonds discussed in Chapter 1 is that here there is a finite probability for default to occur right at maturity, and for default at maturity the recovery fraction on the debt is not fixed, but varies between R and unity.

As when we considered the arbitrage argument for stock option prices in the previous section, we construct a portfolio at time t that evolves forward in time without risk. From our analysis of the stock option case, it is clear that such a portfolio is one that is long a unit of equity and short $\partial E/\partial V$ units of firm value, i.e., $\Pi = E - (\partial E/\partial V)V$. The change in the value of an investment in this portfolio in a time t is the sum of $d\Pi = dE - (\partial E/\partial V)\, dV$ and the dividend payment $qE[1 - (\partial E/\partial V)]\, dt$. Since the portfolio evolves without risk, the total return must equal the risk-free rate of return,

$$dE - \left(\frac{\partial E}{\partial V}\right) dV + qE\,dt - qE\left(\frac{\partial E}{\partial V}\right) dt = y\left[E - \left(\frac{\partial E}{\partial V}\right)V\right] dt$$

$$(3.3.52)$$

Using $dE = (\partial E/\partial V)\, dV + (1/2)(\partial^2 E/\partial V^2)\sigma^2 V^2\, dt + (\partial E/\partial t)\, dt$, this becomes

$$0 = \frac{\partial E}{\partial t} + \frac{1}{2}\sigma^2 V^2 \frac{\partial^2 E}{\partial V^2} + yV\frac{\partial E}{\partial V} - yE + qE\left(1 - \frac{\partial E}{\partial V}\right) \quad (3.3.53)$$

A similar arbitrage argument can be constructed for a portfolio of firm value and debt, and it gives a similar differential equation for the debt. Alternatively, we can just plug $E = V - D$ into Equation 3.3.53 and use $(\partial V/\partial t) = 0$ to get

$$0 = \frac{\partial D}{\partial t} + \frac{1}{2}\sigma^2 V^2 \frac{\partial^2 D}{\partial V^2} + V(y - q)\frac{\partial D}{\partial V} - yD + qD\frac{\partial D}{\partial V} \quad (3.3.54)$$

This is a nonlinear differential equation because of the last term $qD\,\partial D/\partial V$.

We now solve Equation 3.3.53 with the dividend rate set to zero. This gives the equity price today $E(V_0, 0)$, where V_0 is the firm value today. From that we reconstruct the value of the debt using $D(V_0, 0) = V_0 - E(V_0, 0)$. Equation 3.3.53 is the same as Equation 3.2.19 when $V \to S$ and $E \to O$. Hence, in this model, the equity is an option on the firm value. Given the similarity with European call options, we make the same changes of variables,

$$V = de^x \qquad t = T - 2\frac{\tau}{\sigma^2} \qquad E = dv(x, \tau) \qquad (3.3.55)$$

and get the differential equation (cf. Equation 3.2.25)

$$\frac{\partial v}{\partial \tau} = \frac{\partial^2 v}{\partial x^2} + (k - 1)\frac{\partial v}{\partial x} - kv \qquad (3.3.56)$$

where $k = 2y/\sigma^2$. As in the stock options case, we make the further change of variables

$$E(x, \tau) = de^{-\frac{1}{2}(k-1)x - \frac{1}{4}(k+1)^2\tau}u(x, \tau) \qquad (3.3.57)$$

resulting in the simple diffusion equation in Equation 3.2.32. However, the variables x and τ are not the most natural ones for this problem because of the boundary condition $E[V_d(t), t] = 0$, which has no analog in the European stock option case. In terms of the variables x and τ, this boundary condition is $E(x = \log R - k\tau, \tau) = 0$, and the "initial condition" is $E(x, \tau = 0) = d(e^x - 1)\theta(x)$. We would like a boundary condition that does not depend on our time variable. So instead of x and τ, we use $z = x + k\tau$ and τ, and view u as a function of z and τ. Note that at $\tau = 0$, the variable z is equal to x. The boundary condition and initial condition for $u(z, \tau)$ now become

$$u(\log R, \tau) = 0 \qquad u(z, 0) = \left(e^{\frac{1}{2}(k+1)z} - e^{\frac{1}{2}(k-1)z}\right)\theta(z) \qquad (3.3.58)$$

and using

$$\frac{\partial^2 u(x, \tau)}{\partial x^2} = \frac{\partial^2 u(z, \tau)}{\partial z^2} \qquad \frac{\partial u(x, \tau)}{\partial \tau} = \frac{\partial u(z, \tau)}{\partial \tau} + k\frac{\partial u(z, \tau)}{\partial z}$$

$$(3.3.59)$$

the diffusion equation for $u(x, \tau)$ becomes the following partial differential equation:

$$\frac{\partial u}{\partial \tau} - \frac{\partial^2 u}{\partial z^2} + k\frac{\partial u}{\partial z} = 0 \qquad (3.3.60)$$

for $u(z, \tau)$. We found a solution to this differential equation with the appropriate boundary condition when we considered the survival probability density for random walks with a drift term in Chapter 2: the function

$$K(z, s; \tau) = \frac{1}{\sqrt{4\pi\tau}} \left\{ \exp\left(-\frac{(z - k\tau - s)^2}{4\tau}\right) \right.$$
$$\left. - \exp\left[-\frac{(z - k\tau - 2\log R + s)^2}{4\tau} - k(s - \log R)\right] \right\}$$

$$(3.3.61)$$

This function satisfies the differential equation

$$\frac{\partial K}{\partial \tau} = -k\frac{\partial K}{\partial z} + \frac{\partial^2 K}{\partial z^2} \qquad (3.3.62)$$

and the boundary condition

$$K(\log R, s; \tau) = 0 \qquad (3.3.63)$$

and has the initial value

$$K(z, s; 0) = \delta(z - s) - \delta(z + s - 2\log R)e^{-k(s - \log R)} \qquad (3.3.64)$$

The second Dirac delta function is never satisfied in the region $z >$ $\log R$ if $s > \log R$. So a solution that satisfies the initial condition at $\tau = 0$ and boundary conditions is

$$u(z, \tau) = \int_{\log R}^{\infty} ds\, K(z, s; \tau) u(s, 0) \qquad (3.3.65)$$

Using the explicit form for $u(s, 0)$ in Equation 3.3.58 and the fact that $\log R < 0$, this is equal to

$$u(z, \tau) = \int_{0}^{\infty} ds\, K(z, s; \tau) \left(e^{\frac{1}{2}(k+1)s} - e^{\frac{1}{2}(k-1)s} \right) \qquad (3.3.66)$$

Putting in the explicit expression for K,

$$\begin{aligned}
u(z, \tau) = {} & \frac{1}{\sqrt{4\pi\tau}} \int_{0}^{\infty} ds\, e^{\frac{1}{2}(k+1)s} \exp\left(-\frac{(z - k\tau - s)^2}{4\tau} \right) \\
& - \frac{1}{\sqrt{4\pi\tau}} \int_{0}^{\infty} ds\, e^{\frac{1}{2}(k-1)s} \exp\left(-\frac{(z - k\tau - s)^2}{4\tau} \right) \\
& - \frac{1}{\sqrt{4\pi\tau}} \int_{0}^{\infty} ds\, e^{\frac{1}{2}(k+1)s} \exp\left[-\frac{(z - k\tau - 2\log R + s)^2}{4\tau} - k(s - \log R) \right] \\
& + \frac{1}{\sqrt{4\pi\tau}} \int_{0}^{\infty} ds\, e^{\frac{1}{2}(k-1)s} \exp\left[-\frac{(z - k\tau - 2\log R + s)^2}{4\tau} - k(s - \log R) \right]
\end{aligned}$$

$$(3.3.67)$$

The four integrals over s are done by changing variables and completing the square in the argument of the exponential. After expanding out the arguments of the exponentials, all the integrals that need to be done are of the form

$$\begin{aligned}
I(a, b, c) &= \frac{1}{\sqrt{2\pi}} \int_{c}^{\infty} ds\, \exp\left(-\frac{s^2}{2b} + as \right) \\
&= \exp\left(\frac{a^2 b}{2} \right) \frac{1}{\sqrt{2\pi}} \int_{c}^{\infty} ds\, \exp\left[-\frac{(s - ab)^2}{2b} \right] \qquad (3.3.68)
\end{aligned}$$

Changing variables to $u = (s - ab)/\sqrt{b}$, this becomes

$$I(a, b, c) = \exp\left(\frac{a^2 b}{2}\right)\sqrt{\frac{b}{2\pi}}\int_{(c-ab)/\sqrt{b}}^{\infty} du\, \exp\left(-\frac{u^2}{2}\right)$$

$$= \sqrt{b}\, \exp\left(\frac{a^2 b}{2}\right)\Phi\left(\frac{ab - c}{\sqrt{b}}\right) \qquad (3.3.69)$$

For the first integral, rearranging the argument of the exponential to put the integral in a form proportional to $I(a, b, c)$ gives

$$I_1 = \frac{1}{\sqrt{4\pi\tau}}\int_0^{\infty} ds\, e^{\frac{1}{2}(k+1)s}\exp\left(-\frac{(z - k\tau - s)^2}{4\tau}\right)$$

$$= \frac{1}{\sqrt{4\pi\tau}}\int_0^{\infty} ds\, \exp\left[-\frac{s^2}{4\tau} + \frac{s}{2\tau}(z + \tau) - \frac{(z - k\tau)^2}{4\tau}\right] \quad (3.3.70)$$

Using Equation 3.3.69 with $a = (z + \tau)/2\tau$, $b = 2\tau$, and $c = 0$, we get

$$I_1 = \exp\left[\frac{1}{2}(k + 1)\left(z - \frac{(k - 1)\tau}{2}\right)\right]\Phi\left(\frac{z + \tau}{\sqrt{2\tau}}\right) \quad (3.3.71)$$

The second integration is done similarly. Putting it in the form proportional to $I(a, b, c)$,

$$I_2 = \frac{1}{\sqrt{4\pi\tau}}\int_0^{\infty} ds\, e^{\frac{1}{2}(k-1)s}\exp\left(-\frac{(z - k\tau - s)^2}{4\tau}\right)$$

$$= \frac{1}{\sqrt{4\pi\tau}}\int_0^{\infty} ds\, \exp\left[-\frac{s^2}{4\tau} + \frac{s}{2\tau}(z - \tau) - \frac{(z - k\tau)^2}{4\tau}\right]$$

$$(3.3.72)$$

In this case, $a = (z - \tau)/2\tau$, $b = 2\tau$, and $c = 0$. Hence,

$$I_2 = \exp\left[\frac{1}{2}(k-1)\left(z - \frac{(k+1)\tau}{2}\right)\right] \Phi\left(\frac{z - \tau}{\sqrt{2\tau}}\right) \quad (3.3.73)$$

Next we consider

$$I_3 = \frac{1}{\sqrt{4\pi\tau}} \int_0^\infty ds\, e^{\frac{1}{2}(k+1)s} \exp\left[-\frac{(z - k\tau - 2\log R + s)^2}{4\tau} - k(s - \log R)\right]$$

$$= \frac{1}{\sqrt{4\pi\tau}} \int_0^\infty ds\, \exp\left[\frac{-s^2}{4\tau} + \frac{s}{2\tau}(-z + \tau + 2\log R)\right.$$

$$\left. - \frac{(z - k\tau - 2\log R)^2}{4\tau} + k\log R\right] \quad (3.3.74)$$

In this case, $a = (-z + \tau + 2\log R)/2\tau$, $b = 2\tau$, and $c = 0$, and so we get

$$I_3 = R\exp\left[\frac{1}{2}(k-1)\left(z - \frac{(k+1)\tau}{2}\right)\right] \Phi\left(\frac{\tau - z + 2\log R}{\sqrt{2\tau}}\right)$$

$$(3.3.75)$$

Finally,

$$I_4 = \frac{1}{\sqrt{4\pi\tau}} \int_0^\infty ds\, e^{\frac{1}{2}(k-1)s} \exp\left[-\frac{(z - k\tau - 2\log R + s)^2}{4\tau} - k(s - \log R)\right]$$

$$= \frac{1}{\sqrt{4\pi\tau}} \int_0^\infty ds\, \exp\left[\frac{-s^2}{4\tau} + \frac{s}{2\tau}(-z - \tau + 2\log R)\right.$$

$$\left. - \frac{(z - k\tau - 2\log R)^2}{4\tau} + k\log R\right] \quad (3.3.76)$$

In this case, $a = (-z - \tau + 2 \log R)/2\tau$, $b = 2\tau$, and $c = 0$, and we arrive at

$$I_4 = \frac{1}{R} \exp\left[\frac{1}{2}(k+1)\left(z - \frac{(k-1)\tau}{2}\right)\right] \Phi\left(\frac{-\tau - z + 2 \log R}{\sqrt{2\tau}}\right)$$

(3.3.77)

Combining these results using $u = I_1 - I_2 - I_3 + I_4$,

$$u(z, \tau) = \exp\left[\frac{1}{2}(k+1)\left(z - \frac{(k-1)\tau}{2}\right)\right]\left[\Phi\left(\frac{z+\tau}{\sqrt{2\tau}}\right)\right.$$
$$+ \frac{1}{R}\Phi\left(\frac{-\tau - z + 2 \log R}{\sqrt{2\tau}}\right)\right]$$
$$- \exp\left[\frac{1}{2}(k-1)\left(z - \frac{(k+1)\tau}{2}\right)\right]\left[\Phi\left(\frac{z-\tau}{\sqrt{2\tau}}\right)\right.$$
$$+ R\Phi\left(\frac{\tau - z + 2 \log R}{\sqrt{2\tau}}\right)\right]$$

(3.3.78)

Using Equation 3.3.57 and $z = x + k\tau$, we find that the equity is

$$E(x, \tau) = de^x\left[\Phi\left(\frac{x}{\sqrt{2\tau}} + \frac{k+1}{2}\sqrt{2\tau}\right) + \frac{1}{R}\Phi\left(\frac{-x + 2 \log R}{\sqrt{2\tau}} - \frac{k+1}{2}\sqrt{2\tau}\right)\right]$$
$$- de^{-k\tau}\left[\Phi\left(\frac{x}{\sqrt{2\tau}} + \frac{k-1}{2}\sqrt{2\tau}\right) + R\Phi\left(\frac{-x + 2 \log R}{\sqrt{2\tau}} - \frac{k-1}{2}\sqrt{2\tau}\right)\right]$$

(3.3.79)

Using the definitions $x = \log(V/d)$, $\tau = \sigma^2(T - t)/2$, and $k = 2y/\sigma^2$, we express the value of the equity in terms of the firm value,

$$E(V, t) = V\left\{\Phi[d_1(t)] + \frac{1}{R}\Phi\left[-d_1(t) + 2 \log R/\sqrt{\sigma^2(T - t)}\right]\right\}$$
$$- de^{-y(T-t)}\left\{\Phi[d_2(t)] + R\Phi\left[-d_2(t) + 2 \log R/\sqrt{\sigma^2(T - t)}\right]\right\}$$

(3.3.80)

where

$$d_1(t) = \frac{1}{\sigma\sqrt{T-t}}\left[\log\left(\frac{V}{d}\right) + \left(y + \frac{1}{2}\sigma^2\right)(T-t)\right] \quad (3.3.81)$$

and

$$d_2(t) = \frac{1}{\sigma\sqrt{T-t}}\left[\log\left(\frac{V}{d}\right) + \left(y - \frac{1}{2}\sigma^2\right)(T-t)\right] \quad (3.3.82)$$

At any time t, V takes some value; this determines E and hence the debt, $D = V - E$. In other words, the value of the debt can be expressed in terms of the value of the equity. At the initial time $t = 0$, the previous equations simplify to

$$
\begin{aligned}
E_0 = E(V_0, 0) = V_0 &\left\{ \Phi\left[\frac{1}{\sqrt{\sigma^2 T}}\log(V_0/d) + \left(\frac{y}{\sigma^2} + \frac{1}{2}\right)\sqrt{\sigma^2 T}\right] \right.\\
&\left. + \frac{1}{R}\Phi\left[-\frac{1}{\sqrt{\sigma^2 T}}\log(V_0/dR^2) - \left(\frac{y}{\sigma^2} + \frac{1}{2}\right)\sqrt{\sigma^2 T}\right] \right\}\\
- de^{-yT} &\left\{ \Phi\left[\frac{1}{\sqrt{\sigma^2 T}}\log(V_0/d) + \left(\frac{y}{\sigma^2} - \frac{1}{2}\right)\sqrt{\sigma^2 T}\right] \right.\\
&\left. + R\,\Phi\left[\frac{-1}{\sqrt{\sigma^2 T}}\log(V_0/dR^2) - \left(\frac{y}{\sigma^2} - \frac{1}{2}\right)\sqrt{\sigma^2 T}\right] \right\} \quad (3.3.83)
\end{aligned}
$$

In the limit $R \to 0$, default can occur only at maturity of the debt, and the previous equation becomes

$$
\begin{aligned}
E_0|_{R=0} = E(V_0, 0)|_{R=0} = V_0\Phi&\left[\frac{1}{\sqrt{\sigma^2 T}}\log(V_0/d) + \left(\frac{y}{\sigma^2} + \frac{1}{2}\right)\sqrt{\sigma^2 T}\right]\\
- de^{-yT}\Phi&\left[\frac{1}{\sqrt{\sigma^2 T}}\log(V_0/d) + \left(\frac{y}{\sigma^2} - \frac{1}{2}\right)\sqrt{\sigma^2 T}\right]
\end{aligned}
$$

$$(3.3.84)$$

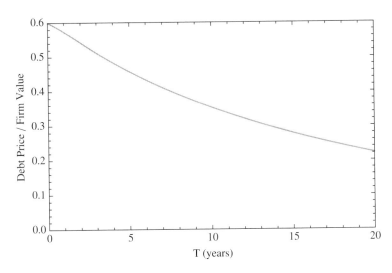

Figure 3.4 Price of the debt today in units of the total firm value, D_0/V_0, as a function of the maturity of the debt T using $d/V_0 = 0.6$, $\sigma = 0.3$, $R = 0.5$, and $y = 4$ percent.

We now consider the dependence of the present value of the corporate debt, $D_0 = D(V_0, 0) = V_0 - E_0$, on the various parameters in the simple structural model introduced in this section. Equation 3.3.83 is used for E_0. In Figure 3.4 we plot D_0/V_0 as a function of the maturity of the zero coupon bonds in years. For this plot, we used $d/V_0 = 0.6$, $y = 0.04$, $\sigma = 0.3$, and $R = 0.5$. The price decreases with maturity for two reasons. First, even if there were no chance of default, the present price would be a decreasing function of maturity, $d \exp(-yT)$. Second, the probability of a default occuring before maturity increases with T, which also reduces D_0. In Figure 3.5 we plot D_0/V_0 as a function of the recovery fraction R using $d/V_0 = 0.6$, $\sigma = 0.3$, $T = 10$ years, and $y = 0.04$. Note that when the recovery fraction is unity, $R = 1$, there is no default risk and $D_0/V_0 = (d/V_0) \exp(-yT)$, which for the parameters used here is equal to about 0.40.

Finally we plot in Figure 3.6 the dependence of the price of the debt today, D_0/V_0, on the volatility σ using $d/V_0 = 0.6$, $R = 0.5$,

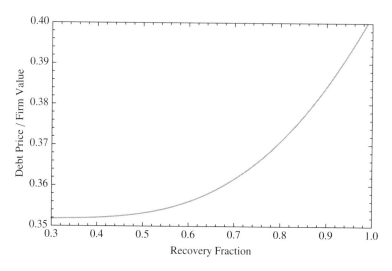

Figure 3.5 Price of the debt today in units of the total firm value, D_0/V_0, as a function of the recovery fraction R using $d/V_0 = 0.6$, $\sigma = 0.3$, $T = 10$ years, and $y = 4$ percent.

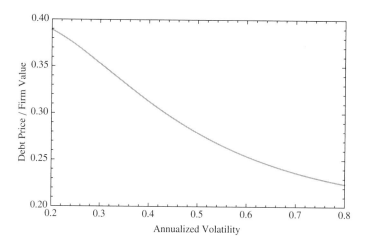

Figure 3.6 Price of the debt today in units of the total firm value, D_0/V_0, as a function of the firm value volatility σ using $d/V_0 = 0.6$, $R = 0.5$, $T = 10$ years, and $y = 4$ percent.

$T = 10$ years, and $y = 0.04$. The value of the debt D_0/V_0 decreases as the volatility σ increases, since the probability of the firm value fluctuating down to the default threshold increases as σ increases.

3.4 Risk-Neutral Default Probabilities

We have seen in the simple model introduced here that the values of the debt and the equity are related by an arbitrage argument. There is another way to derive the expression for the equity or the debt in this model. We introduce the risk-neutral survival (default) probability, which is the probability that the firm survives (defaults) when the firm value evolves not with the real value of the drift term μ but rather with the drift set equal to the risk-free rate, $\mu = y$. Neglecting the dividend payments, the firm value then evolves according to

$$dV = \mu V \, dt + \sigma V \, dw \qquad (3.4.85)$$

Let us change from V to the normal variable

$$z' = [\log V/V_0 - y(t - T)] \qquad (3.4.86)$$

where V_0 is the firm value today. The initial value is $z_0' = z'(0) = yT$. Default occurs before maturity of the debt if z' falls below the time-independent default threshold

$$z_d' = \log (dR/V_0) \qquad (3.4.87)$$

and, following familiar steps, z' obeys the evolution equation

$$dz' = \eta \, dt + \sigma \, dw \qquad (3.4.88)$$

where

$$\eta = \mu - y - \frac{1}{2}\sigma^2 \qquad (3.4.89)$$

In Chapter 2, we found the probability $p_S(z', t)\, dz'$ for the firm value to be between z' and $z' + dz'$ at some time t for precisely this case. It was, after making the replacement $\mu \to \eta$,

$$p_S(z';t) = \frac{1}{\sqrt{2\pi\sigma^2 t}} \left[\exp\left(-\frac{(z' - \eta t - z_0')^2}{2\sigma^2 t} \right) \right.$$
$$\left. - \exp\left(\frac{2\eta(z_d' - z_0')}{\sigma^2} \right) \exp\left(-\frac{(z' - \eta t + z_0' - 2z_d')^2}{2\sigma^2 t} \right) \right]$$

$$(3.4.90)$$

The survival probability is

$$P_S(t) = \int_{z_d'}^{\infty} dz'\, p_S(z, t) = \Phi\left(\frac{\eta t + (z_0' - z_d')}{\sqrt{\sigma^2 t}} \right)$$
$$- e^{2\eta(z_d' - z_0')/\sigma^2} \Phi\left(\frac{\eta t - (z_0' - z_d')}{\sqrt{\sigma^2 t}} \right) \qquad (3.4.91)$$

The risk-neutral survival probability density, $p_S^{RN}(z';t)$, and the risk-neutral survival probability, $P_S^{RN}(t)$, are given by

$$p_S^{RN}(z';t) = p_S(z';t)|_{\mu=y} \qquad P_S^{RN}(t) = P_S(t)|_{\mu=y} \quad (3.4.92)$$

The risk-neutral survival probability plays an important role in the pricing of corporate bonds. Consider, for example, a corporation with $d/V_0 = 0.5$ and $\sigma = 0.35$. We assume that the debt matures in 10 years and that the Treasury rate is fixed at 3 percent. Then, with a recovery fraction $R = 1$, the 5-year risk-neutral survival probability is $P_S^{RN}(5\ \text{years}) = 67.9$ percent. The 10-year risk-neutral survival probability is $P_S^{\mathrm{RN}}(10 \text{ years}) = 43.6 \text{ percent}$. Decreasing the recovery fraction to $R = 0.5$, the 5- and 10-year risk-neutral survival probabilities become $P_S^{\mathrm{RN}}(5 \text{ years}) = 93.2 \text{ percent}$ and $P_S^{\mathrm{RN}}(10 \text{ years}) = 73.2 \text{ percent}$.

It can be shown that the price of the debt that we derived in the previous section using an arbitrage argument is the same as the one we would deduce by discounting the expected cash flows back using the risk-free rate and calculating the expected values using the risk-neutral default probability and probability density instead of the real ones.[5] This is analogous to what happened in the pricing of options or forward contracts on stocks. The value of the debt today, i.e., its price, is the sum of three terms:

$$
\begin{aligned}
D_0 = D(V_0, 0) = e^{-yT} \Bigg[& \int_0^T dt \left(-\frac{dP_S^{\mathrm{RN}}(t)}{dt} \right) Rd \\
& + \int_{z_d'}^{z_d' - \log R} dz' \, p_S^{\mathrm{RN}}(z', T) \left(V_0 e^{z'} \right) + \int_{z_d' - \log R}^{\infty} dz' \, p_S^{\mathrm{RN}}(z', T) d \Bigg]
\end{aligned}
$$

$$(3.4.93)$$

The first term takes into account the possibility of default before maturity. The risk-neutral probability of default occuring in the time interval dt is $-dP_S^{\mathrm{RN}}/dt$, and if default occurs, the value of the recovered principal after discounting it by $\exp(-yt)$ is $Rd \exp(-yT)$. The second arises from the possibility that the firm survives to maturity but defaults at that time. The recovery fraction is R if default occurs before maturity, but at maturity the recovery fraction varies between R and 1, depending on the value of V at that time. Finally, the third term arises from the possibility that the firm does not default at all. The first integral over time of default is easy to perform, and so, using $P_S(0) = 1$, the

---

[5]Shortly we will show this explicitly in the limit where the recovery fraction goes to zero, $R \to 0$.

equation simplifies to

$$D_0 = D(V_0, 0) = e^{-yT} \left\{ [1 - P_S^{\mathrm{RN}}(T)] Rd \right.$$
$$\left. + \int_{z_d'}^{z_d' - \log R} dz' \, p_S^{\mathrm{RN}}(z', T) \left(V_0 e^{z'} \right) + \int_{z_d' - \log R}^{\infty} dz' \, p_S^{\mathrm{RN}}(z', T) d \right\} \tag{3.4.94}$$

Taking the limit as $R \to 0$, the first term vanishes, since default cannot occur before maturity, and the remaining terms become

$$D_0|_{R=0} = D(V_0, 0)|_{R=0} = e^{-yT} \left[\int_{-\infty}^{\log(d/V_0)} dz' \, p^{\mathrm{RN}}(z', T) \left(V_0 e^{z'} \right) \right.$$
$$\left. + \int_{\log(d/V_0)}^{\infty} dz' \, p^{\mathrm{RN}}(z', T) d \right] \tag{3.4.95}$$

where the risk-neutral random walk with drift probability $p^{\mathrm{RN}}(z', t)$ is given by setting $\mu = y$ in the expression for $p(z', t)$ given in Chapter 2. Hence,

$$p^{\mathrm{RN}}(z', T) = \frac{1}{\sqrt{2\pi\sigma^2 T}} \exp\left(-\frac{(z' - yT + \sigma^2 T/2)^2}{2\sigma^2 T} \right) \tag{3.4.96}$$

The integrals in Equation 3.4.95 can be performed explicitly, since they are proportional to $I(a, b, c)$:

$$\int_{-\infty}^{\log(d/V_0)} dz' \, p^{\mathrm{RN}}(z', T) \left(V_0 e^{z'} \right) = \frac{V_0 e^{yT}}{\sqrt{2\pi\sigma^2 T}} \int_{-\infty}^{\log(d/V_0)} dz'$$
$$\times \exp\left(-\frac{(z' - yT - \sigma^2 T/2)^2}{2\sigma^2 T} \right) \tag{3.4.97}$$

Changing variables from z' to $x = (z' - yT - \sigma^2 T/2)/\sqrt{\sigma^2 T}$, we have that

$$
e^{-yT} \int_{-\infty}^{\log(d/V_0)} dz'\, p^{\mathrm{RN}}(z', T)\left(V_0 e^{z'}\right)
$$

$$
= V_0 \Phi\left[\frac{1}{\sqrt{\sigma^2 T}} \log(d/V_0) - \left(\frac{y}{\sigma^2} + \frac{1}{2}\right)\sqrt{\sigma^2 T}\right]
$$

$$
= V_0 - V_0 \Phi\left[\frac{1}{\sqrt{\sigma^2 T}} \log(V_0/d) + \left(\frac{y}{\sigma^2} + \frac{1}{2}\right)\sqrt{\sigma^2 T}\right] \quad (3.4.98)
$$

Similarly,

$$
e^{-yT} d \int_{\log(d/V_0)}^{\infty} dz'\, p^{\mathrm{RN}}(z', T) = e^{-yT} d\, \Phi\left[\frac{1}{\sqrt{\sigma^2 T}} \log(V_0/d)\right.
$$

$$
\left. + \left(\frac{y}{\sigma^2} - \frac{1}{2}\right)\sqrt{\sigma^2 T}\right] \quad (3.4.99)
$$

Combining these results,

$$
D_0|_{R=0} = V_0 - V_0 \Phi\left[\frac{1}{\sqrt{\sigma^2 T}} \log(V_0/d) + \left(\frac{y}{\sigma^2} + \frac{1}{2}\right)\sqrt{\sigma^2 T}\right]
$$

$$
+ e^{-yT} d\, \Phi\left[\frac{1}{\sqrt{\sigma^2 T}} \log(V_0/d) + \left(\frac{y}{\sigma^2} - \frac{1}{2}\right)\sqrt{\sigma^2 T}\right]
$$

$$
(3.4.100)
$$

Comparing this with Equation 3.3.84 and recalling that $E = V - D$, we indeed see that Equation 3.4.95 agrees with the price derived using an arbitrage argument in the previous section. Similarly, it can be verified that Equation 3.4.94 is the correct expression for the price of the debt when the recovery fraction R is not zero.[6]

---

[6]We refrain from explicitly verifying this in the text.

3.5   The Risk Premium

Continuing our discussion of the structural model for pricing corporate bonds introduced in Section 3.3, in the simplified $R = 0$
case, we write the ratio of the expected value of an investment in a
corporate zero coupon bond at maturity $V_c(T)$ divided by its price
$V_c(0) = D(V_0, T)|_{R=0}$ as

$$\left(\frac{V_c(T)}{V_c(0)} \right) = e^{(y+\mu_{risk})T} \tag{3.5.101}$$

where μ_{risk} is the risk premium.[7] Recall that when $R = 0$, default cannot
occur before maturity, and so the debt investor receives payment only
at the time $t = T$. If $\mu_{risk} = 0$, then on average an investment in the
debt of the corporation returns the same as an investment in risk-free
Treasury bonds. Using the results of the previous section, we have that

$$e^{\mu_{risk}T} = \frac{\int_{-\infty}^{\log(d/V_0)} dz'\, p(z', T)\left(V_0 e^{z'}\right) + \int_{\log(d/V_0)}^{\infty} dz'\, p(z', T)d}{\int_{-\infty}^{\log(d/V_0)} dz'\, p^{RN}(z', T)\left(V_0 e^{z'}\right) + \int_{\log(d/V_0)}^{\infty} dz'\, p^{RN}(z', T)d} \tag{3.5.102}$$

Note that $V_c(T)$, the expected value of debt at maturity T, is calculated
using the "real-world" probability density $p(z', T)$, while the value of
the debt today is calculated using the risk-neutral probability density
$p^{RN}(z', T)$. It is this difference that gives rise to the risk premium. We
have already done the integrals in the denominator. Writing

$$p(z', T) = \frac{1}{\sqrt{2\pi\sigma^2 T}} \exp\left(-\frac{(z' - yT + \sigma^2 T/2 - \Delta\mu\, T)^2}{2\sigma^2 T} \right) \tag{3.5.103}$$

---

[7] Here we are using the notation of Chapter 1 except that we have added a subscript
"risk" to the risk premium to distinguish it from the drift term in the evolution
equation for the company firm value.

we see that $p(z', T)$ differs from $p^{\text{RN}}(z', T)$ by the presence of the terms involving $\Delta\mu$, where

$$\Delta\mu = \mu - y \qquad (3.5.104)$$

The factor $\Delta\mu$ should be positive, since on average the return on an investment in firm value should be greater than the return on an investment in Treasuries. The integrations in the numerator of Equation 3.5.102 can be performed analytically. It is instructive to consider the case of small $\Delta\mu$ and hence small μ_{risk}, expanding the right-hand side of Equation 3.5.102 to linear order in $\Delta\mu$ and the left-hand side to linear order in μ_{risk}. Then since

$$p(z', T) = p^{\text{RN}}(z', T) - \Delta\mu\, T \frac{\partial p^{\text{RN}}(z', T)}{\partial z'} + \cdots \qquad (3.5.105)$$

after integrating by parts, Equation 3.5.102 becomes

$$\mu_{\text{risk}} = \Delta\mu \frac{\int_{-\infty}^{\log(d/V_0)} dz'\, p^{\text{RN}}(z', T)\left(V_0 e^{z'}\right)}{\int_{-\infty}^{\log(d/V_0)} dz'\, p^{\text{RN}}(z', T)\left(V_0 e^{z'}\right) + \int_{\log(d/V_0)}^{\infty} dz'\, p^{\text{RN}}(z', T)d} + \cdots$$

$$(3.5.106)$$

where the ellipses denote higher-order terms in $\Delta\mu$. Using the integrals in Equations 3.4.98 and 3.4.99, this becomes

$$\mu_{\text{risk}} = \Delta\mu \frac{V_0 \Phi\left[\frac{\log(d/V_0)}{\sqrt{\sigma^2 T}} - \left(\frac{y}{\sigma^2} + \frac{1}{2}\right)\sqrt{\sigma^2 T}\right]}{V_0 \Phi\left[\frac{\log(d/V_0)}{\sqrt{\sigma^2 T}} - \left(\frac{y}{\sigma^2} + \frac{1}{2}\right)\sqrt{\sigma^2 T}\right] + de^{-yT}\Phi\left[\frac{\log(V_0/d)}{\sqrt{\sigma^2 T}} + \left(\frac{y}{\sigma^2} - \frac{1}{2}\right)\sqrt{\sigma^2 T}\right]}$$

$$(3.5.107)$$

Since $\Phi(z)$ is positive, the risk premium is positive when $\Delta\mu$ is positive. In Figure 3.7 we use Equation 3.5.107 to plot μ_{risk} in percent as a function of time for T between 2 and 10 years. The parameters used are $\Delta\mu = 4$ percent, $d/V_0 = 0.5$, $y = 4$ percent, and $\sigma = 35$ percent.

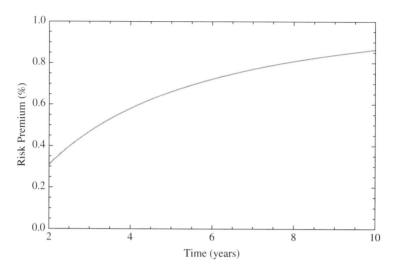

Figure 3.7 Risk premium μ_{risk} in percent plotted as a function of time T in years.

The risk premium is an increasing function of T.

The model we have introduced has too many simplifying assumptions (e.g., all the debt in zero coupon bonds matures on the same date) for the risk premium in Equation 3.5.107 to be useful for real corporate bonds. However, it provides a simple example where the risk premium can be calculated and thus enhances our understanding of its origin. Returning to the approach used to price corporate bonds in Chapter 1, we conclude that if λ^* is determined using the risk-neutral survival probability, then the risk premium is zero. However, if the real-world survival probability is used to determine λ^*, then the risk premium is nonzero.

3.6   Including Dividends

Equation 3.4.94 can be used to price zero coupon bonds in the structural model we have introduced even when the company pays dividends. In that case, the firm value evolves according to

$$dV = \mu V \, dt + \sigma V \, dw - qE \, dt \tag{3.6.108}$$

Making the change of variables as before,

$$V = V_0 \exp \left[z' - y(T - t) \right] \tag{3.6.109}$$

the evolution equation for firm value takes the form

$$dz' = \eta \, dt + \sigma \, dw - q\xi(z', t) \, dt \tag{3.6.110}$$

where

$$\xi(z', t) = \frac{E(V, t)e^{-[z' + y(t - T)]}}{V_0} \tag{3.6.111}$$

This is an evolution equation with a drift term that depends on z' and t. Using the results of Chapter 2, we have that, in this case, the risk-neutral survival probability satisfies the differential equation

$$\left[\frac{\partial}{\partial t} + \eta \frac{\partial}{\partial z'} - q\xi(z', t) \frac{\partial}{\partial z'} - q \frac{\partial \xi(z', t)}{\partial z'} - \frac{\sigma^2}{2} \frac{\partial^2}{\partial z'^2} \right] p_S^{RN}(z', t) = 0$$

$$\tag{3.6.112}$$

where, since we have set $\mu = y$, the drift is $\eta = -\sigma^2/2$. The survival probability density satisfies the intitial condition

$$p(z', 0) = \delta(z' - z_0') \tag{3.6.113}$$

where $z_0' = yT$ and the boundary conditions

$$p_S^{RN}(z_d', t) = 0 \qquad p_S^{RN}(\infty, t) = 0 \tag{3.6.114}$$

where $z'_d = \log(dR/V_0)$. We will treat q as small and include the effects of dividends only at linear order in q. Writing

$$p_S^{RN} = p_S^{RN}\Big|_{q=0} + q \Delta p_S^{RN} + \cdots \qquad (3.6.115)$$

it is Δp_S^{RN} that is needed to include the effects of dividends at linear order in q. Plugging this expansion into Equation 3.6.112, we see that Δp_S^{RN} satisfies

$$\left(\frac{\partial}{\partial t} + \eta \frac{\partial}{\partial z'} - \frac{\sigma^2}{2}\frac{\partial^2}{\partial z'^2}\right) \Delta p_S^{RN}(z', t) = \frac{\partial}{\partial z'}\left[\xi(z', t) p_S^{RN}(z', t)\right]\Big|_{q=0}$$

$$(3.6.116)$$

The right-hand side of this equation is known, since we already solved for $p_S^{RN}(z, t)$ and $E(V, t)$ in the case when there are no dividends. There is a standard way to solve a differential equation like this. We can introduce the Green's function $G(z', w; t, \tau)$, which satisfies the differential equation

$$\left(\frac{\partial}{\partial t} + \eta \frac{\partial}{\partial z'} - \frac{\sigma^2}{2}\frac{\partial^2}{\partial z'^2}\right) G(z', w; t, \tau) = \delta(t - \tau)\delta(z' - w)$$

$$(3.6.117)$$

If one can find a G with the appropriate boundary conditions, then a solution is

$$\Delta p_S^{RN}(z', t) = \int_0^\infty d\tau \int_{z'_d}^\infty dw' G(z', w'; t, \tau) \frac{\partial}{\partial w'}$$

$$\times \left[\xi(w', \tau) p_S^{RN}(w', \tau)\right]\Big|_{q=0}$$

$$(3.6.118)$$

The lower limit of integration over w' is z'_d because the Green's function vanishes there and is defined only for w' greater than this value. One way to check that this is indeed a solution is to act on it with the differential equation

$$\left(\frac{\partial}{\partial t} + \eta \frac{\partial}{\partial z'} - \frac{\sigma^2}{2} \frac{\partial^2}{\partial z'^2} \right) \Delta p_S^{RN}(z', t)$$

$$= \int_{-\infty}^{\infty} d\tau \int_{z'_d}^{\infty} dw' \left(\frac{\partial}{\partial t} + \eta \frac{\partial}{\partial z'} - \frac{\sigma^2}{2} \frac{\partial^2}{\partial z'^2} \right) G(z', w'; t, \tau) \frac{\partial}{\partial w'} \left[\xi(w', \tau) p_S^{RN}(w', \tau) \right] \Big|_{q=0}$$

$$= \int_{-\infty}^{\infty} d\tau \int_{z'_d}^{\infty} dw' \delta(t-\tau) \delta(z' - w') \frac{\partial}{\partial w'} \left[\xi(w', \tau) p_S^{RN}(w', \tau) \right] |_{q=0}$$

$$= \frac{\partial}{\partial z'} \left[\xi(z', t) p_S^{RN}(z', t) \right] \Big|_{q=0} \qquad (3.6.119)$$

We have already found a solution to Equation 3.6.117 with the right-hand side set to zero. It is the survival probability with drift set to η,

$$K(z, w; t) = \frac{1}{\sqrt{2\pi t}} \left(e^{-(z-w-\eta t)^2/(2\sigma^2 t)} - e^{-(z+w-2z_d-\eta t)^2/(2\sigma^2 t)+2\eta(z_d-w)/\sigma^2} \right)$$

$$(3.6.120)$$

It satisfies, for $z > z_d$, the intial boundary condition $K(z, w; 0) = \delta(z - w)$ and the boundary condition $K(z_d, w; t) = 0$. From this we construct the appropriate Green's function

$$G(z, w; t, \tau) = \theta(t - \tau) K(z, w; t - \tau) \qquad (3.6.121)$$

It satisfies Equation 3.6.117 because K satisfies Equation 3.6.117 with the right-hand side set equal to zero, $d\theta(t - \tau)/dt = \delta(t - \tau)$ and $K(z, w; 0) = \delta(z - w)$. It also satisfies the appropriate boundary condition, since K does.

The risk-neutral survival probability has an expansion,

$$P_S^{RN}(t) = P_S^{0,RN}(t) + q \, \Delta P_S^{RN} + \cdots \qquad (3.6.122)$$

where $P_S^{0,\mathrm{RN}}(t)$ is the risk-neutral survival probability when dividends are neglected and the ellipses denote terms of higher order in the dividend yield q. We have that

$$\Delta P_S^{\mathrm{RN}}(t) = \int_{z'_d}^{\infty} \Delta p_S^{\mathrm{RN}}(z', t) \qquad (3.6.123)$$

where $\Delta p_S^{\mathrm{RN}}(z', t)$ is given by Equation 3.6.118. Consider a case where $R = 1$. Then $E(V, t)|_{q=0} = V - d\exp[-y(T - t)]$, which implies that $\xi(z', t)|_{q=0} = 1 - (d/V_0)\exp(-z')$. For a company with debt $d/V_0 = 0.5$ that matures in $T = 10$ years and has firm value volatility $\sigma = 0.35$, performing the integrations numerically, we find that, with the risk-free rate $y = 3$ percent, $\Delta P_S^{\mathrm{RN}}(5 \text{ years}) = -0.348$ and $\Delta P_S^{\mathrm{RN}}(10 \text{ years}) = -0.588$. These are negative because dividends issued by the company to the stockholders increase the probability of default.

4

Bond Portfolio Management

4.1 Investor Preferences and Utility Functions

Most investment portfolios consist of more than one security. In most cases, portfolios consist of bonds, stocks, alternatives, and long or short positions in derivatives such as options. For this reason, it is not sufficient to understand the risk and reward characteristics of an individual security alone. The process by which one systematically constructs an investment portfolio requires an understanding of the investor's preferences or risk profile, the expected risk and return of various securities under consideration, and the relationships between the return distributions of the securities. The investor is faced with two major questions: first, what is the value added to the portfolio from investing in a given security or collection of securities, and second, what is the best security to invest in given the risk and reward desired? In an ideal world in which there are no transaction costs and any derivative can be replicated by a position in underlying securities, it is possible to do away with the reference to investor preferences, since it is always possible to hedge away the risks of any derivative instrument. However, if there are no arbitrage opportunities that exist over the investment time horizon, then the expected return from a hedged portfolio is the risk-free return.

Furthermore, in practice, it is not possible to hedge fundamental fixed-income investments. Hence an understanding of the investor's preferences is almost always critical to making investment decisions. In the first part of this chapter, we will discuss investors' preferences using the concept of a utility function. In a later part, we will highlight the concept of hedging, which naturally leads to relative valuation of securities—one should always select securities that have a higher expected return for the same amount of risk.

How should an investor choose between possible investments? For example, suppose an investor could purchase for one dollar an investment that after a year had a 99 percent chance of having no value but a 1 percent chance of having a value of $100. After many such investments, the average, or expected final value, of this investment would be $1. Since on average the investor does not make money and takes the risk of losing his money, he probably would not make this investment. But suppose instead of a 1 percent chance of having a final value of $100, the winning outcome has a 1 percent chance of having a final value of $200. Then on average the investor doubles his money after one year. This is much more than he would be likely to receive from investing in a risk-free asset, so an investor may allocate part of his investment portfolio to this investment. However, almost any investor would not invest a significant part of his wealth in such an investment, since there is a large chance that he would lose it all, leaving him in a disastrous financial position.

This investor is risk-averse; he cannot take the chance of investing a large part of his wealth in such a risky investment. To decide how an investor chooses to allocate his wealth among possible investments, one usually introduces a nonlinear function $U(W)$ of wealth W that characterizes the investor's preferences. The investor's optimal portfolio allocation over some investment horizon is determined by maximizing $E[U(W)]$ at the end of the investment horizon.

In this chapter, we will, for convenience, usually take the investment horizon to be one year. $U(W)$ is called the investors' *utility function*.

Clearly it should be an increasing function of W, since greater wealth is preferred over less wealth.

Consider an initial investment of W_0 that has, after a year, the value FW_0 with probability P and the value 0 with probability $1 - P$. We suppose that this investment returns more on average than the risk-free Treasury rate Y_1, so $PF > 1 + Y_1$. If an investor allocates all of his initial wealth W_0 to this investment, his expected utility of wealth after a year is $E[U(W)] = PU(FW_0) + (1 - P)U(0)$. On the other hand, if the investor puts all his wealth in risk-free zero coupon Treasury bonds, $E[U(W)] = U[W_0(1 + Y_1)]$. For investors who will never make an investment that puts all of their wealth at risk, $U[W_0(1 + Y_1)] > PU(FW_0) + (1 - P)U(0)$, or equivalently,

$$U(0) < \frac{U[W_0(1 + Y_1)] - PU(W_0F)}{1 - P} \qquad (4.1.1)$$

This holds for arbitrary P. Since $F > (1 + Y_1)$ and $U(W)$ is an increasing function, the difference $U[W_0(1 + Y_1)] - U(W_0F)$ is negative. Hence, taking the limit as P goes to unity of Equation 4.1.1, we deduce that $U(0) = -\infty$.

Next we suppose that the investor can make a risky investment that has return $\hat{r}$ after one year. The random variable $\hat{r}$ has mean $E[\hat{r}] = \bar{r}$ and variance $E[(\hat{r} - \bar{r})^2] = \sigma^2$. He invests a small fraction $\alpha > 0$ of his initial wealth W_0 in this risky investment and puts the remainder in risk-free zero coupon Treasury bonds. His expected utility of wealth after one year is

$$
\begin{aligned}
E[U(W)] &= E[U[(1 - \alpha)W_0(1 + Y_1) + \alpha W_0(1 + \hat{r})]] \\
&= E[U\{W_0[1 + Y_1 + \alpha(\hat{r} - Y_1)]\}] \\
&= U + \alpha U' W_0 E[\hat{r} - Y_1] + \frac{1}{2}\alpha^2 U'' W_0^2 E[(\hat{r} - Y_1)^2] + \cdots
\end{aligned}
$$

$$(4.1.2)$$

where the primes on the utility function denote derivatives. In the power series expansion of the expected utility of wealth, the utility function and its derivatives are evaluated at $W_0(1 + Y_1)$. We suppress this dependence in this section and the next two to simplify the equations. Taking the expected values and neglecting the ellipses, since α is very small, gives

$$E[U(W)] = U + \alpha U' W_0(\bar{r} - Y_1) + \frac{1}{2}\alpha^2 U'' W_0^2 \left[(\bar{r} - Y_1)^2 + \sigma^2\right]$$

(4.1.3)

The second term on the right-hand side of Equation 4.1.3 is positive, since $U' > 0$ and the risky investment returns, on average, more than risk-free Treasuries, $\bar{r} > Y_1$.

Suppose that the investor has a choice between two such risky investments with returns $\hat{r}_1$ and $\hat{r}_2$ and that the expected return of both is the same, $E[\hat{r}_1] = E[\hat{r}_2] = \bar{r}$, but their volatilities differ, i.e., $E[(\hat{r}_1 - \bar{r})^2] = \sigma_1^2, E[(\hat{r}_2 - \bar{r})^2] = \sigma_2^2$ with $\sigma_1 > \sigma_2$. Both these investments have the same expected return, and the first (with return $\hat{r}_1$) is more volatile than the second (with return $\hat{r}_2$). So a risk-averse investor would prefer to allocate the fixed fraction α of his initial wealth to the second investment, since it has lower volatility. We denote the value after one year of a portfolio that allocates a fraction α of the investor's initial wealth W_0 to the first (second) risky investment (and the remainder to risk-free zero coupon Treasury bonds) by $W_{1(2)}$. Equation 4.1.3 implies that

$$E[U(W_2)] - E[U(W_1)] = \frac{1}{2}\alpha^2 U'' W_0^2 \left(\sigma_2^2 - \sigma_1^2\right) \quad (4.1.4)$$

Since the risk-averse investor prefers the second investment, $E[U(W_2)] > E[U(W_1)]$, we conclude that $U''(W) < 0$. The utility function is increasing (positive first derivative) but has a negative second derivative because the investor is risk-averse. Simple utility functions that satisfy all the criteria we have deduced are the power law utility functions,

$$U_\gamma(W) = -\frac{1}{\gamma} W^{-\gamma} \qquad (4.1.5)$$

where the power is $\gamma \geq 0$. The case $\gamma = 0$ is handled by taking the limit as $\gamma \to 0$, which, after discarding an infinite term that is independent of W, gives $U_0(W) = \log W$. For these utility functions, $U'_\gamma(W) = W^{-\gamma-1} > 0$ and $U''_\gamma(W) = -(\gamma+1)W^{-\gamma-2} < 0$. The larger γ is, the more risk-averse the investor is. In Figure 4.1 we plot $U_\gamma(W)$ as a function of W for $\gamma = 1, 3$, and 5.

The absolute and relative risk aversion, $A(W)$ and $R(W)$, are defined to be

$$A(W) = -\frac{U''(W)}{U'(W)} \qquad R(W) = -\frac{WU''(W)}{U'(W)} \qquad (4.1.6)$$

For power law utility functions, $A(W) = (1+\gamma)/W$ and $R(W) = (1+\gamma)$.

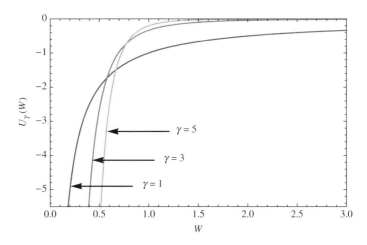

Figure 4.1 Plot of power law utility function in Equation 4.1.5 as a function of W for $\gamma = 1, 3, 5$.

4.2   Mean-Variance Portfolio Allocation

If the investor wants to allocate for one year a fraction α of his initial wealth W_0 to a single risky investment and put the remainder in a risk-free zero coupon Treasury bond, he must decide which risky investment he would prefer and what fraction of his wealth to allocate to that investment. Suppose the fraction of his wealth that he allocates to the risky asset is small enough that expanding the expected utility of wealth in a power series in α is appropriate. Then at quadratic order in the expected utility of wealth is

$$E[U(W)] = U + \alpha U' W_0(\bar{r} - Y_1) + \frac{1}{2}\alpha^2 U'' W_0^2 \left[(\bar{r} - Y_1)^2 + \sigma^2\right]$$

$$(4.2.7)$$

where $\bar{r}$ is the expected one-year return on the risky investment and σ is the volatility of the return. The optimal value of α is the one that maximizes $E[U(W)]$. We find the optimal value of the fraction allocated to risky assets, α_{opt}, by differentiating with respect to α and setting this derivative to zero. This gives

$$U' W_0(\bar{r} - Y_1) + \alpha_{\text{opt}} U'' W_0^2 \left[(\bar{r} - Y_1)^2 + \sigma^2\right] = 0 \quad (4.2.8)$$

Hence,

$$\alpha_{\text{opt}} = \left(\frac{U'}{-U'' W_0}\right) \left(\frac{(\bar{r} - Y_1)}{(\bar{r} - Y_1)^2 + \sigma^2}\right) \quad (4.2.9)$$

For small $\bar{r} - Y_1$, the initial optimal fraction of risky assets, α_{opt}, is small and the power series expansion is valid. This optimal portfolio has utility of wealth

$$E[U(W)]_{\text{opt}} = U - \frac{1}{2}\left(\frac{(U')^2}{U''}\right)\left(\frac{(\bar{r} - Y_1)^2}{(\bar{r} - Y_1)^2 + \sigma^2}\right)$$

$$= U - \frac{1}{2}\left(\frac{(U')^2}{U''}\right)\left(\frac{S^2}{1 + S^2}\right) \quad (4.2.10)$$

where the Sharpe ratio,[1] S, is the risky investment's excess return above the Treasury rate divided by its volatility,

$$S = \frac{\bar{r} - Y_1}{\sigma} \qquad (4.2.11)$$

If an investor is choosing between investments with different excess returns $\bar{r} - Y_1$ and volatilities, then, in the mean-variance approximation, she always chooses the investment that has the largest Sharpe ratio.

In the mean-variance approximation, the fractional allocation to the risky assets α_{opt} is inversely proportional to the relative risk aversion,

$$\alpha_{\text{opt}} = \frac{1}{R[W_0(1 + Y_1)]} \left(\frac{(1 + Y_1)(\bar{r} - Y_1)}{(\bar{r} - Y_1)^2 + \sigma^2} \right) \qquad (4.2.12)$$

and the absolute allocation to the risky assets $\alpha_{\text{opt}} W_0$ is inversely proportional to the absolute risk aversion,

$$\alpha_{\text{opt}} W_0 = \frac{1}{A[W_0(1 + Y_1)]} \left(\frac{(\bar{r} - Y_1)}{(\bar{r} - Y_1)^2 + \sigma^2} \right) \qquad (4.2.13)$$

Investors with the same relative risk aversion allocate the same fraction of their wealth to the risky assets, and investors with the same absolute risk aversion allocate the same absolute amount to the risky assets.

4.3   Beyond Mean-Variance Portfolio Allocation

Now we go beyond mean variance in the portfolio allocation using perturbation theory. In the mean-variance analysis, we found that the

---

[1] W. Sharpe, "The Sharpe Ratio," *Journal of Portfolio Management* 21, no. 1 (1994), p. 49.

optimal fraction of risky assets α_{opt} depends on the excess return,

$$\mu = \bar{r} - Y_1 \tag{4.3.14}$$

and is small when μ is small compared with σ, i.e., when the Sharpe ratio is small. So we expand the optimal fraction of risky assets in a power series in μ:

$$\alpha_{opt} = \alpha_{opt}^{(1)} + \alpha_{opt}^{(2)} + \cdots \tag{4.3.15}$$

where $\alpha_{opt}^{(n)}$ is of order μ^n. We have already found from the mean-variance analysis that

$$\alpha_{opt}^{(1)} = \left(\frac{U'}{-U''W_0} \right) \left(\frac{\mu}{\sigma^2} \right) \tag{4.3.16}$$

Similarly, the expected utility of wealth for the optimal portfolio is expanded in a power series in μ:

$$E[U(W)]|_{opt} = E^{(0)}[U(W)] + E^{(2)}[U(W)] + E^{(3)}[U(W)] + \cdots \tag{4.3.17}$$

We have found that $E^{(0)}[U(W)]_{opt} = U$ and

$$E^{(2)}[U(W)]_{opt} = -\frac{1}{2} \left(\frac{(U')^2}{U''} \right) \frac{\mu^2}{\sigma^2} \tag{4.3.18}$$

Note that for the optimal portfolio, the linear term in μ vanishes because the optimal portfolio is determined by maximizing the expected utility of wealth.

To make a power series expansion of the expected utility of wealth, we assume that the utility function is infinitely differentiable. Furthermore, we have to assume that the probability distribution for the risky asset returns falls off fast enough at $\pm\infty$ so that all its moments exist.

For the problem at hand, the wealth at the end of the investment horizon is $W = W_0[(1 + Y_1) + \alpha(\mu + \delta\hat{r})]$, where $\delta\hat{r} = \hat{r} - \bar{r}$. Recall that $E[\delta\hat{r}] = 0$ and $E[(\delta\hat{r})^2] = \sigma^2$. Expanding the investor's expected utility of wealth to third order in α, the quantity we must maximize is

$$E[U(W)] = U + \alpha U' W_0 \mu + \frac{1}{2}\alpha^2 U'' W_0^2 \left(\mu^2 + \sigma^2\right)$$

$$+ \frac{1}{6}\alpha^3 U''' W_0^3 E[(\mu + \delta\hat{r})^3] \qquad (4.3.19)$$

To this order we also need $E[(\delta\hat{r})^3] = \sigma^3 s$, where s is the skewness of the probability distribution for $\delta\hat{r}$. Differentiating Equation 4.3.19 gives the following equation for α_{opt}:

$$U' W_0 \mu + \alpha_{\text{opt}} U'' W_0^2 \left(\mu^2 + \sigma^2\right) + \frac{1}{2}\alpha_{\text{opt}}^2 U''' W_0^3 (\mu^3 + 3\mu\sigma^2 + s\sigma^3) = 0$$

$$(4.3.20)$$

Next we use the expansion for α_{opt} in Equation 4.3.20 and keep all terms of order μ^2. This gives

$$\alpha_{\text{opt}}^{(2)} U'' W_0^2 \sigma^2 + \frac{1}{2}(\alpha_{\text{opt}}^{(1)})^2 U''' W_0^3 s\sigma^3 = 0 \qquad (4.3.21)$$

which implies that

$$\alpha_{\text{opt}}^{(2)} = \frac{1}{2}(\alpha_{\text{opt}}^{(1)})^2 \left(\frac{U''' W_0}{-U''}\right) s\sigma \qquad (4.3.22)$$

All other things being held fixed, a more positive skewness shifts the risky asset return distribution to one that has a larger probability for large positive returns and should result in a greater allocation to the risky asset. Hence we deduce that for a risk-averse investor, the third derivative of the utility function is positive. Finally, we put this back in the expression for the utility of wealth and get at order μ^3 that

$$E^{(3)}[U(W)]|_{\text{opt}} = \alpha_{\text{opt}}^{(2)} W_0 \mu U' + \alpha_{\text{opt}}^{(2)} \alpha_{\text{opt}}^{(1)} W_0^2 \sigma^2 U'' + \frac{1}{6} (\alpha_{\text{opt}}^{(1)})^3 W_0^3 s \sigma^3 U'''$$

$$= \frac{1}{6} (\alpha_{\text{opt}}^{(1)})^3 W_0^3 s \sigma^3 U''' = -\frac{1}{6} \left(\frac{(U')^3 U'''}{(U'')^3} \right) s \left(\frac{\mu}{\sigma} \right)^3$$

$$(4.3.23)$$

At this order of our expansion in μ, the expected utility of wealth of the optimal portfolio depends on the Sharpe ratio and the skewness of the probability distribution for the risky asset. At a fixed Sharpe ratio, a risky asset with larger skewness is preferred.

To determine the optimal portfolio allocation at third order in μ and the expected utility of wealth at fourth order in μ, we expand the utility of wealth to fourth order in α. Higher-order terms do not contribute to α_{opt} and $E[U(W)]|_{\text{opt}}$ at the order we are working. Hence we need

$$E[U(W)] = U + \alpha U' W_0 \mu + \frac{1}{2} \alpha^2 U'' W_0^2 \left(\mu^2 + \sigma^2 \right)$$

$$+ \frac{1}{6} \alpha^3 U''' W_0^3 (\mu^3 + 3\sigma^2 \mu + s\sigma^3) + \frac{1}{24} \alpha^4 U'''' W_0^4 E[(\mu + \delta \hat{r})^4]$$

$$(4.3.24)$$

At this order, we need to use $E[(\delta \hat{r})^4] = 3\sigma^4 + k\sigma^4$, where k is the excess kurtosis. Differentiating Equation 4.3.24 gives the following equation for α_{opt}:

$$U' W_0 \mu + \alpha_{\text{opt}} U'' W_0^2 (\mu^2 + \sigma^2) + \frac{1}{2} \alpha_{\text{opt}}^2 U''' W_0^3 (\mu^3 + 3\mu\sigma^2 + s\sigma^3)$$

$$+ \frac{1}{6} \alpha_{\text{opt}}^3 U'''' W_0^4 (\mu^4 + 6\mu^2 \sigma^2 + 4s\mu\sigma^3 + 3\sigma^4 + k\sigma^4) = 0$$

$$(4.3.25)$$

Keeping only terms of order μ^3, this becomes

$$\alpha_{opt}^{(1)} U'' W_0^2 \mu^2 + \alpha_{opt}^{(3)} U'' W_0^2 \sigma^2 + \frac{1}{2}(\alpha_{opt}^{(1)})^2 U''' W_0^3 (3\mu\sigma^2)$$

$$+ \alpha_{opt}^{(1)}\alpha_{opt}^{(2)} U''' W_0^3 (\sigma^3 s) + \frac{1}{6}(\alpha_{opt}^{(1)})^3 U'''' W_0^4 (3\sigma^4 + \sigma^4 k) = 0$$

$$(4.3.26)$$

Hence, the order μ^3 term in the power series expansion of the optimal fraction of the investor's wealth allocated to risky assets is

$$\alpha_{opt}^{(3)} = -\alpha_{opt}^{(1)} \left(\frac{\mu^2}{\sigma^2}\right) - \frac{3}{2}(\alpha_{opt}^{(1)})^2 \left(\frac{U''' W_0}{U''}\right) \mu$$

$$- \alpha_{opt}^{(1)}\alpha_{opt}^{(2)} \left(\frac{U''' W_0}{U''}\right) \sigma s - \frac{1}{6}(\alpha_{opt}^{(1)})^3 \left(\frac{U'''' W_0^2}{U''}\right)(3\sigma^2 + \sigma^2 k)$$

$$(4.3.27)$$

For fixed μ, σ, and s, a larger k corresponds to a return distribution with fatter tails. Hence a risk-averse investor should allocate less to the risky asset as k increases. We conclude that $U'''' < 0$. Finally, we find for the order μ^4 contribution to the optimal portfolio's expected utility

$$E^{(4)}[U(W)]|_{opt} = -\frac{1}{8}\left(\frac{(U')^4 U'''}{(U'')^5}\right)\left(\frac{\mu}{\sigma}\right)^4 s^2 + \frac{1}{2}\left(\frac{(U')^2}{U''}\right)\left(\frac{\mu}{\sigma}\right)^4$$

$$- \frac{1}{2}\left(\frac{(U')^3 U'''}{(U'')^3}\right)\left(\frac{\mu}{\sigma}\right)^4 + \frac{1}{8}\left(\frac{U''''(U')^4}{(U'')^4}\right)\left(\frac{\mu}{\sigma}\right)^4\left(1 + \frac{k}{3}\right)$$

$$(4.3.28)$$

For the power law utility functions U_γ, all the derivatives can easily be computed:

$$W^{\gamma+n}\frac{d^n U_\gamma(W)}{dW^n} = \left(-\frac{1}{\gamma}\right)(-\gamma)\cdots(-\gamma - n + 1) \qquad (4.3.29)$$

We were able to use the results of this section to deduce the fact that the first four derivatives of the utility function alternate in sign. Investors prefer high and positive odd moments in the portfolio return distribution, such as the mean and the skewness. And, they prefer smaller even moments in the return distribution (such as variance and kurtosis). However, the usefulness of this for actual calculations of the optimal utility of wealth is limited somewhat by the fact that the power series expansion does not always converge rapidly. Suppose we have a risky asset with an excess return $\mu = 4$ percent and an annualized volatility of 20 percent, and we assume that the risky asset is normally distributed. In this case, the Sharpe ratio $S = 0.2$. We take for the utility function a power law with $\gamma = 8$ and assume that the asset is normally distributed. In this case, $\alpha_{\text{opt}}^{(1)} = 0.111(1 + Y_1)$, $\alpha_{\text{opt}}^{(2)} = 0$, and $\alpha_{\text{opt}}^{(3)} = -5(1 + Y_1) \times 10^{-5}$. So the leading term is very accurate. For $\gamma = 3$, the optimal allocation to these risky assets is $\alpha_{\text{opt}}^{(1)} = 0.250(1 + Y_1), \alpha_{\text{opt}}^{(2)} = 0$, and $\alpha_{\text{opt}}^{(3)} = -6(1 + Y_1) \times 10^{-4}$. Now the optimal allocation is about 25 percent. Finally, for $\gamma = 1$, we have that $\alpha_{\text{opt}}^{(1)} = 0.500(1 + Y_1), \alpha_{\text{opt}}^{(2)} = 0, \alpha_{\text{opt}}^{(3)} = -0.005(1 + Y_1)$, and the optimal allocation to the risky asset is about 50 percent.

4.4 Three Exactly Solvable Portfolio Allocation Problems

We first consider portfolio allocation to a normally distributed risky asset using an exponential utility function,

$$U_b[W] = -\frac{1}{b}e^{-bW} \qquad (4.4.30)$$

Note that $U_b[0]$ is finite. Hence an investor with this utility function would consider allocating all of his portfolio to a risky asset that can fluctuate to zero value. This utility function has constant absolute risk aversion, $A = b$. A plot of $U_b(W)$ as a function of W for $b = 1, 2$, and 3 is presented in Figure 4.2.

The expected utility of wealth for a portfolio with a fraction of assets α in normally distributed risky assets with excess return μ and

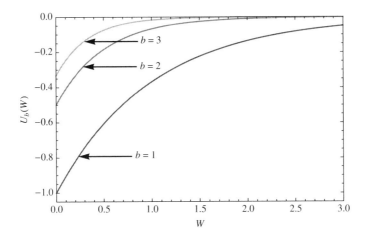

Figure 4.2 Plot of the exponential utility function in Equation 4.4.30 as a function of W for $b = 1, 2,$ and 3.

volatility σ is

$$
\begin{aligned}
E[U_b(W)] &= -\frac{1}{b}E\left[\exp\left[-bW_0(1 + Y_1 + \alpha\mu + \alpha\delta\hat{r})\right]\right] \\
&= -\frac{1}{b}\exp\left[-bW_0(1 + Y_1 + \alpha\mu) + \frac{b^2 W_0^2 \alpha^2 \sigma^2}{2}\right]
\end{aligned}
$$
(4.4.31)

In this case, the optimal fraction of risky assets is

$$
\alpha_{\text{opt}} = \frac{\mu}{bW_0\sigma^2}
$$
(4.4.32)

and the expected utility of wealth for the investor is

$$
E[U_b(W)]|_{\text{opt}} = -\frac{1}{b}\exp\left[-bW_0(1 + Y_1) - \frac{\mu^2}{2\sigma^2}\right]
$$
(4.4.33)

When comparing the optimal utility of wealth between two such risky assets, the one with the higher Sharpe ratio is preferred. One difference between using this utility function and the power law utility functions is that the optimal fraction of risky assets depends on the total initial wealth W_0. This is not true for the power law utility functions. The relative level of risk aversion for the power law utility functions is a constant independent of the total wealth of the investor.

Next, we consider the case of an investor whose investment choices are risk-free Treasuries, a risky asset with a normally distributed return, and a risky "lottery ticket"-like investment. For the risky assets, his choices are:

1. Securities whose returns are normally distributed with some expected return[2] μ and standard deviation σ.
2. Securities that can return some large return r_u with probability p or a negative return r_d with some probability $(1 - p)$.

For α in the normal asset and β in the lottery ticket security, an elegant way to determine the moments of the return on the risky part of the portfolio is to introduce the moment generating function,

$$\Psi(t) = \sum_{k=0,1} \int_{-\infty}^{\infty} e^{[\alpha x + \beta r_u (\frac{r_d}{r_u})^k] t} p^{1-k} (1 - p)^k \mathcal{P}(x)\, dx \qquad (4.4.34)$$

where

$$\mathcal{P}(x) = \frac{1}{\sqrt{2\pi}\sigma} e^{-\frac{1}{2}\frac{(x-\mu)^2}{\sigma^2}} \qquad (4.4.35)$$

is the standard normal probability distribution. From the form of $\Psi(t)$, it is clear that the nth derivative of Ψ with respect to t, evaluated at $t = 0$, gives the expected value of the return on the risky assets raised to the nth power. Performing the x integration, we find that

$$\Psi(t) = p e^{(\alpha\mu + \beta r_u)t + \frac{1}{2}\alpha^2\sigma^2 t^2} + (1 - p)e^{(\alpha\mu + \beta r_d)t + \frac{1}{2}\alpha^2\sigma^2 t^2} \qquad (4.4.36)$$

---

[2]Note that here we are using μ for the expected return, not the excess expected return.

We can easily show that for the risky part of the portfolio,

$$\text{Expected return} = \alpha\mu + \beta[r_u p + r_d(1 - p)]$$
$$\text{Variance} = \alpha^2\sigma^2 + \beta^2(1 - p)p(r_u - r_d)^2$$
$$\text{Skewness} = \frac{\beta^3 p(1 - p)(1 - 2p)(r_u - r_d)^3}{[\alpha^2\sigma^2 + \beta^2(1 - p)p(r_u - r_d)^2]^{3/2}}$$

$$(4.4.37)$$

Keeping all other things fixed, the expected "risk" or standard deviation from playing the lottery trade scales linearly with the difference $r_u - r_d$, but as the square root of p. As long as $r_u - r_d$ and β are positive and $p < 1/2$, the combined portfolio has a large positive skew. In particular, expanding the skewness around $p = 0$, we obtain that

$$\text{Skewness} = \frac{\beta^3}{\sigma^3\alpha^3}(r_u - r_d)^3 p + \cdots \qquad (4.4.38)$$

where the ellipses denote terms proportional to higher powers of p.

To determine the optimal allocation, we will assume that the investor has a one-year investment horizon and a utility function $U(W)$ that depends on the stochastic wealth W, specified by

$$W = W_0[1 + \alpha x + \beta r_l + (1 - \alpha - \beta)Y_1] \qquad (4.4.39)$$

where W_0 is the initial wealth, α is the fraction of the initial wealth invested in risky normally distributed assets, β is the fraction of the initial wealth invested in the binomial (lottery ticket) distributed risky asset, x is the annual return on the normal risky asset, r_l is the annual return on the binomial (lottery) investment, and Y_1 is the risk-free annual return. Now we must choose the utility function for the investor.

We again take the exponential utility function (see Equation 4.4.30) with absolute risk aversion b.

Writing $b = B/W_0$, the expected utility of wealth is

$$E[U_b(W)] = -\frac{W_0}{B} \exp\left\{-B[1+(1-\alpha)Y_1]+\frac{B\alpha}{2}\left(-2\mu+B\alpha\sigma^2\right)\right\}$$
$$\times \left\{p\exp\left[-B\beta(r_u-Y_1)\right] + (1-p)\exp\left[-B\beta(r_d-Y_1)\right]\right\}$$

$$(4.4.40)$$

Because the normal and binomial risky asset returns are uncorrelated and we have used an exponential utility function, the expected utility of wealth can be factored into one factor that involves α and one factor that involves β. So the portfolio allocation problem can be factored, and differentiating the expected utility of wealth with respect to α and β and setting those derivatives to zero gives

$$\alpha_{\text{opt}} = \frac{\mu - Y_1}{B\sigma^2} \qquad (4.4.41)$$

and

$$\beta_{\text{opt}} = \frac{1}{B(r_u - r_d)}\log\left(\frac{p(r_u - Y_1)}{(1 - p)(Y_1 - r_d)}\right) \qquad (4.4.42)$$

The risk-averse investor allocates more to the lottery trade when $Y_1 - r_d$ is smaller or p is closer to unity.

The fair value for p, i.e., the one that gives the market expectation of the binomial trade return equal to zero, is $p = r_d/(r_d - r_u)$. Using this value for p, we have that $p/(1 - p) = -r_d/r_u$ and the argument of the logarithm in Equation 4.4.42 is less than unity. Hence the lottery trade is shorted. Suppose we fix B by demanding that $\alpha_{\text{opt}} = 0.6$ for the case when $Y_1 = 3$ percent, $\sigma = 0.25$, and $\mu = 7$ percent. This gives $B = 1.07$. In Figure 4.3 we show the allocation to the lottery trade when this value of B is used, $Y_1 = 3$ percent, $p = 1/3$, and $r_d = -0.1$.

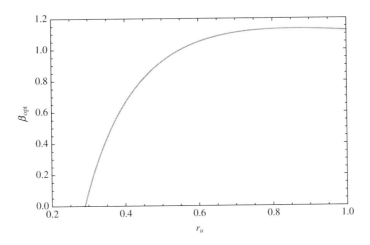

Figure 4.3 Plot of β_{opt} as a function of r_u using $B = 1.07$, $Y_1 = 3$ percent, $p = 1/3$, and $r_d = -0.1$.

It is worth considering what would happen if we repeated this asset allocation problem with a utility function that has constant relative risk aversion that is greater than unity. A risk-averse investor with such a power law utility function will not allocate any of his wealth to the risky asset that is normally distributed because $U(0) = -\infty$. If the investor allocated a fraction α of his wealth to this asset, it puts all of his wealth at risk from fluctuations that have $x = Y_1 - (1/\alpha)(1 + Y_1)$. Of course the normal distribution is certainly inappropriate for very large negative returns. Furthermore, returns less than -1 are not possible if the investor cannot lose more than the original investment. This problem can be approached numerically by using a modified probability distribution for the returns x. Say, for example,

$$\mathcal{P}(x) = \frac{1}{\sqrt{2\pi}\sigma} \left(\frac{1}{\Phi[(1 + \mu)/\sigma]} \right) \exp\left(-\frac{(x - \mu)^2}{2\sigma^2} \right) \theta(x + 1)$$

$$(4.4.43)$$

which vanishes for $x < -1$. Now μ is not exactly the expected return, but the difference between μ and $E[x]$ is very small for many reasonable choices of μ and σ.

In Figure 4.3 the value of β_{opt} is increasing with r_u for most of the plot; however, it will decrease like $1/r_u$ for very large r_u, as is evident from Equation 4.4.42. This seems rather perplexing. If all other things are held fixed and the upside from the lottery ticket investment is increased, shouldn't the allocation to this investment increase? The answer is no because the utility function we have chosen asymptotes to zero. For very large W, a further increase in W has only a small impact on $U_b(W)$, and so the investor prefers to lower her risk by reducing β_{opt}. Obviously the same thing happens with power law utility functions that asymptote to zero when the investor allocates her wealth among Treasuries and the lottery ticket investment. There are power law utility functions that correspond to a risk-averse investor that do not asymptote to zero, but rather increase without bound. These have $-1 < \gamma \leq 0$. For many investors, a power law utility function that grows without bound may be appropriate for very large $W > W_*$, but one with a larger value of γ may apply for $W < W_*$. It is not difficult to construct such a hybrid power law utility function by matching the value of the utility function and its first derivative at the transition point, $W = W_*$. For example, the utility function

$$U(W) = -\frac{1}{\gamma'} W_*^{\gamma'-\gamma} W^{-\gamma'} + \left(\frac{1}{\gamma'} - \frac{1}{\gamma} \right) W_*^{-\gamma} \qquad W > W_*$$

$$U(W) = -\frac{1}{\gamma} W^{-\gamma} \qquad W < W_* \tag{4.4.44}$$

is a power law utility function with power γ for $W < W_*$ and a power law utility function with power γ' for $W > W_*$.

Finally, consider an investor with a power law utility function, but take as the risky asset a zero coupon corporate bond with zero recovery fraction. The reason that this bond is risky is because, unlike the Treasury zero coupon bond, an investor in this corporate bond can lose the principal. Again we choose an investment horizon of one year. As with the lottery ticket investment in the previous example, there are two possible outcomes for the excess return, $\hat{r}_e = \hat{r} - Y_1$, depending on whether the firm defaults or not. The probability distribution for the excess return can be written as

$$\mathcal{P}(r_e) = P_D \delta(r_e + 1 + Y_1) + P_S \delta \left(r_e - \frac{\mu + (1 + Y_1)P_D}{P_S} \right)$$

(4.4.45)

where P_D is the one-year default probability and $P_S = 1 - P_D$ is the one-year survival probability. Since $P_S + P_D = 1$, this probability distribution is properly normalized. If the firm defaults, the excess return is $r_e = -1 - Y_1$, and so this is the argument of the first delta function. At this point, it is probably not clear what μ is in the argument of the second delta function. We gain an understanding of this by calculating the expected value of r_e that follows from this probability distribution. Since

$$E[\hat{r}_e] = \int_{-\infty}^{\infty} dr_e \mathcal{P}(r_e) r_e = -P_D(1 + Y_1) + \mu + P_D(1 + Y_1) = \mu$$

(4.4.46)

μ is the expected value of the excess return. The variance for the probability distribution for $\hat{r}_e$ is

$$\sigma^2 = E[(\hat{r}_e - \mu)^2] = P_S \left(\frac{\mu + (1 + Y_1)P_D}{P_S} - \mu \right)^2$$

$$+ P_D[-(1 + Y_1) - \mu]^2 = (\mu + 1 + Y_1)^2 \frac{P_D}{P_S}$$

(4.4.47)

So with an excess return of $\mu = 1$ percent a one-year default probability of $P_D = 2$ percent, and an annualized one-year Treasury yield of $Y_1 = 4$ percent, the volatility is $\sigma = 15$ percent. Hence the Sharpe ratio for this investment is small, $S = 0.06$. We can expect the leading term in the perturbative approach, introduced in Section 4.3, to be a very good approximation. However, that is not the case, since the probability distribution is very far from normal. According to the results in Chapter 2, the skewness of the probability distribution for $\delta \hat{r}$ is

$$s = \frac{E[(r_e - \mu)^3]}{\sigma^3} = \frac{2P_D - 1}{\sqrt{P_D P_S}} \qquad (4.4.48)$$

and so with $P_D = 2$ percent, the skewness of the probability distribution for the excess return $\hat{r}_e$ is $s = -6.86$. In the perturbative approach of the previous section for a risky asset that is a zero coupon corporate bond with an excess return of $\mu = 1$ percent and a one-year default probability of $P_D = 2$ percent, when the risk-free rate is $Y_1 = 4$ percent for a power law utility function with $\gamma = 3$, we have $\alpha_{opt}^{(1)} = 11.6$ percent and $\alpha_{opt}^{(2)} = -3.3$ percent. In perturbation theory, the large skewness has a significanct impact on the optimal fraction of risky assets. Unlike in the previous examples considered in this chapter, the higher-order terms in the perturbative expansion for the optimal fraction of risky assets are important.

Comparing the variance of the probability distribution for corporate bond returns given in Chapter 2 with that in Equation 4.4.47 implies that

$$\mu = P_S \exp\left[\int_0^{1\,\mathrm{year}} d\tau\, y_c(\tau)\right] - (1 + Y_1) \qquad (4.4.49)$$

Hence, μ is essentially[3] the risk premium introduced in Chapter 1.

With a fraction α of the investor's initial wealth W_0 allocated to the corporate bond, the wealth at the end of a year is $W = W_0[(1 +$

---

[3]There is a small difference, since in Chapter 1 we used continuous compounding.

$Y_1) + \alpha \hat{r}_e]$ and the expected utility of wealth is

$$E[U_\gamma(W)] = -\frac{W_0^{-\gamma}}{\gamma} \left\{ P_S \left[(1 + Y_1) + \alpha \frac{\mu + (1 + Y_1)P_D}{P_S} \right]^{-\gamma} \right.$$

$$\left. + P_D \left[(1 + Y_1) - \alpha(1 + Y_1) \right]^{-\gamma} \right\} \qquad (4.4.50)$$

For $\mu > 0$, we expect a maximum at some positive value of α. Differentiating with respect to α, we find the following equation for the optimal portfolio allocation to this corporate bond:

$$\left[1 + Y_1 + \alpha_{\text{opt}} \left(\frac{\mu + (1 + Y_1)P_D}{P_S} \right) \right]^{-\gamma - 1} [\mu + (1 + Y_1)P_D]$$

$$- \left[1 + Y_1 - \alpha_{\text{opt}}(1 + Y_1) \right]^{-\gamma - 1} (1 + Y_1)P_D = 0 \qquad (4.4.51)$$

Introducing the variable

$$\epsilon = \left(\frac{(1 + Y_1)P_D}{\mu + (1 + Y_1)P_D} \right)^{\frac{1}{\gamma + 1}} \qquad (4.4.52)$$

the optimal fraction of risky assets satisfies the linear equation

$$\left[1 + Y_1 + \alpha_{\text{opt}} \left(\frac{\mu + (1 + Y_1)P_D}{P_S} \right) \right] \epsilon = \left[1 + Y_1 - \alpha_{\text{opt}}(1 + Y_1) \right]$$

$$(4.4.53)$$

Equation 4.4.53 has the solution

$$\alpha_{\text{opt}} = \frac{(1 + Y_1)(1 - \epsilon)}{1 + Y_1 + \epsilon[\mu + (1 + Y_1)P_D]/P_S} \qquad (4.4.54)$$

Note that as the probability of default goes to zero, $\epsilon \to 0$, and so $\alpha_{\text{opt}} \to 1$. A value of $\alpha_{\text{opt}} > 1$ corresponds to a portfolio that is leveraged by borrowing at the risk-free rate to invest in the risky asset. The average return on the corporate bond is greater than the risk-free Treasury return Y_1; however, even when the probability of default is very small, the investor will never use leverage because it puts all of his wealth at risk.

Consider a zero coupon corporate bond with zero recovery fraction and expected excess average return of $\mu = 1$ percent and a one-year default probability $P_D = 2$ percent. Furthermore, we assume the annualized Treasury return is $Y_1 = 4$ percent. For an investor with $\gamma = 3$, the parameter ϵ in Equation 4.4.52 is equal to 0.9065 and the optimal fraction of the portfolio to allocate to this risky asset is $\alpha_{opt} = 9.10$ percent. Recall that the perturbative approach including the skewness gave $\alpha_{opt} \simeq 8.3$ percent.

4.5   Portfolio Allocation to a CDO

In this section, we consider the problem of finding the optimal allocation of investments when the portfolio consists of risk-free assets that have an annual return Y_1 and a risky asset with return $\hat{r}$. The risky asset consists of a fixed collection of zero coupon corporate bonds. This risky asset is a very simple example of a collateralized debt obligation (CDO), i.e., a collection of debt instruments bundled together and sold off as a single object. We suppose that the CDO consists of N bonds and that the ith bond is initially a fraction, f_i, of the CDO value, so

$$\sum_{i=1}^{N} f_i = 1 \tag{4.5.55}$$

Finally, for simplicity, we take the recovery fraction on each of the bonds to be zero. Suppose the bond for company i would return $r_i(t)$ over the investment horizon t if the company does not default in that time period. In this case, after a time t, the return on an investment in the CDO is

$$\hat{r} = \sum_{i=1}^{N} f_i[1 + r_i(t)][1 - \hat{n}_i(t)] - 1 = \sum_{i=1}^{N} f_i r_i(t) - \hat{l}(t) \tag{4.5.56}$$

where $\hat{l}(t)$ is the fractional default loss variable. It is given by

$$\hat{l}(t) = \sum_{i=1}^{N} f_i[1 + r_i(t)]\hat{n}_i(t) \qquad (4.5.57)$$

where, as in Chapter 2, $\hat{n}_i(t)$ is a random variable that takes the value 1 if the company defaults in the time period t and is 0 otherwise. In Chapter 1 we wrote

$$r_i(t) = \exp\left[\int_0^t d\tau\, y_{ic}(\tau)\right] - 1 \qquad (4.5.58)$$

where $y_{ic}(t)$ is the promised short corporate rate of return for company i. Because of the factor of $[1 + r_i(t)]$ multiplying f_i in Equation 4.5.57, it is convenient to introduce $\bar{f}_i = [1 + r_i(t)]f_i$. Note that even though we don't explicitly display it, the $\bar{f}_i$ have dependence on the time horizon t.

The expected fractional loss is

$$E[\hat{l}(t)] = \sum_{i=1}^{N} \bar{f}_i P_D(i;t) \qquad (4.5.59)$$

Here, $P_D(i;t)$ is the probability that company i defaults in the time horizon t. The variance of the probability distribution for the fractional loss is

$$
\begin{aligned}
v^{(2)} = \sigma^2 &= E\left[\{\hat{l}(t) - E[\hat{l}(t)]\}^2\right] = E[\hat{l}(t)^2] - E[\hat{l}(t)]^2 \\
&= \sum_{i,j} \bar{f}_i \bar{f}_j E[\hat{n}_i(t)\hat{n}_j(t)] - \sum_{i,j} \bar{f}_i \bar{f}_j P_D(i;t) P_D(j;t) \\
&= \sum_{i \neq j} \bar{f}_i \bar{f}_j [P_D(i,j;t) - P_D(i;t) P_D(j;t)] \\
&\quad + \sum_i \bar{f}_i^2 P_D(i;t)[1 - P_D(i;t)] \qquad (4.5.60)
\end{aligned}
$$

where, using the notation of Chapter 2, $P_D(i,j;t) = E[\hat{n}_i(t)\hat{n}_j(t)]$ is the joint default probability for firms i and j. Note also that we used the fact that $\hat{n}_i(t)^2 = \hat{n}_i(t)$. The volatility for the return $\hat{r}(t)$ on the CDO is $\sigma = \sqrt{v^{(2)}}$. The third moment of the fractional loss probability distribution is

$$v^{(3)} = E\left[\{\hat{l}(t) - E[\hat{l}(t)]\}^3\right] = E[\hat{l}(t)^3] - 3E[\hat{l}(t)^2]E[\hat{l}(t)] + 2E[\hat{l}(t)]^3$$

$$= \sum_{i,j,k} \bar{f}_i \bar{f}_j \bar{f}_k E[\hat{n}_i(t)\hat{n}_j(t)\hat{n}_k(t)] - 3 \sum_{i,j,k} \bar{f}_i \bar{f}_j \bar{f}_k E[\hat{n}_i(t)\hat{n}_j(t)] P_D(k;t)$$

$$+ 2 \sum_{i,j,k} \bar{f}_i \bar{f}_j \bar{f}_k P_D(i;t) P_D(j;t) P_D(k;t) \qquad (4.5.61)$$

Using

$$\sum_{i,j,k} \bar{f}_i \bar{f}_j \bar{f}_k E[\hat{n}_i(t)\hat{n}_j(t)\hat{n}_k(t)]$$

$$= \sum_{i\neq j\neq k} \bar{f}_i \bar{f}_j \bar{f}_k P_D(i,j,k;t) + 3 \sum_{i\neq j} \bar{f}_i^2 \bar{f}_j P_D(i,j;t) + \sum_i \bar{f}_i^3 P_D(i;t)$$

$$(4.5.62)$$

$$\sum_{i,j,k} \bar{f}_i \bar{f}_j \bar{f}_k E[\hat{n}_i(t)\hat{n}_j(t)] P_D(k;t)$$

$$= \sum_{i\neq j\neq k} \bar{f}_i \bar{f}_j \bar{f}_k P_D(i,j;t) P_D(k;t) + 2 \sum_{i\neq j} \bar{f}_i^2 \bar{f}_j P_D(i,j;t) P_D(i;t)$$

$$+ \sum_{i\neq k} \bar{f}_i^2 \bar{f}_k P_D(i;t) P_D(k;t) + \sum_i \bar{f}_i^3 P_D(i;t)^2 \qquad (4.5.63)$$

and

$$\sum_{i,j,k} \bar{f}_i \bar{f}_j \bar{f}_k P_D(i;t) P_D(j;t) P_D(k;t)$$

$$= \sum_{i\neq j\neq k} \bar{f}_i \bar{f}_j \bar{f}_k P_D(i;t) P_D(j;t) P_D(k;t)$$

$$+ 3 \sum_{i\neq j} \bar{f}_i^2 \bar{f}_j P_D(i;t)^2 P_D(j;t) + \sum_i \bar{f}_i^3 P_D(i;t)^3 \qquad (4.5.64)$$

Equation 4.5.61 becomes

$$
\begin{aligned}
v^{(3)} = \sum_{i \neq j \neq k} \bar{f}_i \bar{f}_j \bar{f}_k \{ & [P_D(i, j, k; t) - P_D(i; t) P_D(j; t) P_D(k; t)] \\
& - 3 P_D(k; t)[P_D(i, j; t) - P_D(i; t) P_D(j; t)] \} \\
+ 3 \sum_{i \neq j} \bar{f}_i^2 \bar{f}_j & [1 - 2 P_D(i; t)][P_D(i, j; t) - P_D(i; t) P_D(j; t)] \\
+ \sum_i \bar{f}_i^3 P_D(i; t) & [1 - 3 P_D(i; t) + 2 P_D(i; t)^2] \qquad (4.5.65)
\end{aligned}
$$

The skewness of the returns is $s = -v^{(3)}/\sigma^3$, where the minus sign arises because $v^{(3)}$ is the third moment of the loss distribution, not the return distribution. Using these results and higher-order moments if necessary, we can approximately find the optimal allocation to the CDO using the perturbative results of Section 4.3.

Now let's consider the case where $f_i = 1/N$, so all the bonds are equally weighted, and furthermore suppose that they all have the same promised rate of return $r_i(t) = r_c(t)$ over the investment horizon. Finally, we assume that there are no correlations between corporate defaults. Then $P_D(i, j; t) = P_D(i; t) P_D(j; t)$ and $P_D(i, j, k; t) = P_D(i; t) P_D(j; t) P_D(k; t)$. To further simplify the problem, suppose that all the bonds have equal default probabilities, so that $P_D(i; t) = P_D(t)$. Then over the time horizon t the variance of the return is

$$
\sigma^2 = \{[1 + r_c(t)]^2/N\} P_D(t)[1 - P_D(t)] \qquad (4.5.66)
$$

The volatility falls like $1/\sqrt{N}$ as the number of bonds in the CDO increases. Diversification by increasing N reduces the investors' risk. The skewness of the return distribution is

$$
s = - \frac{1 - 3 P_D(t) + 2 P_D(t)^2}{\sqrt{N P_D(t)(1 - P_D)^3}} \qquad (4.5.67)
$$

The skewness falls like $1/\sqrt{N}$, consistent with the results of Chapter 2, and the central limit theorem implies that the probability distribution for the returns approaches a normal distribution as $N \to \infty$. Suppose $N = 100$, $t = 1$ year, and $P_D(1\text{ year}) = 2$ percent; then $\sigma = 1.4[1 + r(1\text{ year})]$ percent and $s = -0.69$.

Now we relax the assumption that the defaults are uncorrelated. We have some information on $P_D(i, j; t)$ from historical default correlations, but for the skewness, we need the joint default probability for three firms. Furthermore, if we went to even higher order in perturbation theory for the portfolio allocation problem, the joint default probability for even more firms is required. We will use the default model based on a multivariate normal copula function to handle this difficulty. Recall from Chapter 2 that in this model, the joint default probabilities are

$$
P_D(i_1, \cdots, i_n; t) = \frac{1}{(2\pi)^{1/2}\sqrt{\det \xi}} \int_{-\infty}^{\chi_{i_1}(t)} dx_1 \ldots \int_{-\infty}^{\chi_{i_n}(t)} dx_n
$$

$$
\times \exp\left[-\frac{1}{2} \sum_{ij} x_i \xi_{ij}^{(-1)} x_j \right] \tag{4.5.68}
$$

where the sum goes over $i, j = 1, \cdots, n$, and $\xi_{ij}^{(-1)}$ is the inverse of the $n \times n$ factor correlation matrix ξ_{ij}. The functions $\chi_i(t)$ are determined by the single-firm default probabilities, $P_D(i; t) = \Phi[\chi_i(t)]$. So in our example where $P_D(i; 1\text{ year}) = P_D(1\text{ year}) = 2$ percent, we find that $\chi_i(1\text{ year}) = \chi(1\text{ year}) = -2.0538$. We model the $n \times n$ correlation matrix with $\xi_{ij} = \xi$ for $i \neq j$. In this case, the correlation matrix has one eigenvalue equal to $1 + (n-1)\xi$ and $n - 1$ equal to $1 - \xi$. We need all the eigenvalues to be positive for any natural number $n < N$, and so $1 > \xi > -1/(N - 1)$. The correlation matrix has determinant $\det \xi = (1 - \xi)^{n-1}[1 + (n-1)\xi]$. Finally, to calculate the joint survival probabilities, we need the inverse of the correlation matrix. It is not hard to verify that the inverse has elements

$$\xi_{ii}^{(-1)} = \frac{1 + (n-2)\xi}{1 + (n-2)\xi - (n-1)\xi^2}$$

$$\xi_{ij}^{(-1)} = \frac{-\xi}{1 + (n-2)\xi - (n-1)\xi^2} \qquad \text{for} \quad i \neq j \qquad (4.5.69)$$

Using these formulas, the joint survival probability for any two of the firms is

$$P_D(i, j; t) = \frac{1}{(2\pi)\sqrt{1-\xi^2}} \int_{-\infty}^{\chi(t)} dx_1 \int_{-\infty}^{\chi(t)} dx_2$$

$$\times \exp\left[-\frac{1}{2(1-\xi^2)}\left(x_1^2 + x_2^2 - 2\xi x_1 x_2\right)\right] \qquad (4.5.70)$$

and the joint default probability for any three firms is

$$P_D(i, j, k; t) = \frac{1}{(2\pi)^{(3/2)}(1-\xi)\sqrt{1+2\xi}} \int_{-\infty}^{\chi(t)} dx_1 \int_{-\infty}^{\chi(t)} dx_2 \int_{-\infty}^{\chi(t)} dx_3$$

$$\times \exp\left\{-\frac{1}{2(1+\xi-2\xi^2)}\left[(1+\xi)(x_1^2 + x_2^2 + x_3^2)\right.\right.$$

$$\left.\left. - 2\xi(x_1 x_2 + x_1 x_3 + x_2 x_3)\right]\right\} \qquad (4.5.71)$$

These integrals can be performed numerically. Using $\chi(1 \text{ year}) = -2.0538$ [which corresponds to $P_D(1 \text{ year}) = 2$ percent] and the factor correlation $\xi = 0.2$, we find that the two-firm joint default probability is $P_D(i, j; 1 \text{ year}) = 1.10 \times 10^{-3}$. Using results from Chapter 2, this implies a one-year default correlation $d_{ij} = 3.57$ percent. In this example, the three-firm joint default probability is $P_D(i, j, k; 1 \text{ year}) = 1.13 \times 10^{-4}$. For the CDO with 100 bonds, Equation 4.5.60 gives for the volatility $\sigma = 2.98[1 + r_c(1 \text{ year})]$ percent. The correlations have increased the volatility by about a factor of 2, and in leading order in perturbation theory, this amounts to a reduction in the optimal amount allocated to the CDO by a factor of 4! Obviously, understanding correlations between the assets in the CDO is crucial to correctly assigning its optimal weight in any portfolio. Furthermore, the correlations increase the magnitude of the skewness, and we find that $s = -3.12$, which is roughly five times the skewness in the uncorrelated case.

The importance of correlations between risky assets for the portfolio allocation problem and the fact that they sometimes cannot be accurately extracted from historical data present a problem for determining the optimal portfolio. However, there is an even more serious issue. In times of market stress, which usually arise from a liquidity crisis, the correlations of most risky assets go to near their extreme values, ± 1, and depart radically from their historical norms.

4.6   Portfolio Allocation with Many Risky Assets

So far we have mostly considered cases in which the portfolio consists of risk-free assets and a single risky asset. The problem has been to determine the fraction of the investor's portfolio that she allocates to those risky assets. In this section, we use the mean-variance approximation to determine the portfolio allocation when there are several risky assets and the investor has to decide not only how much of her wealth to put in the risky assets, but also how to allocate it among those risky assets. We start by considering n risky assets, which we distinguish by subscripts, $i = 1, \cdots, n$. Suppose they have annualized returns $\hat{r}_i$ with mean $E[\hat{r}_i] = \bar{r}_i$ and annualized excess returns $\mu_i = \bar{r}_i - Y_1$. The annualized returns have variances $\sigma_i^2 = E[(\hat{r}_i - \bar{r}_i)^2]$ and a covariance matrix c_{ij}. Suppose the investor allocates a fraction α_i of her initial wealth W_0 to the risky asset with return $\hat{r}_i$. After the one-year investment horizon, the investor's wealth is

$$W = W_0 \left[(1 + Y_1) \left(1 - \sum_{i=1}^{n} \alpha_i \right) + \sum_{i=1}^{n} \alpha_i (1 + \hat{r}_i) \right] \quad (4.6.72)$$

Introducing $\delta\hat{r}_i = \hat{r}_i - \bar{r}_i$, the expression for W becomes

$$W = W_0 \left[(1 + Y_1) + \sum_{i=1}^{n} \alpha_i(\mu_i + \delta\hat{r}_i) \right] \qquad (4.6.73)$$

The Sharpe ratio for the risky assets is

$$S(\alpha_1, \cdots, \alpha_n) = \frac{\sum_{i=1}^{n} \mu_i\alpha_i}{\sqrt{\sum_{i,j=1}^{n} \alpha_i c_{ij}\alpha_j}} \qquad (4.6.74)$$

It depends on how the investor divides her assets among the risky assets, but not on the total fraction of the assets allocated to them. More mathematically, if we write $\alpha_i = \alpha x_i$, where $\sum_{i=1}^{n} x_i = 1$, then α is the total fraction of risky assets and it cancels out in the expression for S.

Expanding the expected utility of wealth in the α_i gives

$$E[U(W)] = U + U'W_0 \sum_{i=1}^{n} \alpha_i\mu_i + \frac{1}{2}U''W_0^2 \sum_{i,j=1}^{n} \alpha_i\alpha_j(\mu_i\mu_j + c_{ij}) + \cdots$$
$$(4.6.75)$$

where the utility function and its derivatives are evaluated at $W_0(1 + Y_1)$ and the ellipses represent the terms higher than quadratic order in the α_i. Truncating at quadratic order and differentiating with respect to α_i gives for the optimal allocation

$$U'W_0\mu_i + U''W_0^2 \sum_{j=1}^{n}(c_{ij} + \mu_i\mu_j)\alpha_{j,\text{opt}} = 0 \qquad (4.6.76)$$

which has the solution

$$\alpha_{i,\text{opt}} = -\left(\frac{U'}{U''W_0} \right) \sum_{j=1}^{n} X_{ij}^{-1}\mu_j \qquad (4.6.77)$$

where X^{-1} is the inverse of the $n \times n$ matrix with components $X_{ij} = \mu_i \mu_j + c_{ij}$. The utility of wealth for the optimal portfolio is

$$E[U(W)]_{\text{opt}} = U - \frac{1}{2} \left(\frac{(U')^2}{U''} \right) \sum_{i,j=1}^{n} \mu_i X_{ij}^{-1} \mu_j \quad (4.6.78)$$

Treating the excess returns as small compared with the volatilities gives $X_{ij} \simeq c_{ij}$. In this approximation, the Sharpe ratio for the risky assets in the optimal portfolio is

$$S(\alpha_{1,\text{opt}}, \cdots, \alpha_{n,\text{opt}}) = \sqrt{\sum_{i,j=1}^{n} \mu_i c_{ij}^{-1} \mu_j} \quad (4.6.79)$$

In the same approximation, the expected utility of wealth for the optimal portfolio is

$$E[U(W)]_{\text{opt}} = U - \frac{1}{2} \left(\frac{(U')^2}{U''} \right) S^2 \quad (4.6.80)$$

which is the same expression we had for optimal portfolios with a single risky asset.

If there are just two risky assets, $n = 2$, then (again treating the excess returns as small compared with the volatilities)

$$X \simeq c = \begin{pmatrix} \sigma_1^2 & \xi_{12} \sigma_1 \sigma_2 \\ \xi_{12} \sigma_1 \sigma_2 & \sigma_2^2 \end{pmatrix} \quad (4.6.81)$$

where ξ_{12} is the correlation between the two assets. The inverse of this matrix is

$$X^{-1} \simeq c^{-1} = \frac{1}{\sigma_1^2 \sigma_2^2 - \xi_{12}^2 \sigma_1^2 \sigma_2^2} \begin{pmatrix} \sigma_2^2 & -\xi_{12} \sigma_1 \sigma_2 \\ -\xi_{12} \sigma_1 \sigma_2 & \sigma_1^2 \end{pmatrix} \quad (4.6.82)$$

Using this in Equation 4.6.77 gives

$$\frac{\alpha_{1,\text{opt}}}{\alpha_{2,\text{opt}}} = \frac{\mu_1\sigma_2^2 - \mu_2\xi_{12}\sigma_1\sigma_2}{\mu_2\sigma_1^2 - \mu_1\xi_{12}\sigma_1\sigma_2} \tag{4.6.83}$$

We can use this formula to see how correlations affect the portfolio allocation problem for normal assets. Consider the case where $\mu_1 = 1$ percent, $\sigma_1 = 10$ percent, $\mu_2 = 4$ percent, and $\sigma_2 = 30$ percent. The Sharpe ratios for these risky assets are $S_1 = 0.01/0.1 = 0.10$ and $S_2 = 0.04/0.3 = 0.13$. If there is no correlation between these two risky assets, $\alpha_{1,\text{opt}}/\alpha_{2,\text{opt}} = 2.25$. However, if they are positively correlated with a correlation $\xi_{12} = 0.4$, the ratio of optimal allocations becomes $\alpha_{1,\text{opt}}/\alpha_{2,\text{opt}} = 1.5$. On the other hand, if the correlation is $\xi_{12} = -0.4$, then $\alpha_{1,\text{opt}}/\alpha_{2,\text{opt}} = 2.65$.

4.7 The Efficient Frontier

Suppose an investor would like to make an investment in some risky assets labeled by an index i (that goes from $i = 1, \cdots, n$) but keep the volatility of the return (over some fixed time horizon) on this investment fixed at the value σ_p. In this section, we show what allocation maximizes the investor's return. The curve of maximum return versus volatility is called the *efficient frontier*. The investor can put a fraction $0 < x_i < 1$ of the initial investment in risky asset i and

$$\sum_{i=1}^{n} x_i = 1 \tag{4.7.84}$$

The return on asset i (over the investment time horizon) has expected value $r_i > 0$, and the covariance matrix of risky asset returns is c_{ij}. The expected portfolio return r_p and the portfolio return volatility σ_p are given by

$$r_p = \sum_i x_i r_i \qquad (4.7.85)$$

and

$$\sigma_p^2 = \sum_{i,j} x_i c_{ij} x_j \qquad (4.7.86)$$

In Equations 4.7.85 and 4.7.86, we have dropped the limits on the sums. In this section, all the sums go from 1 to n. Our task is to maximize r_p over the possible values of x_i subject to the constraints in Equations 4.7.84 and 4.7.86. To simplify the analysis, we start by assuming that the assets are uncorrelated with volatilities σ_i. Hence $c_{ij} = 0$ for $i \neq j$. The diagonal elements of the covariance matrix are equal to the return variances, $c_{ii} = \sigma_i^2$. We introduce Lagrange multipliers λ and λ' for these constraints and maximize the function

$$r_p(x_i, \lambda, \lambda') = \sum_i x_i r_i - \lambda \left(\sum_i x_i^2 \sigma_i^2 - \sigma_p^2 \right) - \lambda' \left(\sum_i x_i - 1 \right)$$

$$(4.7.87)$$

treating the x_i's as unconstrained. At the maximum, the partial derivatives of r_p with respect to x_i, λ, and λ' vanish. This gives $n + 2$ equations that can be used to determine these quantities. Setting the derivatives with respect to the Lagrange multipliers to zero gives the constraints in Equations 4.7.85 and 4.7.86. In addition to these equations, we have that

$$\frac{\partial r_p}{\partial x_i} = r_i - 2\lambda x_i \sigma_i^2 - \lambda' = 0 \qquad (4.7.88)$$

Dividing Equation 4.7.88 by σ_i^2, summing over i from 1 to n, and using Equation 4.7.84 gives

$$\sum_i \frac{r_i}{\sigma_i^2} - 2\lambda - \lambda' \sum_i \frac{1}{\sigma_i^2} = 0 \qquad (4.7.89)$$

Multiplying Equation 4.7.88 by x_i, summing over i, and using Equations 4.7.85 and 4.7.86 gives

$$r_p - 2\lambda\sigma_p^2 - \lambda' = 0 \qquad (4.7.90)$$

Equations 4.7.89 and 4.7.90 yield the following expressions for λ and λ':

$$\lambda = \frac{1}{2\left(1 - \sigma_p^2 \sum_i 1/\sigma_i^2\right)} \left(\sum_i \frac{r_i}{\sigma_i^2} - r_p \sum_i \frac{1}{\sigma_i^2}\right) \qquad (4.7.91)$$

and

$$\lambda' = \frac{1}{\left(1 - \sigma_p^2 \sum_i 1/\sigma_i^2\right)} \left(-\sigma_p^2 \sum_i \frac{r_i}{\sigma_i^2} + r_p\right) \qquad (4.7.92)$$

Next we plug the values of x_i determined by Equation 4.7.88 into the expression for r_p in Equation 4.7.85, which yields

$$r_p = \sum_i \left(\frac{r_i - \lambda'}{2\lambda\sigma_i^2}\right) r_i \qquad (4.7.93)$$

This implies that

$$2\lambda r_p = \sum_i \frac{r_i^2}{\sigma_i^2} - \lambda' \sum_i \frac{r_i}{\sigma_i^2} \qquad (4.7.94)$$

Inserting the expressions for λ and λ' from Equations 4.7.91 and 4.7.92 into Equation 4.7.94 gives the quadratic equation for r_p,

$$Ar_p^2 + Br_p + C = 0 \qquad (4.7.95)$$

where

$$A = -\sum_i \frac{1}{\sigma_i^2} \qquad (4.7.96)$$

$$B = 2\sum_i \frac{r_i}{\sigma_i^2} \qquad (4.7.97)$$

and

$$C = -\left[\sigma_p^2\left(\sum_i \frac{r_i}{\sigma_i^2}\right)^2 + \left(1 - \sigma_p^2\sum_i 1/\sigma_i^2\right)\sum_j \frac{r_j^2}{\sigma_j^2}\right] \qquad (4.7.98)$$

Solving the quadratic equation,

$$r_p = \frac{1}{\sum_i 1/\sigma_i^2}\left\{\sum_i \frac{r_i}{\sigma_i^2} + \sqrt{\left(\sum_k \frac{\sigma_p^2}{\sigma_k^2} - 1\right)\left[\sum_i \frac{1}{\sigma_i^2}\sum_j \frac{r_j^2}{\sigma_j^2} - \left(\sum_j \frac{r_j}{\sigma_j^2}\right)^2\right]}\right\} \qquad (4.7.99)$$

It is evident from these equations that r_p is an increasing function of σ_p, though it is not linear in σ_p.

In Figure 4.4 we show a plot of the efficient frontier (i.e., r_p as a function of σ_p) in the case where there are two risky assets with $r_1 = 6$ percent, $\sigma_1 = 20$ percent, $r_2 = 5$ percent, and $\sigma_2 = 15$ percent. In Figure 4.5 we show the values of x_1 and x_2 for the portfolios on the efficient frontier. With two assets, the minimum volatility $\sigma_p^{\min}$ is

$$\sigma_p^{\min} = \frac{\sigma_1\sigma_2}{\sqrt{\sigma_1^2 + \sigma_2^2}} \qquad (4.7.100)$$

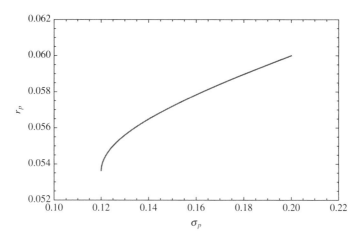

Figure 4.4 Plot of the efficient frontier for a portfolio of two risky assets with $r_1 = 6$ percent, $\sigma_1 = 20$ percent, $r_2 = 5$ percent, and $\sigma_2 = 15$ percent.

and this occurs for a portfolio with

$$x_j = 1 - \frac{\sigma_j^2}{\sigma_1^2 + \sigma_2^2} \qquad (4.7.101)$$

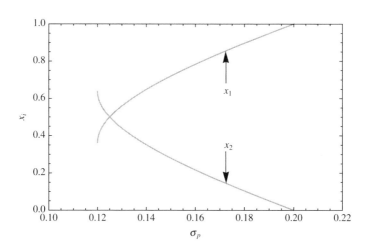

Figure 4.5 Plot of fractions x_1 and x_2 allocated to risky assets 1 and 2 for portfolios on the efficient frontier that have two risky assets with $r_1 = 6$ percent, $\sigma_1 = 20$ percent, $r_2 = 5$ percent, and $\sigma_2 = 15$ percent.

Note that the minimum return for a portfolio on the efficient frontier is greater than the smaller risky asset return r_2, since

$$r_p^{\min} - r_2 = \frac{\sigma_2^2}{\sigma_1^2 + \sigma_2^2}(r_1 - r_2) \qquad (4.7.102)$$

It is not difficult to generalize the analysis in this section to include correlations between the risky assets. Then we can use Equation 4.7.99 provided the substitutions

$$\sum_i \frac{1}{\sigma_i^2} \to \sum_{i,k} c_{ik}^{-1} \qquad (4.7.103)$$

$$\sum_i \frac{r_i}{\sigma_i^2} \to \sum_{i,k} c_{ik}^{-1} r_k \qquad (4.7.104)$$

and

$$\sum_i \frac{r_i^2}{\sigma_i^2} \to \sum_{i,k} r_i c_{ik}^{-1} r_k \qquad (4.7.105)$$

are made. In Figure 4.6 we show the efficient frontier for the same two assets in Figure 4.4, but with a correlation between the two assets of $\xi = -0.5, 0, 0.5$. A negative correlation between the assets allows for lower values of the portfolio volatility and for the same volatility gives a larger return than when the assets are uncorrelated or have a positive correlation.

4.8   Value at Risk

Consider a portfolio with N assets that we label by the subscript $i = 1, \cdots, N$. The portfolio return after an investment horizon of one year is

$$r = \sum_{i=1}^{N} \alpha_i \hat{r}_i \qquad (4.8.106)$$

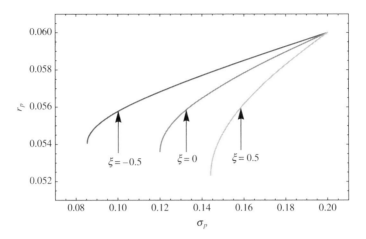

Figure 4.6 Plot of the efficient frontier for the same assets as in Figure 4.4, but with a correlation between assets of $\xi = -0.5, 0, -0.5$.

where α_i is the fraction of this value that was invested in asset i and $\hat{r}_i$ is the return on asset i. The returns are taken to be normally distributed with expected values $\bar{r}_i = E[\hat{r}_i]$ and variances $\sigma_i^2 = E[(\hat{r}_i - \bar{r}_i)^2]$. The correlation matrix for the asset returns has elements $\xi_{ij} = E[(\hat{r}_i - \bar{r}_i)(\hat{r}_j - \bar{r}_j)/\sigma_i\sigma_j]$. The expected return on this portfolio is

$$\bar{r} = \sum_{i=1}^{N} \alpha_i \bar{r}_i \qquad (4.8.107)$$

and the variance of the return is

$$\sigma^2 = \sum_{i,j} \alpha_i \alpha_j \sigma_i \sigma_j \xi_{ij} \qquad (4.8.108)$$

The probability p that the portfolio loses a fraction greater than or equal to f of its value over the investment horizon is

$$p = \frac{1}{\sqrt{2\pi\sigma^2}} \int_{-\infty}^{-f} dr \, \exp\left(-\frac{(r - \bar{r})^2}{2\sigma^2}\right) \qquad (4.8.109)$$

Changing the integration variable to $y = (r - \bar{r})/\sigma$, this becomes

$$p = \frac{1}{\sqrt{2\pi}} \int_{-\infty}^{(-f-\bar{r})/\sigma} dy \exp\left(-\frac{y^2}{2}\right) = \Phi[(-f - \bar{r})/\sigma] \quad (4.8.110)$$

where Φ is the cumulative normal function defined in Chapter 2. The fraction f of the original portfolio value that the investor is at risk of losing, i.e., the value at risk, from a fluctuation that occurs with probability p is $f(p) = -\bar{r} - \sigma\Phi^{-1}(p)$, where Φ^{-1} is the inverse of the cumulative normal distribution function. Note that we are making an approximation here. The return r must be greater than -1, and so we are assuming that the value of p is large enough and σ small enough that the integration region can be extended from -1 to $-\infty$. If for a given value of p the value of f that solves Equation 4.8.110 is negative, it means that a fluctuation of probability p cannot cause a loss that overcomes the expected return $\bar{r}$. In this case, the fraction of the original investment that is at risk is zero. So we write

$$f(p) = \max\left[-\bar{r} - \sigma\Phi^{-1}(p), 0\right] \quad (4.8.111)$$

As an example, consider fluctuations with probability $p = 5$ percent. $\Phi^{-1}(0.05) = -1.645$. So the value at risk from a possible 5 percent fluctuation is

$$f(5\%) = \max\left[-\bar{r} + 1.645\sigma, 0\right] \quad (4.8.112)$$

So if the expected (annualized) return is $\bar{r} = 6$ percent and the (annualized) volatility is $\sigma = 20$ percent, then the value at risk from a fluctuation with probability 5 percent is $f(5\%) = -0.06 + 1.645 \times 0.20 = 26.9$ percent.

Next suppose that the portfolio is equally distributed among the N assets. Then $\alpha_i = 1/N$. Suppose furthermore that the correlation for the returns has a common off-diagonal element $\xi_{ij} = \xi$ and that the returns all have the same average value $\bar{r}_i = \bar{r}$ and the same volatilities $\sigma_i = \bar{\sigma}$. The variance of the portfolio return is then

$$\sigma^2 = \bar{\sigma}^2 \left(\frac{1 + \xi(N - 1)}{N} \right) \qquad (4.8.113)$$

One can see from this equation the dramatic importance of correlations. If the returns are uncorrelated, so that $\xi = 0$, then the variance falls as $1/N$ and the investor will dramatically reduce the value at risk by increasing the number of assets. For example, using $\bar{r} = 6$ percent and $\bar{\sigma} = 20$ percent, we found in the previous paragraph that with one asset (i.e., $N = 1$), the value at risk from a fluctuation with 5 percent probability is $f(5\%) = 26.9$ percent. However, with $N = 5$ uncorrelated assets, the portfolio variance falls to $\sigma = 0.20/\sqrt{5} = 8.944$ percent and the value at risk from a fluctuation with probability 5 percent is $f(5\%) = 8.71$ percent. Now suppose that there is a modest correlation of $\xi = 0.2$ between these assets. Then for $N = 5$ the variance is $\sigma = 0.20 \times \sqrt{1 + 0.2 \times 4}/\sqrt{5} = 12.00$ percent, and the value at risk from a fluctuation with probability of 5 percent is increased from the uncorrelated $\xi = 0$ value of 8.71 percent to 13.74 percent. Next consider the case in which $N = 100$. Then with a correlation of $\xi = 0.2$, the portfolio volatility decreases to $\sigma = 0.2 \times \sqrt{1 + 0.2 \times 99}/\sqrt{100} = 9.12$ percent and the value at risk from a fluctuation with probability 5 percent is 9.00 percent. There is little advantage to adding more assets than 100 when the correlation is $\xi = 0.2$. In the limit as $N \rightarrow \infty$, the volatility of the portfolio becomes $\sigma = 0.2 \times \sqrt{0.2} = 8.94$ percent and the value at risk from a fluctuation with 5 percent probability is $f(5\%) = 8.71$ percent.

The value at risk increases as the probability p decreases. Suppose that instead of a fluctuation that has a 5 percent probability, we consider one that has a $p = 1$ percent probability. Since $\Phi^{-1}(0.01) = -2.326$,

$$f(1\%) = \max\left[-\bar{r} + 2.326\sigma,\, 0\right] \qquad (4.8.114)$$

If the expected (annualized) return is $\bar{r} = 6$ percent and the (annualized) volatility is $\sigma = 10$ percent, then the value at risk from a fluctuation with probability 1 percent is $f(1\%) = -0.06 + 2.326 \times 0.10 = 17.26$ percent.

In times of market stress, correlations and volatilities increase dramatically, and consequently the value at risk also increases. Also, there is no guarantee that the actual distribution of returns will be anywhere close to normal. In fact, market return distributions in periods of stress exhibit empirical behavior that has fat tails (i.e., high kurtosis) and significant skewness. We can exhibit fat tails by mixing two normal distributions. Consider the case of a portfolio that is equally divided among N risky assets with returns r_i. They are not normally distributed, but rather their probability distribution is the sum of two normal distributions. The first has the N assets normally distributed with a common positive correlation between them of ξ_n and common volatilities $\bar{\sigma}_n$. The second probability distribution has the N assets normally distributed with a common positive correlation between them of ξ_s and common volatilities $\bar{\sigma}_s$. These two distributions correspond, respectively, to the return distributions during a normal period and a period of market stress. Let $\bar{r}_n$ be the average portfolio return during the normal period and $\bar{r}_s$ the average portfolio return during the stressed period. Hence the probability distribution for the portfolio return, $r = (1/N) \sum_i r_i$, is

$$\mathcal{P}(r) = (1-\epsilon)\frac{1}{\sqrt{2\pi\sigma_n^2}} \exp\left(-\frac{(r - \bar{r}_n)^2}{\sigma_n^2}\right) + \epsilon\frac{1}{\sqrt{2\pi\sigma_s^2}} \exp\left(-\frac{(r - \bar{r}_s)^2}{\sigma_s^2}\right)$$

$$(4.8.115)$$

where

$$\sigma_{n,s}^2 = \bar{\sigma}^2 \left(\frac{1 + \xi_{n,s}(N-1)}{N} \right) \qquad (4.8.116)$$

The parameter ϵ is small because most of the time the markets are in a normal state. With small ϵ, typical fluctuations in the return r are dominated by the normal environment part of the probability distribution $\mathcal{P}(r)$. Nonetheless, the second term in Equation 4.8.115 can have a dramatic impact on the value at risk. A fluctuation that causes a loss greater than or equal to a fraction f of the portfolio value happens with probability p, given by

$$p = \int_{-\infty}^{-f} dr\, \mathcal{P}(r) = (1-\epsilon)\Phi\left(\frac{-f - \bar{r}_n}{\sigma_n}\right) + \epsilon\Phi\left(\frac{-f - \bar{r}_s}{\sigma_s}\right)$$

$$(4.8.117)$$

Choosing a particular probability p and probability distribution parameters ϵ, $\bar{r}_{n,s}$, $\sigma_{n,s}$, and $\xi_{n,s}$ the value at risk f can be solved for numerically. For example, suppose that $p = 5$ percent, $N = 100$, $\epsilon = 0.1$, $\bar{r}_{n,s} = 6$ percent, $\bar{\sigma}_n = 20$ percent, $\bar{\sigma}_s = 40$ percent, $\xi_n = 0.2$, and $\xi_s = 0.9$. To focus on the impact of the change in the volatilities and correlations of the assets, we have left their expected returns the same in the normal and stressed market environments. The portfolio return volatilities in the normal and stressed environments are $\sigma_n = 0.2 \times \sqrt{1 + 0.2 \times 99}/\sqrt{100} = 9.12$ percent and $\sigma_s = 0.4 \times \sqrt{1 + 0.9 \times 99}/\sqrt{100} = 37.97$ percent. In this case, the value at risk from a 5 percent fluctuation is $f(5\%) = 12.58$ percent. Recall that if the effect of the stressed environment is removed (i.e., $\epsilon = 0$), then $f(5\%) = 9.00$ percent.

Next let's use the same parameters as before, but change the expected return in the part of the probability distribution that comes from the stressed economic environment to $\bar{r}_s = 0$. Then the value at risk is $f(5\%) = 13.65$ percent. If we consider a fluctuation that occurs with probability 1 percent, then the value at risk becomes $f(1\%) = 48.66$ percent. Finally, using the same parameters, but with the contribution of the stressed environment removed (i.e., $\epsilon = 0$), the value at risk from a 1 percent fluctuation is only $f(1\%) = 15.22$ percent.

4.9   Fixed-Income Risk Factors and Hedging

The Treasury yield curve has many bonds corresponding to various maturities. However, for risk management purposes, we do not always need to know the behavior of each point separately. Just as neighboring points on a string tend to move together during string fluctuations, shocks to the yield curve tend to bring about tightly related behavior on different regions of the yield curve. Statistical analysis of yield movement data shows that approximately 75 to 80 percent of the time, all the points on the yield curve tend to move up or down together. The percentage change in the price of a bond with respect to such parallel shifts of the yield curve is called *duration*. The yield curve can also illustrate higher modes of oscillations. When the short end moves up and the long end moves down (or vice versa), the movement is called *yield curve steepening* or *flattening*. This type of yield curve movement statistically happens 15 to 20 percent of the time. Finally, the higher modes, such as the one in which the short end and the long end move in the same direction, but the middle portion moves in the opposite direction, happen 5 to 10 percent of the time. Theoretically, there are as many modes possible as the number of points on the yield curve, but for risk management of fixed-income portfolios, capturing the first few modes usually suffices.

The way to extract these factors is to compute the covariance matrix of yield changes from historical data, then compute the eigenvectors. Since the sum of the eigenvalues has to add up to the total variance by this construction, the eigenvector decomposition automatically ranks the movements of the yield curve in terms of the most dominant orthogonal movements. Note that if we have more complicated asset classes, such as corporate or mortgage bonds, then they are sensitive to the movement of the corporate credit spreads in addition to the shape of the yield curve. In practice, a portfolio manager can manage the risk of her portfolio by managing the exposures to each one of these factors. The factors themselves are simply derivatives of the bond prices with respect to underlying variables such as yields, shape of the yield curve, corporate spreads, and so on.

For most simple fixed-income portfolios, the most important risk measure is the (level) duration, which determines the first-order change in the portfolio value when the yield curve moves up or down in parallel. If this were the only factor that were relevant, we could simply take the duration of the portfolio times the expected volatility of yields to come up with the price volatility of the portfolio. For example, if we expect that yields will fluctuate with an annual standard deviation of 100 bp/year, then a portfolio with a five-year duration would be expected to experience 5 percent price volatility a year. However, while the yield curve moves up or down, it might be accompanied by steepening or flattening, as well as narrowing or widening of corporate spreads. So the correlation of the risk factors can become important in determining the risk of the portfolio. We will now demonstrate the impact of changing correlations on risk factors for portfolios.

For simplicity in this section, we consider only five factors, which are not assumed to be orthogonal: L, the overall level of the yield curve; S_{2-10}, the slope between the 2- and 10-year points on the yield curve; S_{10-30}, the slope between the 10-year and 30-year points on the yield curve; M, the difference or spread between mortgage and Treasury returns and C, the spread between corporate and Treasury returns. We write the market price or value of the portfolio as $P(L, S_{2-10}, S_{10-30}, M, C)$. The duration of the portfolio with respect to level, i.e., the familiar duration defined in Chapter 1, is simply

$$-\frac{1}{P}\frac{dP}{dL} = -\frac{1}{P}\left(\frac{\partial P}{\partial L} + \frac{\partial P}{\partial S_{2-10}}\frac{\partial S_{2-10}}{\partial L} + \frac{\partial P}{\partial S_{10-30}}\frac{\partial S_{10-30}}{\partial L} + \frac{\partial P}{\partial M}\frac{\partial M}{\partial L} + \frac{\partial P}{\partial C}\frac{\partial C}{\partial L}\right)$$

$$(4.9.118)$$

We can estimate the partial derivatives, $\partial S_{2-10}/\partial L$ and so on, from historical data or forecast them. The value of the factors fluctuates in time. Suppose that in a small time period dt the change in a spread factor S depends on the change in the factor L by the simple linear relationship

$$dS = dX_S + \beta_{S,L}\, dL \qquad (4.9.119)$$

where $E[dL] = 0$ and $E[dL\, dL] = \sigma_L^2\, dt$. Here dX_S is not correlated with dL. Multiplying both sides of Equation 4.9.119 by dL and averaging, we get $E[dS \cdot dL] = \beta_{S,L} E[dL \cdot dL] = \beta_{S,L}\sigma_L^2\, dt$. Using the definition of a correlation matrix, $E[dS \cdot dL] = \xi_{S,L}\sigma_S\sigma_L\, dt$, and we obtain

$$\frac{\partial S}{\partial L} = \beta_{S,L} = \xi_{S,L}\frac{\sigma_S}{\sigma_L} \qquad (4.9.120)$$

Repeating this for all the other betas in terms of correlations and volatilities, we obtain that the total duration of a portfolio (with respect to level) is

$$-\frac{1}{P}\frac{dP}{dL} = -\frac{1}{P}\left(\frac{\partial P}{\partial L} + \xi_{S_{2-10},L}\frac{\sigma_{S_{2-10}}}{\sigma_L}\frac{\partial P}{\partial S_{2-10}}\right.$$

$$\left. + \xi_{S_{10-30},L}\frac{\sigma_{S_{10-30}}}{\sigma_L}\frac{\partial P}{\partial S_{10-30}} + \xi_{M,L}\frac{\sigma_M}{\sigma_L}\frac{\partial P}{\partial M} + \xi_{C,L}\frac{\sigma_C}{\sigma_L}\frac{\partial P}{\partial C}\right)$$

$$(4.9.121)$$

Typically fixed-income portfolios are managed against a benchmark or index. A popular fixed-income benchmark is the Lehman Brothers Aggregate Index (now known as the Barclays Aggregate). A portfolio manager will manage her duration and other risk factors against the same risk factor for the index.

Relabeling the total and partial durations on the left- and right-hand sides with the letter D, and using Δ to signify the difference between the portfolio and the index exposures, we can write the over- or underexposure of the total portfolio duration as

$$
\begin{aligned}
\Delta D_{\text{Total}}^{(L)} = {} & \Delta D_L + \xi_{S_{2-10},L} \frac{\sigma_{S_{2-10}}}{\sigma_L} \Delta D_{2-10} \\
& + \xi_{S_{10-30},L} \frac{\sigma_{S_{10-30}}}{\sigma_L} \Delta D_{10-30} \\
& + \xi_{M,L} \frac{\sigma_M}{\sigma_L} \Delta D_M + \xi_{C,L} \frac{\sigma_C}{\sigma_L} \Delta D_C
\end{aligned}
$$

$$(4.9.122)$$

Equation 4.9.122 is the key result for computing the total duration with respect to changes in overall level of the yield curve of portfolios. Note that to calculate the total level duration, we need to know the correlation of the other risk factors with the overall yield curve level factor L as well as the volatilities of the risk factors. We can use historical estimates of correlations and volatilities, but this will underestimate the risk to the portfolio, because in times of market stress, the correlations tend to their extreme values, ± 1, and the volatilities increase. Usually we not only make an estimate using historical values for the correlations and volatilities, but also stress-test the portfolio by calculating the total level duration using forecast volatilities and correlations that the portfolio manager feels would be more appropriate during times of market stress.

In this example, a reasonable expectation for the signs of the elements of the correlation of the five factors is

$$
\begin{array}{c}
\quad\quad \text{Level} \quad \text{Slope}_{2-10} \quad \text{Slope}_{10-30} \quad \text{Mortgage} \quad \text{Corporate} \\
\begin{array}{c}
\text{Level} \\
\text{Slope}_{2-10} \\
\text{Slope}_{10-30} \\
\text{Mortgage} \\
\text{Corporate}
\end{array}
\left(
\begin{array}{ccccc}
1 & - & - & - & - \\
- & 1 & + & + & + \\
- & + & 1 & + & + \\
- & + & + & 1 & + \\
- & + & + & + & 1
\end{array}
\right)
\end{array}
$$

$$(4.9.123)$$

For example, as the yields fall, we expect corporate spreads and mortgage spreads to rise (i.e., a negative correlation of corporate and mortgage spreads with yield level). Similarly, in an easing cycle, as yields fall, we would expect the curve to steepen (again a negative correlation of yield level with the slope parameters). Of course, these correlations can change and do change, depending on the environment. For example, it is entirely possible that as mortgage spreads narrow, corporate spreads narrow in most environments but widen in some. In a typical environment, the correlation of these variables might be

$$
\begin{array}{c}
\quad\quad \text{Level} \quad \text{Slope}_{2-10} \quad \text{Slope}_{10-30} \quad \text{Mortgage} \quad \text{Corporate} \\
\begin{array}{c}
\text{Level} \\
\text{Slope}_{2-10} \\
\text{Slope}_{10-30} \\
\text{Mortgage} \\
\text{Corporate}
\end{array}
\left(
\begin{array}{ccccc}
1 & -0.50 & -0.30 & -0.25 & -0.70 \\
-0.50 & 1 & 0.90 & 0.30 & 0.70 \\
-0.30 & 0.90 & 1 & 0.25 & 0.20 \\
-0.25 & 0.30 & 0.25 & 1 & 0.75 \\
-0.70 & 0.70 & 0.20 & 0.75 & 1
\end{array}
\right)
\end{array}
$$

$$(4.9.124)$$

This correlation matrix contains some large elements with magnitudes near unity and some more modest correlations. The eigenvalues of this matrix are all positive, so it is a consistent correlation matrix.

It is easy to construct a corellation matrix that is more appropriate to stressed environments using the results of Chapter 2. Recall that there we wrote the correlation matrix in the form

$$\xi_{ij} = (vv^T)_{ij} = \sum_k v_{ik}v_{jk} \qquad (4.9.125)$$

where the 5×5 matrix has rows $v_{1k} = (1, 0, 0, 0, 0)$, $v_{2k} = (c_1, s_1, 0, 0, 0)$, $v_{3k} = (c_2, s_2c_3, s_2s_3, 0, 0)$, $v_{4k} = (c_4, s_4c_5, s_4s_5c_6, s_4s_5s_6, 0)$, and $v_{5k} = (c_7, s_7c_8, s_7s_8c_9, s_7s_8s_9c_{10}, s_7s_8s_9s_{10})$. Here we are using the notation $c_j = \cos\theta_j$ and $s_j = \sin\theta_j$. The top row of the correlation matrix is then $v_{11}v_{j1}$. So the first row (and column) would have elements $(1, -1, -1, -1, -1)$ provided that $\theta_1 = \theta_2 = \theta_4 = \theta_7 = \pi$. The other elements of the correlation matrix are equal to unity. For these angles, the matrix ξ is

	Level	Slope$_{2-10}$	Slope$_{10-30}$	Mortgage	Corporate
Level	1	-1	-1	-1	-1
Slope$_{2-10}$	-1	1	1	1	1
Slope$_{10-30}$	-1	1	1	1	1
Mortgage	-1	1	1	1	1
Corporate	-1	1	1	1	1

$$(4.9.126)$$

However, this corresponds to a matrix with four zero eigenvalues. It is not positive definite and hence is not an acceptable correlation matrix. We can get an acceptable correlation matrix that is arbitrarily close to Equation 4.9.126 by choosing the angles θ_j to be very close to the values given earlier. To calculate the total level duration, we do not need to invert the correlation matrix, so we can use Equation 4.9.126 as an estimate of the correlations in times of market stress. For the total level duration, the difference between using this matrix and using an invertible correlation matrix that has elements very close to those in Equation 4.9.126 is negligible. Even though volatilities also increase in times of market stress, the total level duration depends only on the ratios of the volatilities, so the change in the correlations is more important.

Reasonable values of the annualized factor volatilities are (in basis points) $\sigma_L = 100$, $\sigma_{S_{2-10}} = 75$, $\sigma_{S_{10-30}} = 35$, $\sigma_M = 25$, and $\sigma_C = 50$. Consider a portfolio that has only $\Delta D_M = 1.5$ different from zero. In this case $\Delta D_{\text{Total}}^{(L)} = 1.50 \times (25/100)\xi_{M,L} = 0.375\xi_{M,L}$. Using the correlation matrix in Equation 4.9.124, which is appropriate to normal market environments, the total level duration (compared with the benchmark) is $\Delta D_{\text{Total}}^{(L)} = 0.375 \times (-0.25) = -0.094$. However, in a stressed environment, where the correlation matrix is very close to Equation 4.9.126, the total level duration (with respect to the benchmark) is $D_{\text{Total}}^{(L)} = -0.375$. In the normal environment, the total level duration is close to the benchmark. However, in the stressed environment, because of the high mortgage spread duration, this portfolio has a duration that is short the benchmark by about a third of a year.

Most realistic fixed-income portfolios consist of securities whose risk factors such as duration do not remain constant as the yield curve and other market variables fluctuate. This happens either because of explicit nonlinear instruments in the portfolio, such as options, or because of instruments that show positive or negative convexity to yield curve movements (such as mortgages). To deal with these characteristics, we need to know the sensitivities of these securities to the movements of the risk factors as well. In practice, this frequently requires simulating the sensitivity of complex securities using numerical procedures.

5

Term Structure Models

5.1 The Yield Curve

Recall that the yield curve, $Y(T)$, is a term used to describe the spot yields for different maturities as a function of the maturity. The shape and overall level of the yield curve change over time. However, it is empirically observed that just a few types of changes dominate the movements of the yields of individual bonds of all maturities. The most dominant one is the parallel shift of the yield curve, and this happens approximately 75 to 80 percent of the time. This is related to changes in inflation and inflation expectations. The second most dominant movement is steepening or flattening of the yield curve, and this occurs about 15 to 20 percent of the time. This move is related to changes in monetary policy or in the growth of the economy. The remaining movement that is of some importance is bowing of the yield curve. Of course, other movements are also possible, but they are rare relative to these. For this reason, most yield curve models use a two- or three-factor model to describe the yield movements of all the bonds.

Since not every maturity of the yield curve has a bond associated with it, to draw out a smooth curve, we need to come up with some interpolation scheme between the bonds that do exist. Furthermore, the investor may feel that some bonds are more fairly priced by the market than others. A yield curve determined by a fit to the prices of the these fairly priced bonds can be used to determine if other bonds are "rich" (overpriced) or "cheap" (underpriced). There are two ways of constructing a continuous yield curve: we can assume a curve-fitting function with no dynamic content, or we can create a dynamic term structure model, which will be described later in this chapter. The parameters that drive the nondynamic models have little economic content, but the ones in the dynamic models carry quite a bit of content.

Because of the ease of implementation, a widely used curve-fitting algorithm in the nondynamic class is the Nelson-Siegel model.[1] In it the yield for a maturity T is given by

$$Y(T) = \beta_1 + \left(\frac{1 - e^{-\lambda T}}{\lambda T} \right) \beta_2 + \left(\frac{1 - e^{-\lambda T}}{\lambda T} - e^{-\lambda T} \right) \beta_3 \quad (5.1.1)$$

where the parameters may be extracted by fitting to known bond yields for each time t. Since the yield curve $Y(T)$ changes with time t, the parameters $\beta_{1,2,3}$ and λ have implicit t dependence.

The parameter λ is a decay constant; the larger it is, the faster the exponential decay. The first factor β_1 is a long-term factor that describes parallel shifts of the yield curve, since $Y(\infty) = \beta_1$. The term multiplying β_2 decays from 1 to 0 very quickly; hence β_2 is a factor that describes short-maturity effects. It also describes the steepness of the yield curve, since $Y(\infty) - Y(0) = \beta_2$. The term multiplying β_3 first rises and then falls; hence it is a medium-term or curvature factor.

---

[1] C. Nelson and A. Siegel, "Parsimonious Modeling of Yield Curves," *Journal of Business* 60, no. 4 (1987), p. 473.

This approach is an excellent way to quickly fit the yield curve; however, it does not tell us anything about the underlying dynamics of the economy. So in the next sections we discuss dynamic term structure models.

5.2 One- and Two-Factor Vasicek Models for the Yield Curve

We now begin the study of dynamic models for the time dependence, i.e., term structure, of the spot yield. These models give a stochastic evolution for the short rate $y(t)$. The resulting short rate is then compounded to get the spot yield. The evolution of the short rate with time has a randomness, and it is assumed that $y(t + dt)$ depends on $y(t)$ but not on the short rate at earlier times. The spot yield $Y(t)$ is calculated by averaging a zero coupon bond price over all possible stochastic paths for the short rate,

$$\text{Price} = \exp\left[-Y(T)T\right] P = E\left[\exp\left[-\int_0^T dt\, y(t)\right]\right] P \quad (5.2.2)$$

where P is the principal and $t = T$ is the time the bond matures. Such a model for the spot yield is called a *term structure model*.

One of the simplest term structure models is the one-factor Vasicek model, which we briefly introduced in Chapter 2. It takes the short Treasury rate to evolve in time according to the mean reverting random walk,

$$dy(t) = \alpha[\gamma - y(t)]\, dt + \sigma\, dw \quad (5.2.3)$$

Negative yields should not occur, except possibly in a period of extreme risk aversion when investors are willing to pay for the security of Treasury bonds. The evolution in Equation 5.2.3 allows for negative y. However, as long as the fluctuations that correspond to negative y are very low probability events, this feature is of no practical consequence. In Chapter 7 we will introduce term structure models that do not allow negative yields. In these models, bond prices cannot be calculated analytically.

We are interested in the price of a zero coupon bond when the short rate evolves according to Equation 5.2.3. The price is given by averaging the value of a zero coupon bond over possible interest-rate paths as in Equation 5.2.2. Hence the spot yield is given by

$$\exp\left[-Y(T)T\right] = E\left[\exp\left[-\int_0^T dt\, y(t)\right]\right] \qquad (5.2.4)$$

To evaluate the spot yield $Y(T)$, we divide the short rate into an average value $\bar{y} = E[y]$ and a fluctuating part $\tilde{y}$:

$$y = \bar{y} + \tilde{y} \qquad (5.2.5)$$

where $E[\tilde{y}] = 0$. Since y is a normal variable, we can use Equation 2.1.8 from Chapter 2, which implies that

$$Y(T) = \frac{1}{T}\int_0^T dt\, \bar{y}(t) - \frac{1}{2T}\int_0^T dt \int_0^T dt'\, E[\tilde{y}(t)\tilde{y}(t')] \qquad (5.2.6)$$

In Chapter 2, we integrated Equation 5.2.3 and found that

$$\bar{y}(t) = e^{-\alpha t} y(0) + \gamma\left(1 - e^{-\alpha t}\right) \qquad (5.2.7)$$

and

$$\tilde{y}(t) = \sigma e^{-\alpha t}\int_0^t d\tau\, e^{\alpha \tau}\left(\frac{dw(\tau)}{d\tau}\right) \qquad (5.2.8)$$

To calculate the spot yield, the needed integrals are

$$\int_0^T dt\, \bar{y}(t) = \left(\frac{y(0) - \gamma}{\alpha}\right)\left(1 - e^{-\alpha T}\right) + \gamma T \qquad (5.2.9)$$

and

$$\int_0^T dt \int_0^T dt' \, E[\bar{y}(t)\bar{y}(t')] = \sigma^2 \int_0^T dt \, e^{-\alpha t} \int_0^T dt' \, e^{-\alpha t'} \int_0^t d\tau$$
$$\times \, e^{\alpha\tau} \int_0^{t'} d\tau' e^{\alpha\tau'} E\left[\frac{dw(\tau)}{d\tau}\frac{dw(\tau')}{d\tau'}\right]$$

$$(5.2.10)$$

The final expected value is $\delta(\tau - \tau')$, and we use this to do the τ' integration,

$$\int_0^t d\tau \int_0^{t'} d\tau' \, e^{\alpha(\tau+\tau')}\delta(\tau - \tau') = \theta(t - t') \int_0^{t'} d\tau \, e^{2\alpha\tau}$$
$$+ \, \theta(t' - t) \int_0^t d\tau \, e^{2\alpha\tau} \quad (5.2.11)$$

Performing the τ integration then gives

$$\int_0^T dt \int_0^T dt' \, E[\bar{y}(t)\bar{y}(t')]$$
$$= \frac{\sigma^2}{2\alpha} \int_0^T dt \, e^{-\alpha t} \int_0^T dt' \, e^{-\alpha t'} \left[\theta(t-t')\left(e^{2\alpha t'} - 1\right) + \theta(t'-t)\left(e^{2\alpha t} - 1\right)\right]$$

$$(5.2.12)$$

The term in the square brackets proportional to the step function $\theta(t - t')$ contributes the same as the term proportional to $\theta(t' - t)$, and so

$$\int_0^T dt \int_0^T dt' \, E[\bar{y}(t)\bar{y}(t')] = \frac{\sigma^2}{\alpha} \int_0^T dt \, e^{-\alpha t} \int_0^t dt' \left(e^{\alpha t'} - e^{-\alpha t'}\right)$$

$$(5.2.13)$$

Performing the remaining integrals gives

$$\int_0^T dt \int_0^T dt' \, E[\bar{y}(t)\bar{y}(t')] = \frac{\sigma^2}{\alpha^2} \int_0^T dt \left(1 + e^{-2\alpha t} - 2e^{-\alpha t}\right)$$

$$= \frac{\sigma^2}{\alpha^2}\left[T + \frac{1}{2\alpha}\left(1 - e^{-2\alpha T}\right) - \frac{2}{\alpha}\left(1 - e^{-\alpha T}\right)\right]$$

$$(5.2.14)$$

Putting these results together, the spot yield in the one-factor Vasicek model is

$$Y(T) = \gamma + \left(\frac{y(0) - \gamma}{\alpha T}\right)\left(1 - e^{-\alpha T}\right)$$

$$- \frac{\sigma^2}{2\alpha^2}\left[1 + \frac{1}{2\alpha T}\left(1 - e^{-2\alpha T}\right) - \frac{2}{\alpha T}\left(1 - e^{-\alpha T}\right)\right]$$

$$(5.2.15)$$

Note that in the limit as $\alpha \to 0$, the spot yield goes to $Y(T) \to y(0) - \sigma^2 T^2/6$. In this limit, for late times the spot yield becomes negative, which is clearly nonsensical. The mean reversion term cures this problem. For late times (i.e., $T \gg 1/\alpha$), Equation 5.2.15 goes to the finite value $Y(T) \to \gamma - \sigma^2/(2\alpha^2)$.

There is another way to derive this result. At any time t before maturity, the short rate has some value y, and at time t we can write the price of a zero coupon bond maturing at time T as $\text{Price}(t) = Q(y, t)P$, where P is the principal and Q is the price of the zero coupon bond divided by its principal. In a time dt, this price changes by

$$dQ = Q_y \, dy + \frac{1}{2}Q_{yy}\sigma^2 \, dt + Q_t \, dt \qquad (5.2.16)$$

where we have adopted the notation,

$$Q_y = \frac{\partial Q}{\partial y} \qquad Q_{yy} = \frac{\partial^2 Q}{\partial y^2} \qquad Q_t = \frac{\partial Q}{\partial t} \qquad (5.2.17)$$

and kept only terms to linear order in dt. On average, the price of a zero coupon bond increases at the risk-free rate of return, $E[d\,\text{Price}(t)] = y\,\text{Price}(t)\,dt$, and so $E[dQ(t)] = yQ(t)\,dt$. Taking the expected value (at time t) of Equation 5.2.16, using the one-factor Vasicek model for dy, $E[dw] = 0$, and $E[(dw)^2] = dt$, gives

$$Q_y\alpha(\gamma - y) + \frac{1}{2}Q_{yy}\sigma^2 + Q_t = yQ \qquad (5.2.18)$$

To solve this partial differential equation, we use the ansatz

$$Q = \exp\left[A(t)y + C(t)\right] \qquad (5.2.19)$$

At maturity, the price of the zero coupon bond is equal to the principal P, and so $Q(y, T) = 1$. To satisfy this, we adopt the "initial" conditions $A(T) = C(T) = 0$. Since the price of the zero coupon bond at $t = 0$ is $\text{Price}(0) = \exp\left[-Y(T)T\right]P$, we have that $Q[y = y(0), 0] = \exp\left[-Y(T)T\right]$. Hence, the yield to maturity T is

$$Y(T) = -\left(\frac{C(0) + y(0)A(0)}{T}\right) \qquad (5.2.20)$$

The partial differential equation for Q implies that

$$A\alpha(\gamma - y) + \frac{1}{2}\sigma^2 A^2 + \frac{dA}{dt}y + \frac{dC}{dt} = y \qquad (5.2.21)$$

Since y is arbitrary, this is solved by setting the term independent of y to zero and the coefficient of y to zero,

$$A\alpha\gamma + \frac{1}{2}\sigma^2 A^2 + \frac{dC}{dt} = 0 \qquad -A\alpha + \frac{dA}{dt} = 1 \qquad (5.2.22)$$

To solve the differential equation for A, we make the substitution $A = \exp(\alpha t)F$; then the differential equation for F is $dF/dt = \exp(-\alpha t)$. Solving this with the "initial value" $F(T) = 0$ and using the relation between F and A yields

$$A(t) = -\frac{1}{\alpha}\left(1 - e^{\alpha(t-T)}\right) \qquad (5.2.23)$$

Then the solution to the differential equation for C with the initial value $C(T) = 0$ is

$$C(t) = \int_t^T dt \left[A(t)\alpha\gamma + \frac{1}{2}\sigma^2 A(t)^2\right] \qquad (5.2.24)$$

Performing this integration and using the values of $A(0)$ and $C(0)$ in the expression for the yield in Equation 5.2.20 gives the result for the yield we found previously in Equation 5.2.15.

We can also calculate the yield curve $Y(T)$ with a simulation using the methods introduced in Chapter 2. The function given here calls the function, shortrate[ ], defined in Chapter 2, and returns a list of coordinates $T, Y(T)$ for the yield curve for T between zero and nyears. The yield curve is calculated using the one-factor Vasicek model with parameters $\alpha = $ alpha, $\sigma = $ sigma, $y(0) = $ y0, and $\gamma = $ gamma by averaging over nPaths mean reverting paths.

```
avgSpotYield[nPaths_, alpha_, sigma_, y0_, gamma_,
  deltaT_, nYears_] :=
 Module[{n = 1, nMax = nPaths, path, avg, nSteps =
  Floor[nYears/deltaT]},
SeedRandom[n];
```

```
path = NestList[shortrate[alpha, gamma, #, sigma,
 deltaT] &, y0, nSteps];
avg = Exp[-(Table[Sum[path[[j + 1]]*deltaT,
 {j, 0, i}], {i, 0, nSteps}])]/nMax;
n = 2;
While[n <= nMax, SeedRandom[n];
 path = NestList[shortrate[alpha, gamma, #, sigma,
 deltaT] &, y0, nSteps];
 avg += Exp[-(Table[Sum[path[[j + 1]]*deltaT,
 {j, 0, i}], {i, 0, nSteps}])]/nMax;
 n = n + 1];
 Transpose[{Table[x, {x, 0, nYears, deltaT}],
 Table[-Log[avg[[i + 1]]]/((i + 1)*deltaT),
 {i, 0, nSteps}]}]
]
```

In Figure 5.1 the yield curve is calculated by averaging over 1,000 sample interest-rate paths, and in Figure 5.2 the yield curve is calculated by averaging over 10,000 sample interest-rate paths. The parameters of the model were taken to be $\alpha = 0.1$, $\gamma = 0.065$, $\sigma = 0.01$, and

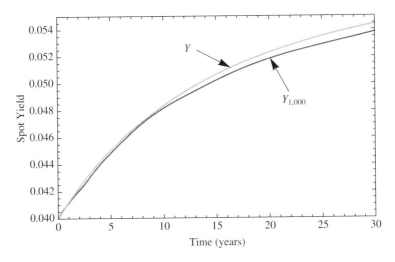

Figure 5.1 Spot yield curve calculated by averaging over 1,000 paths, $Y_{1,000}(T)$, and the analytic spot yield curve $Y(T)$.

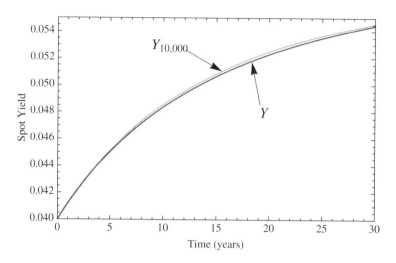

Figure 5.2 Spot yield curve calculated by averaging over 10,000 paths, $Y_{10,000}(T)$, and the analytic spot yield curve $Y(T)$.

$y(0) = 0.04$. We can see the improved convergence toward the analytic result as the number of interest-rate paths increases.

In practice, the parameters in a term structure model that gives the time evolution of the short rate are fit to the prices of some bonds or Treasury spot yields that the investor feels are most fairly priced by the market. The resulting yield curve is then used to price other bonds, which are classified as rich or cheap depending on whether their traded prices are higher or lower than what the model gives. Treasury bonds that are cheap are attractive investment opportunities. These models can also be used to price derivatives of bonds. We will discuss that in Chapter 6. The parameters of the term structure model are fit daily to the traded prices of the most fairly priced bonds and change significantly when the investment environment changes dramatically.

Models with one stochastic factor of the type we have just described do not have enough freedom to describe all the possible shapes of the yield curve. Models with two factors are much more realistic. The two-factor Vasicek model introduces stochastic factors $x(t)$ and $z(t)$

that evolve with time according to

$$dx(t) = \alpha_x[\gamma_x - x(t)]\,dt + \sigma_x\,dw_x$$

$$dz(t) = \alpha_z[\gamma_z - z(t)]\,dt + \sigma_z\,dw_z \qquad (5.2.25)$$

The two Brownian motions are correlated and satisfy

$$E\left[\frac{dw_x(t)}{dt}\frac{dw_x(t')}{dt'}\right] = \delta(t - t') \qquad E\left[\frac{dw_z(t)}{dt}\frac{dw_z(t')}{dt'}\right] = \delta(t - t')$$

$$E\left[\frac{dw_x(t)}{dt}\frac{dw_z(t')}{dt'}\right] = \rho\delta(t - t')$$

$$(5.2.26)$$

The correlation between the Brownian motions dw_x and dw_z is denoted by ρ. Taking the Treasury short rate to be

$$y(t) = b + x(t) + z(t) \qquad (5.2.27)$$

where b is a new parameter, the spot yield can be calculated using the same methods that were applied to the one-factor model. The result is

$$Y(T) = b + \gamma_x + \gamma_z + \frac{(1 - e^{-\alpha_x T})}{\alpha_x T}[x(0) - \gamma_x] + \frac{(1 - e^{-\alpha_z T})}{\alpha_z T}[z(0) - \gamma_z]$$

$$- \frac{\sigma_x^2}{2\alpha_x^2}\left(1 - 2\frac{1 - e^{-\alpha_x T}}{\alpha_x T} + \frac{1 - e^{-2\alpha_x T}}{2\alpha_x T}\right)$$

$$- \frac{\sigma_z^2}{2\alpha_z^2}\left(1 - 2\frac{1 - e^{-\alpha_z T}}{\alpha_z T} + \frac{1 - e^{-2\alpha_z T}}{2\alpha_z T}\right)$$

$$- \frac{\rho\sigma_x\sigma_z}{\alpha_x\alpha_z}\left(1 - \frac{1 - e^{-\alpha_x T}}{\alpha_x T} - \frac{1 - e^{-\alpha_z T}}{\alpha_z T} + \frac{1 - e^{-(\alpha_x + \alpha_z)T}}{(\alpha_x + \alpha_z)T}\right)$$

$$(5.2.28)$$

The differential equation method can also be used to solve for the yield in the two-factor Vasicek model. At any time t before maturity, the stochastic variables x and z have some values, and so in this case we write the price of a zero coupon bond with principal P at a time t before maturity as $\text{Price}(t) = Q(x, z, t)P$. The partial differential equation for $Q(x, z, t)$ is derived as in the one-factor Vasicek model. We find, using a notation for partial derivatives, as in Equation 5.2.17, that Q satisfies the partial differential equation

$$Q_x \alpha_x (\gamma_x - x) + Q_z \alpha_z (\gamma_z - z) + \frac{1}{2} \sigma_x^2 Q_{xx} + \frac{1}{2} \sigma_z^2 Q_{zz} + \rho \sigma_x \sigma_z Q_{xz}$$
$$+ Q_t = yQ = (b + x + z)Q \qquad (5.2.29)$$

In this case, we make the following ansatz for the solution:

$$Q = \exp\left[A(t)x + B(t)z + C(t)\right] \qquad (5.2.30)$$

The appropriate "initial values" are $A(T) = B(T) = C(T) = 0$, and the yield in the two-factor Vasicek model is

$$Y(T) = -\left(\frac{C(0) + x(0)A(0) + z(0)B(0)}{T}\right) \qquad (5.2.31)$$

Using our ansatz, the partial differential equation for Q implies that

$$A\alpha_x(\gamma_x - x) + B\alpha_z(\gamma_z - z) + \frac{1}{2}\sigma_x^2 A^2 + \frac{1}{2}\sigma_z^2 B^2$$
$$+ \rho\sigma_x\sigma_z AB + \frac{dA}{dt}x + \frac{dB}{dt}z + \frac{dC}{dt} = (b + x + z)$$
$$(5.2.32)$$

Since at time t the variables x and z can take on arbitrary values, their coefficients must vanish, and Equation 5.2.32 is equivalent to the system of coupled ordinary differential equations,

$$\frac{dA}{dt} - \alpha_x A = 1$$

$$\frac{dB}{dt} - \alpha_z B = 1$$

$$\frac{dC}{dt} + \alpha_x \gamma_x A + \alpha_z \gamma_z B + \frac{1}{2}\sigma_x^2 A^2 + \frac{1}{2}\sigma_z^2 B^2 + \rho \sigma_x \sigma_z A B = b$$

$$(5.2.33)$$

We now proceed as in the one-factor model, solving for A and B,

$$A(t) = -\frac{1}{\alpha_x}\left(1 - e^{\alpha_x(t-T)}\right) \qquad B(t) = -\frac{1}{\alpha_z}\left(1 - e^{\alpha_z(t-T)}\right) \quad (5.2.34)$$

and plugging these into the integral

$$C(t) = b(t - T)$$
$$+ \int_t^T dt \left(\alpha_x \gamma_x A + \alpha_z \gamma_z B + \frac{1}{2}\sigma_x^2 A^2 + \frac{1}{2}\sigma_z^2 B^2 + \rho \sigma_x \sigma_z A B\right)$$

$$(5.2.35)$$

to get C.

5.3   Spot Yield Volatility

In a term structure model, the spot yield $Y(T)$ is not a random variable. The short Treasury rate at future times is a random variable; however, the spot yield as defined in Equation 5.2.4 is an expected value. As time moves forward, the fit values of the parameters in the term structure model change, and this results in a fluctuating value for $Y(T)$. Fitting Treasury bonds at different times to the traded bond prices results in a spot yield volatility $\sigma_{Y(T)}$. Even if the parameters in the Vasicek model that determine the evolution of the short rate do not change with time, the initial values $x(0)$ and $z(0)$ do because of the stochastic nature of their evolution. This leads us to define a yield volatility in the following way:

$$E\left[dY(T)\,dY(T)\right] = \sigma_{Y(T)}^2\,dt \qquad (5.3.36)$$

where t is the time at which the fit is performed.

In the two-factor Vasicek model, the expected value in Equation 5.3.36 is taken by treating the initial values $x(0)$ and $z(0)$ as normal random variables. Their variance is determined by the stochastic evolution equations $E[dx(0)^2] = \sigma_x^2\,dt$, $E[dz(0)^2] = \sigma_z^2\,dt$, and $E[dx(0)\,dz(0)] = \rho\sigma_x\sigma_z\,dt$. Hence the spot yield variance is

$$\sigma_{Y(T)}^2 = \left(\frac{\partial Y(T)}{\partial x(0)}\right)^2\sigma_x^2 + \left(\frac{\partial Y(T)}{\partial z(0)}\right)^2\sigma_z^2 + 2\left(\frac{\partial Y(T)}{\partial x(0)}\right)\left(\frac{\partial Y(T)}{\partial z(0)}\right)\rho\sigma_x\sigma_z$$

$$(5.3.37)$$

Using Equation 5.2.28, the partial derivatives that are needed to compute the spot yield volatility are

$$\frac{\partial Y(T)}{\partial x(0)} = \frac{(1 - e^{-\alpha_x T})}{\alpha_x T} \qquad \frac{\partial Y(T)}{\partial z(0)} = \frac{(1 - e^{-\alpha_z T})}{\alpha_z T} \qquad (5.3.38)$$

5.4   The Taylor Rule

The value of the short rate is set at Federal Reserve meetings, which occur roughly once per month. At these meetings, the central bankers try to set the short Treasury rate (i.e., the fed funds rate) so that inflation is near a target value π^* ($\pi^* \sim 1.5-2$ percent) and so the real economic output is near a desired trend level. If the economic output is too low, there is high unemployment and economic hardship. If the economic output is too high, this will result in a high demand for labor and goods, resulting in rising prices and hence an undesirable level of inflation. Inflation that is too high distorts economic activity and furthermore erodes the value of savings, particularly the savings of citizens who are no longer in the workforce and have moved their investments into fixed-income securities, a large fraction of which may not be inflation-protected real return bonds. In addition to adjusting the short rate, the Federal Reserve has other tools at its disposal. In times of extreme economic weakness, it can buy long-dated Treasuries (or other bonds) to drive down long-dated Treasury yields[2] (and reduce spreads). We will not consider this possible Federal Reserve action in this chapter.

Let $\pi(t)$ denote the inflation rate at time t and $o(t)$ denote the real economic output relative to the desired trend level. The precise definition of the output gap $o(t)$ in terms of gross domestic product (GDP[3]) is not important for us.

If the Federal Reserve increases the short rate y at its meeting, then this makes borrowing more expensive, slowing the economy and lowering inflation. If it decreases the value of y, then borrowing becomes cheaper and economic activity is stimulated, which results in a higher inflation rate. Expanding the real value of the short rate [i.e., $y(0) - \pi(0)$] that the Federal Reserve sets at its meeting (at $t = 0$) in a power series in $\pi(0) - \pi^*$ and $o(0)$ and neglecting terms of order $(\pi - \pi^*)^2$ and $o(0)^2$ and higher results in the Taylor rule,[4]

$$y(0) = r^* + \theta_1 [\pi(0) - \pi^*] + \theta_2 o(0) + \pi(0) = \hat{c} + \hat{\theta}_1 \pi(0) + \theta_2 o(0)$$

$$(5.4.39)$$

where[5]

$$\hat{c} = r^* - \theta_1 \pi^* \qquad \hat{\theta}_1 = \theta_1 + 1 \qquad (5.4.40)$$

---

[2]This happened in 2009.

[3]GDP is the total value of the goods and services produced. For the United States in 2008, it was about \$14 trillion.

[4]J. Taylor, "Discretion versus Policy Rules in Practice," *Carnegie-Rochester Conference Series on Public Policy* 39(1993), p. 195.

[5]Note that we use the symbol $\hat{c}$ in Equation 5.4.39 even though this is not a random variable.

Period	$\hat{c}$	$\hat{\theta}_1$	θ_2
Third quarter 1987–Fourth quarter 2005	1.9[1.3, 2.5]	1.3[1.1, 1.5]	0.86[0.72, 0.99]

Table 5.1 Estimates of the parameters of the standard Taylor rule. The 90 percent confidence intervals of the estimates are shown in brackets. The data used are from the third quarter of 1987 to the fourth quarter of 2005.

The motivation for the Taylor rule is analogous to the motivation for Hooke's law for the force from a displaced spring. Hooke's law results from expanding the force in a power series about the equilibrium point of the spring, where the force vanishes, and the Taylor rule results from expanding the real short rate in a power series about the displacement of inflation from its target value and about the output gap. We expect the Taylor rule to be a reasonable approximation as long as inflation is near π^* and the output gap is near zero. The results of a fit of the Taylor rule to data[6] are shown in Table 5.1. Annualized units are used there. A comparison of this fit with the historical values of the fed funds rate is shown in Figure 5.3. We can derive the Taylor rule if we adopt a quantitative model for how the economy evolves with time and a model for how the Federal Reserve sets the short rate. We take the economy to be described by two stochastic differential equations that give the evolution of inflation, $\pi(t)$, and the output gap, $o(t)$, with time t:

$$d\pi(t) = \mu_\pi \, dt + \alpha_1 \pi(t) \, dt + \alpha_2 o(t) \, dt + \sigma_\pi \, dw_\pi$$

$$do(t) = \mu_o \, dt + \beta_1 o(t) \, dt - \beta_2 \left[y(t) - \pi(t) \right] \, dt + \sigma_o \, dw_o \quad (5.4.41)$$

Here w_π and w_o are standard uncorrelated Brownian motions and $y(t)$ is the short rate adjusted by the Federal Reserve at discrete times t_n

---

[6]This fit was performed by Matthew P. Dorsten.

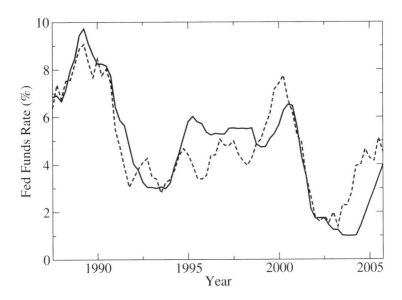

Figure 5.3 Taylor rule fit to historical data from the third quarter of 1987 to the fourth quarter of 2005. The solid line is the historical interest rate, and the dashed line is the predicted value of the interest rate given the best-fit values of its parameters in Table 5.1.

separated by intervals Δt. Hence, with $t = 0$ the present time, then $y(0) = y_0$ for $0 < t < t_1 = \Delta t$, $y(t) = y_1$ for $t_1 < t < t_2 = t_1 + \Delta t$, and so on. The coefficients α_1 and β_1 are negative, so the random walks for inflation and output gap are mean reverting to values determined in part by the drifts μ_π and μ_o. The coefficient α_2 is positive, since a positive output gap is a driver of inflation, and similarly the coefficient β_2 is positive, since a fed funds rate less than the inflation rate increases the output gap. Using the evolution determined by Equation 5.4.41, the inflation and output gap at any time $t > t_0$ are determined by the initial values $\pi(0)$, $o(0)$; the fed funds rate $y(\tau)$ for $0 < \tau < t$; the constants α_1, α_2, β_1, β_2, μ_π, and μ_o; and the standard deviations σ_π and σ_o of inflation and the output gap, respectively.

This coupled set of stochastic differential equations can be integrated formally without knowing the functional form of the short rate $y(t)$. To simplify the notation, we introduce two-element column vectors $\mathbf{v}(t)$, $d\mathbf{s}(t)$, $\boldsymbol{\mu}$, and $\mathbf{n}$, defined by

$$\mathbf{v}(t) = \begin{pmatrix} \pi(t) \\ o(t) \end{pmatrix} \qquad d\mathbf{s}(t) = \begin{pmatrix} \sigma_\pi\, dw_\pi(t) \\ \sigma_o\, dw_o(t) \end{pmatrix}$$

$$\boldsymbol{\mu} = \begin{pmatrix} \mu_\pi \\ \mu_o \end{pmatrix} \qquad\qquad \mathbf{n} = \begin{pmatrix} 0 \\ 1 \end{pmatrix} \qquad\qquad (5.4.42)$$

and the 2×2 matrix

$$M = \begin{pmatrix} \alpha_1 & \alpha_2 \\ \beta_2 & \beta_1 \end{pmatrix} \qquad\qquad (5.4.43)$$

In terms of these quantities, the solution of Equation 5.4.41 is the vector

$$\mathbf{v}(t) = e^{Mt}\mathbf{v}(0) + \left(e^{Mt} - 1\right)M^{-1}\boldsymbol{\mu} - \beta_2 \int_0^t y(\tau)e^{M(t-\tau)}\mathbf{n}\, d\tau$$

$$+ \int_0^t e^{M(t-\tau)}\, d\mathbf{s}(\tau) \qquad\qquad (5.4.44)$$

It is easy to verify that Equation 5.4.44 is indeed a solution to Equations 5.4.41. Differentiating with respect to time,

$$\frac{d\mathbf{v}(t)}{dt} = M\mathbf{v}(t) + \boldsymbol{\mu} - \beta_2 y(t)\mathbf{n} + \frac{d\mathbf{s}(t)}{dt} \qquad\qquad (5.4.45)$$

where the last two terms come from differentiating the limits of integration in Equation 5.4.44 and we have assembled the results of differentiating the time dependence of $\exp{(Mt)}$ into the first two terms of the equation. Equation 5.4.45 is Equations 5.4.41 written in vector form.

At time $t = 0$, we assume that the Federal Reserve adjusts the short rate y_0 and the possible future values of the short rate y_j, $j = 1, \ldots$, in an attempt to minimize the loss function

$$L_{\text{Taylor}} = \frac{1}{2} E \left[\sum_{n=0}^{\infty} \gamma e^{-dn\Delta t} (y_{n+1} - y_n)^2 \right.$$
$$\left. + \int_0^{\infty} dt\, e^{-d't} \left\{ [\pi(t) - \pi^*]^2 + \lambda o(t)^2 \right\} \right] \quad (5.4.46)$$

Without loss of generality, we have fixed the coefficient of $[\pi(t) - \pi^*]^2$ to be unity. The first term in the loss function L_{Taylor} is an inertia term that expresses the Federal Reserve's aversion to making large changes in the short rate. The larger γ is, the more the Federal Reserve is concerned about making large changes in the short rate. The last two terms reflect the Federal Reserve's desire to simultaneously have inflation at the targeted value π^* and the output gap minimized. The larger the value of λ, the more the Federal Reserve is concerned about economic growth. The constants d and d' are a measure of how much the Federal Reserve discounts the impact of events in the future. For example, the Federal Reserve cares more about inflation next year than about inflation 20 years from now. We assume that d and d' are large enough that the sum and integral over time converge.

Plugging the solution for $\pi(t)$ and $o(t)$ given in Equation 5.4.44 into Equation 5.4.46 and taking the expected value gives an expression for L_{Taylor} that is a quadratic polynomial in the y_i's, since $\pi(t)$ and $o(t)$ are linearly dependent upon the y_i's. The values of y_j are determined by minimizing the loss function with respect to them, i.e., by solving the equations $dL_{\text{Taylor}}/dy_k = 0$. These equations have the form

$$\sum_{j=0}^{\infty} X_{kj} y_j + Y_k^{\pi} \pi(0) + Y_k^{o} o(0) + Z_k = 0 \quad (5.4.47)$$

where the quantities X_{kj}, Y_k^{π}, Y_k^{o}, and Z_k are independent of the y_k, $\pi(0)$, and $o(0)$. The linear dependence on $o(0)$ and $\pi(0)$ comes from the fact that $\pi(t)$ and $o(t)$ are linearly dependent on these initial values and that the loss function is quadratic in $\pi(t)$ and $o(t)$. Viewing X_{kj} as an infinite dimensional matrix, we invert it, multiply Equation 5.4.47 by X_{0k}^{-1}, and sum over k to get the Taylor rule,

$$y(0) + \sum_{k=0} X_{0k}^{-1} Y_k^\pi \pi(0) + \sum_{k=0} X_{0k}^{-1} Y_k^o o(0) + \sum_{k=0} X_{0k}^{-1} Z_k = 0 \quad (5.4.48)$$

The linear Taylor rule arose because we took the loss function to be quadratic. To push the analogy with a spring further, recall that the linear force law results because the potential energy is quadratic in the spring's displacement; the quadratic loss function we have used is analogous to the quadratic potential energy for a spring.

There is a subtle point in this analysis that we have glossed over. The Federal Reserve cannot set a negative value for the short rate. Hence, if the solution to Equation 5.4.48 for $y(0)$ is negative, the Federal Reserve actually sets the rate to zero, which gives the rule

$$y(0) = \max \left[\hat{c} + \hat{\theta}_1 \pi(0) + \theta_2 o(0), 0 \right] \quad (5.4.49)$$

The parameters $\hat{c}$, $\hat{\theta}_1$, and θ_2 depend on the parameters in the economic model (i.e., $\alpha_{1,2}$, $\beta_{1,2}$, $\mu_{\pi,o}$, and $\sigma_{\pi,o}$) and the parameters in the Federal Reserve's loss function (i.e., γ, d, d', π^*, and λ).

Since the Federal Reserve cannot make the short Treasury rate negative, if the rate reaches zero, the Federal Reserve cannot make further adjustments (of the short rate) to help stimulate the economy. That is what makes periods with very low inflation and a very low (or negative) output gap so dangerous. If the Federal Reserve runs out of ammunition, it is possible to enter a sustained era of deflation and negative output gap. This economic catastrophe (sustained deflation and negative output gap) happened in Japan for roughly 20 years.

5.5   A Macroeconomic Two-Factor Model

We can use the results of the previous section to derive a two-factor model[7] for the time evolution of the short rate $y(t)$. First, we neglect the

---

[7]This model was developed in collaboration with Matthew Dorstan.

max function in Equation 5.4.49. This should be a good approximation for the U.S. economy, where minimizing the loss function should not result in a negative $y(0)$. Second, we make the approximation that at each time t, the Federal Reserve is continuously adjusting the short rate according to the Taylor rule,

$$y(t) = \hat{c} + \hat{\theta}_1 \pi(t) + \theta_2 o(t) \qquad (5.5.50)$$

Putting this into Equations 5.4.41 for the evolution of the economy gives

$$d\pi(t) = \mu_\pi \, dt + \alpha_1 \pi(t) \, dt + \alpha_2 o(t) \, dt + \sigma_\pi \, dw_\pi$$
$$do(t) = \hat{\mu}_o \, dt + \hat{\beta}_1 o(t) \, dt + \hat{\beta}_2 \pi(t) \, dt + \sigma_o \, dw_o \qquad (5.5.51)$$

Here $\hat{\beta}_1 = \beta_1 - \theta_2\beta_2$, $\hat{\beta}_2 = \beta_2(1 - \hat{\theta}_1)$, and $\hat{\mu}_o = \mu_o - \beta_2\hat{c}$. Equations 5.5.51 and 5.5.50 are analogous to Equations 5.2.25 and 5.2.27 of the Vasicek model.[8] Equations 5.5.51 and 5.5.50 are a two-factor model for the evolution of the Treasury short rate $y(t)$ where the two factors are inflation and output gap. Two-factor models are reasonable models for the Treasury short rate because the economy is mostly driven by inflation and output gap.

The solution to Equations 5.5.51 is

$$\mathbf{v}(t) = e^{\widehat{M}t}\mathbf{v}(0) + \left(e^{\widehat{M}t} - 1\right)\widehat{M}^{-1}\hat{\mu} + \int_0^t e^{\widehat{M}(t-\tau)} \, d\mathbf{s}(\tau) \qquad (5.5.52)$$

where

$$\widehat{M} = \begin{pmatrix} \alpha_1 & \alpha_2 \\ \hat{\beta}_2 & \hat{\beta}_1 \end{pmatrix} \qquad (5.5.53)$$

---

[8] In fact we will show, in the next section, that for a range of parameters the two-factor Vasicek model is the same as this model.

and

$$\hat{\boldsymbol{\mu}} = \begin{pmatrix} \mu_\pi \\ \hat{\mu}_o \end{pmatrix} \tag{5.5.54}$$

The vectors $\mathbf{v}(t)$ and $d\mathbf{s}(\tau)$ are defined as in the previous section.

It is convenient to introduce the vector Θ with components $\Theta_1 = \hat{\theta}_1$ and $\Theta_2 = \theta_2$, so that the Taylor rule is $y(t) = \hat{c} + \hat{\theta}_1 \pi(t) + \theta_2 o(t) = \hat{c} + \Theta^\top \mathbf{v}$. Here the symbol $\top$ denotes the transpose. Inflation and output gap are normal random variables, and so writing $\mathbf{v} = \bar{\mathbf{v}} + \tilde{\mathbf{v}}$, where $E[\mathbf{v}] = \bar{\mathbf{v}}$ and $E[\tilde{\mathbf{v}}] = 0$, the yield is

$$Y(T) = \hat{c} + \frac{1}{T} \int_0^T dt\, \Theta^\top \bar{\mathbf{v}}(t)$$

$$- \frac{1}{2T} \sum_{a,b=1}^2 \Theta_a \Theta_b \int_0^T dt \int_0^T dt'\, E\left[\bar{v}(t)_a \bar{v}(t')_b \right] \tag{5.5.55}$$

We will not perform the integrations explicitly here. Rather, in the next section we show how this model can be mapped onto the two-factor Vasicek model.

5.6   Relationship between the Macroeconomic and Vasicek Models

So far in this chapter, we have introduced two two-factor models. The Vasicek model was motivated by simplicity. In this model, the Treasury short rate is $y(t) = b + x(t) + z(t)$, and the two factors $x(t)$ and $z(t)$ evolve in time according to the stochastic differential equations

$$d\mathbf{v}_V(t) = \boldsymbol{\mu}_V \, dt + M_V \mathbf{v}_V(t) \, dt + d\mathbf{s}_V(t) \tag{5.6.56}$$

where

$$\boldsymbol{\mu}_V = \begin{pmatrix} \alpha_x \gamma_x \\ \alpha_z \gamma_z \end{pmatrix} \qquad \mathbf{v}_V(t) = \begin{pmatrix} x(t) \\ z(t) \end{pmatrix}$$

$$M_V = \begin{pmatrix} -\alpha_x & 0 \\ 0 & -\alpha_z \end{pmatrix} \quad d\mathbf{s}_V(t) = \begin{pmatrix} \sigma_x \, dw_x \\ \sigma_z \, dw_z \end{pmatrix} \quad (5.6.57)$$

The correlated Brownian motions w_x and w_y satisfy $E[dw_x(t) \, dw_x(t)] = dt$, $E[dw_z(t) \, dw_z(t)] = dt$, and $E[dw_x(t) \, dw_z(t)] = \rho \, dt$.

The macroeconomic two-factor model was motivated by a consideration of Federal Reserve policy and the role that inflation and economic growth play in the economy. In this model, the Treasury short rate is $y(t) = \hat{c} + \hat{\theta}_1 \pi(t) + \theta_2 o(t)$, and the two factors (inflation and output gap) $\pi(t)$ and $o(t)$ evolve in time according to the stochastic differential equations

$$d\mathbf{v}(t) = \hat{\boldsymbol{\mu}} \, dt + \widehat{M}\mathbf{v}(t) \, dt + d\mathbf{s}(t) \quad (5.6.58)$$

where

$$\hat{\boldsymbol{\mu}} = \begin{pmatrix} \mu_\pi \\ \hat{\mu}_o \end{pmatrix} \quad \mathbf{v}(t) = \begin{pmatrix} \pi(t) \\ o(t) \end{pmatrix}$$

$$\widehat{M} = \begin{pmatrix} \alpha_1 & \alpha_2 \\ \hat{\beta}_2 & \hat{\beta}_1 \end{pmatrix} \quad d\mathbf{s}(t) = \begin{pmatrix} \sigma_\pi \, dw_\pi(t) \\ \sigma_o \, dw_o(t) \end{pmatrix} \quad (5.6.59)$$

Now the Brownian motions $w_\pi(t)$ and $w_o(t)$ are uncorrelated and satisfy $E[dw_\pi(t) \, dw_\pi(t)] = dt$, $E[dw_o \, dw_o] = dt$, and $E[dw_\pi \, dw_o] = 0$.

The goal of this section is to express the parameters in the Vasicek model in terms of those in the macroeconomic model. The form of these two-factor models suggests that $b = \hat{c}$ and that $x(t)$ and $z(t)$ are linear combinations of $\pi(t)$ and $o(t)$. The matrix M_V is diagonal, while $\widehat{M}$ is not. However, $\widehat{M}$ can be diagonalized by a transformation U,

$$\widehat{M} = U \begin{pmatrix} \lambda_+ & 0 \\ 0 & \lambda_- \end{pmatrix} U^{-1} \quad (5.6.60)$$

The eigenvalues of $\widehat{M}$ are

$$\lambda_{\pm} = \frac{\alpha_1 + \hat{\beta}_1 \pm \delta}{2} \tag{5.6.61}$$

and

$$\delta^2 = (\alpha_1 + \hat{\beta}_1)^2 - 4(\alpha_1 \hat{\beta}_1 - \hat{\beta}_2 \alpha_2) = \alpha_1^2 - 2\alpha_1 \hat{\beta}_1 + \hat{\beta}_1^2 + 4\hat{\beta}_2 \alpha_2 \tag{5.6.62}$$

The transformation that diagonalizes $\widehat{M}$, and its inverse U^{-1}, is given in terms of the parameters in the macroeconomic model by

$$U = \frac{1}{\alpha_2(\lambda_- - \lambda_+)} \begin{pmatrix} \alpha_2 & \alpha_2 \\ \lambda_+ - \alpha_1 & \lambda_- - \alpha_1 \end{pmatrix}$$

$$U^{-1} = \begin{pmatrix} \lambda_- - \alpha_1 & -\alpha_2 \\ \alpha_1 - \lambda_+ & \alpha_2 \end{pmatrix} \tag{5.6.63}$$

Let F be a diagonal matrix with entries $F_{11} = e$ and $F_{22} = f$. Let's consider the quantity $FU^{-1}\mathbf{v}(t)$. Using the evolution equation, Equation 5.6.58, and the definitions of the various quantities,

$$d(FU^{-1}\mathbf{v}) = FU^{-1}\hat{\boldsymbol{\mu}}\, dt + \begin{pmatrix} \lambda_+ & 0 \\ 0 & \lambda_- \end{pmatrix} FU^{-1}\mathbf{v}(t)\, dt + FU^{-1}\, d\mathbf{s}(t) \tag{5.6.64}$$

This is equivalent to the Vasicek model evolution in Equation 5.6.56, provided that we identify

$$\mathbf{v}_V(t) = FU^{-1}\mathbf{v}(t) \qquad M_V = \begin{pmatrix} \lambda_+ & 0 \\ 0 & \lambda_- \end{pmatrix}$$

$$\boldsymbol{\mu}_V = FU^{-1}\hat{\boldsymbol{\mu}} \qquad d\mathbf{s}(t)_V = FU^{-1}\, d\mathbf{s}(t) \tag{5.6.65}$$

We immediately conclude from the expression for M_V that $\alpha_x = -\lambda_+$ and $\alpha_z = -\lambda_-$. The relationship between $\boldsymbol{\mu}_V$ and $\hat{\boldsymbol{\mu}}$ implies that

$$\gamma_x = -\frac{e}{\lambda_+}[(\lambda_- - \alpha_1)\mu_\pi - \alpha_2\hat{\mu}_o] \tag{5.6.66}$$

$$\gamma_z = -\frac{f}{\lambda_-}[(\alpha_1 - \lambda_+)\mu_\pi + \alpha_2\hat{\mu}_o] \tag{5.6.67}$$

The components of the equation relating $\mathbf{v}_V$ and $\mathbf{v}$ are

$$x(t) = e[(\lambda_- - \alpha_1)\pi(t) - \alpha_2 o(t)] \tag{5.6.68}$$

$$z(t) = f[(\alpha_1 - \lambda_+)\pi(t) + \alpha_2 o(t)] \tag{5.6.69}$$

Using these equations to compute $E[dx(t)^2]$, $E[dz(t)^2]$, and $E[dx(t)\,dz(t)]$ implies that

$$\sigma_x = e\sqrt{(\lambda_- - \alpha_1)^2\sigma_\pi^2 + \alpha_2^2\sigma_o^2} \tag{5.6.70}$$

$$\sigma_z = f\sqrt{(\alpha_1 - \lambda_+)^2\sigma_\pi^2 + \alpha_2^2\sigma_o^2} \tag{5.6.71}$$

and

$$\rho = \frac{\sigma_\pi^2\alpha_2\hat{\beta}_2 - \sigma_o^2\alpha_2^2}{\sqrt{(\lambda_- - \alpha_1)^2\sigma_\pi^2 + \alpha_2^2\sigma_o^2}\sqrt{(\alpha_1 - \lambda_+)^2\sigma_\pi^2 + \alpha_2^2\sigma_o^2}} \tag{5.6.72}$$

It remains to determine the parameters e and f. We find them by noting that $x(t) + z(t) = y(t) - b = y(t) - \hat{c} = \hat{\theta}_1\pi(t) + \theta_2 o(t)$. Plugging in the expressions that give x and z in terms of π and o gives $e[(\lambda_- - \alpha_1)\pi(t) - \alpha_2 o(t)] + f[(\alpha_1 - \lambda_+)\pi(t) + \alpha_2 o(t)] = \hat{\theta}_1\pi(t) + \theta_2 o(t)$. This must hold for all $\pi(t)$ and $o(t)$, which implies the two equations

$$e(\lambda_- - \alpha_1) + f(\alpha_1 - \lambda_+) = \hat{\theta}_1 \tag{5.6.73}$$

$$\alpha_2(f - e) = \theta_2 \tag{5.6.74}$$

Hence,

$$e = \frac{\theta_2(\lambda_+ - \alpha_1) + \hat{\theta}_1\alpha_2}{\alpha_2(\lambda_- - \lambda_+)} \tag{5.6.75}$$

$$f = \frac{\theta_2(\lambda_- - \alpha_1) + \hat{\theta}_1\alpha_2}{\alpha_2(\lambda_- - \lambda_+)} \tag{5.6.76}$$

This completes the derivation of the relationship of the Vasicek and macroeconomic two-factor models. All the parameters of the Vasicek model have been expressed in terms of those in the macroeconomic model.

5.7   Another Two-Factor Model

We discuss in this section one more two-factor term structure model. In this model, the two factors evolve according to

$$dx = \mu\, dt + \sigma_x\, dw_x \qquad dz = -\alpha z\, dt + \sigma_z\, dw_z \quad (5.7.77)$$

The two random walks for the x and z factors are uncorrelated,

$$E\left[\frac{dw_x}{dt}\frac{dw_x}{dt'}\right] = \delta(t - t') \quad E\left[\frac{dw_z}{dt}\frac{dw_z}{dt'}\right] = \delta(t - t') \quad E\left[\frac{dw_x}{dt}\frac{dw_z}{dt'}\right] = 0$$

$$\tag{5.7.78}$$

Unlike in the Vasicek two-factor model, the short rate y is driven by its evolution to $x + z$ at large times, but it can be different at any given time:

$$dy = k(x + z - y)\, dt \tag{5.7.79}$$

   In this model, the long-term factor x is not mean reverting and represents the fundamental structure of the economy, while the mean reverting factor z represents transitory fluctuations about this long-term behavior. The calculation of the yield and other quantities in this model is similar to that for the two-factor Vasicek model. We briefly sketch the calculation of the yield in this model. It is straightforward to integrate the evolution equation for the x factor. This gives

$$x(t) = x_0 + \mu t + \sigma_x \int_0^t d\tau \left(\frac{dw_x}{d\tau} \right) \tag{5.7.80}$$

where $x_0 = x(0)$. For the mean reverting factor z, we perform the usual change of variables and then integrate the equation. This procedure gives

$$z(t) = z_0 e^{-\alpha t} + e^{-\alpha t} \sigma_z \int_0^t d\tau \, e^{\alpha \tau} \left(\frac{dw_z}{d\tau} \right) \tag{5.7.81}$$

Now we must integrate Equation 5.7.79. We make the change of variables,

$$y = e^{-kt} \Omega_y(t) \tag{5.7.82}$$

Now

$$\frac{dy}{dt} = -ky + e^{-kt} \frac{d\Omega_y}{dt} \tag{5.7.83}$$

Plugging this into the evolution equation for y implies that

$$\frac{d\Omega_y}{dt} = e^{kt} k [x(t) + z(t)] \tag{5.7.84}$$

which after integrating and changing back to the variable y gives

$$y(t) = y_0 e^{-kt} + e^{-kt} k \int_0^t d\tau \, e^{k\tau} [x(\tau) + z(\tau)] \tag{5.7.85}$$

We break the variables x, z, and y into the sum of their expected values and a fluctuating part that has zero expected value: $x = \bar{x} + \tilde{x}$, $z = \bar{z} + \tilde{z}$, $y = \bar{y} + \tilde{y}$, where $\bar{x} = E[x]$, and so on. The expressions for these quantities are

$$\bar{x}(t) = x_0 + \mu t$$

$$\bar{z}(t) = z_0 e^{-\alpha t}$$

$$\tilde{x}(t) = \sigma_x \int_0^t d\tau \left(\frac{dw_x}{d\tau}\right)$$

$$\tilde{z}(t) = e^{-\alpha t} \sigma_z \int_0^t d\tau\, e^{\alpha \tau} \left(\frac{dw_z}{d\tau}\right) \tag{5.7.86}$$

The short rate $y(t) = \bar{y}(t) + \tilde{y}(t)$ is given in terms of them by

$$\bar{y}(t) = y_0 e^{-kt} + e^{-kt} k \int_0^t d\tau\, e^{k\tau} [\bar{x}(\tau) + \bar{z}(\tau)]$$

$$\tilde{y}(t) = e^{-kt} k \int_0^t d\tau\, e^{k\tau} [\tilde{x}(\tau) + \tilde{z}(\tau)] \tag{5.7.87}$$

The spot yield to maturity T, $Y(T)$, is defined by

$$e^{-Y(T)T} = E\left[\exp\left[-\int_0^T d\phi\, y(\phi)\right]\right] \tag{5.7.88}$$

Since y is normal, we have that

$$Y(T) = \frac{1}{T} \int_0^T d\phi\, \bar{y}(\phi) - \frac{1}{2T} \int_0^T d\phi \int_0^T d\phi'\, E[\tilde{y}(\phi)\tilde{y}(\phi')] \tag{5.7.89}$$

Using the expression for $\tilde{y}$ in terms of $\tilde{x}$ and $\tilde{z}$ gives

$$E[\tilde{y}(\phi)\tilde{y}(\phi')] = k^2 e^{-k(\phi+\phi')} \int_0^\phi d\tau\, e^{k\tau} \int_0^{\phi'} d\tau\, e^{k\tau'} \{E[\tilde{x}(\tau)\tilde{x}(\tau')]$$

$$+ E[\tilde{z}(\tau)\tilde{z}(\tau')]\} \tag{5.7.90}$$

We break the spot yield up into its component pieces,

$$Y(T) = Y_0(T) + \Delta Y_x(T) + \Delta Y_z(T) \tag{5.7.91}$$

where

$$Y_0(T) = \frac{1}{T} \int_0^T d\phi \, \bar{y}(\phi) \tag{5.7.92}$$

$$\Delta Y_x(T) = -\frac{1}{2T} \int_0^T d\phi \int_0^T d\phi' \, k^2 e^{-k(\phi+\phi')} \int_0^{\phi} d\tau \, e^{k\tau} \int_0^{\phi'} d\tau' e^{k\tau'} \, E[\bar{x}(\tau) E\bar{x}(\tau')] \tag{5.7.93}$$

and

$$\Delta Y_z(T) = -\frac{1}{2T} \int_0^T d\phi \int_0^T d\phi' \, k^2 e^{-k(\phi+\phi')} \int_0^{\phi} d\tau \, e^{k\tau} \int_0^{\phi'} d\tau \, e^{k\tau'} \, E[\bar{z}(\tau) E\bar{z}(\tau')] \tag{5.7.94}$$

It is straightforward to integrate the expected short rate to get

$$Y_0(T) = y_0 \left(\frac{1 - e^{-kT}}{kT} \right) + x_0 \left(\frac{-1 + e^{-kT}}{kT} + 1 \right)$$
$$+ \mu \left(\frac{1 - e^{-kT}}{k^2 T} + \frac{T}{2} - \frac{1}{k} \right) + z_0 \left(\frac{1 - e^{-kT}}{T(\alpha - k)} - \frac{(1 - e^{-\alpha T})k}{T\alpha(\alpha - k)} \right) \tag{5.7.95}$$

In Chapter 2 we showed that

$$E[\bar{x}(\tau)\bar{x}(\tau')] = \sigma_x^2 [\tau'\theta(\tau - \tau') + \tau\theta(\tau' - \tau)] \tag{5.7.96}$$

Putting this into Equation 5.7.93 and performing the four integrations gives

$$\Delta Y_x(T) = \sigma_x^2 \left[-\frac{T^2}{6} + \frac{T}{2k} - \frac{1}{2k^2} \left(1 - 2e^{-kT} \right) - \frac{1}{4k^3 T} \left(1 - e^{-2kT} \right) \right] \tag{5.7.97}$$

The evolution of z is the same as the short rate in the one-factor Vasicek model with $\gamma = 0$. Using Equation 5.2.12,

$$E[\bar{z}(\tau)\bar{z}(\tau')] = \frac{\sigma_z^2}{2\alpha} e^{-\alpha(\tau+\tau')} \left[\left(e^{2\alpha\tau'} - 1 \right) \theta(\tau - \tau') \right.$$
$$\left. + \left(e^{2\alpha\tau} - 1 \right) \theta(\tau' - \tau) \right] \tag{5.7.98}$$

Putting this into Equation 5.7.94 and performing the four integrations gives

$$\Delta Y_z(T) = \sigma_z^2 \left[-\frac{1}{2\alpha^2} + \frac{k^2}{4T\alpha^3(k-\alpha)^2} \left(1 - e^{-\alpha T} \right) \left(3 - e^{-\alpha T} \right) \right.$$
$$+ \frac{1}{4kT(k-\alpha)^2} \left(1 - e^{-kT} \right) \left(3 - e^{-kT} \right)$$
$$- \frac{k}{T\alpha(k+\alpha)(k-\alpha)^2} \left(1 - e^{-\alpha T} \right) \left(1 - e^{-kT} \right)$$
$$- \frac{k^2}{T\alpha^2(k+\alpha)(k-\alpha)^2} \left(1 - e^{-\alpha T} \right)$$
$$\left. - \frac{1}{T(k+\alpha)(k-\alpha)^2} \left(1 - e^{-kT} \right) \right] \tag{5.7.99}$$

In Figure 5.4 we plot the yield curve $Y(T)$ for the choice of parameters $k = 1.06$, $\mu = 0.003$, $\alpha = 0.21$, $\sigma_x = 0.009$, $\sigma_z = 0.015$, $x_0 = 0.045$, $z_0 = -0.021$, and $y_0 = 0.029$. These are in annualized units, so, for example, a drift $\mu = 0.003$ means a drift of 0.3 percent per year and an initial short rate $y_0 = 0.029$ means a short rate of 2.9 percent per year. The yield $Y(T)$ first falls and then rises.

Next consider the same parameters as are used in Figure 5.4, but change the initial value of the z factor to $z_0 = 0.029$. The resulting (spot) yield curve $Y(T)$ is plotted in Figure 5.5. In this case, the yield curve is an increasing function of T for all maturities. Finally we

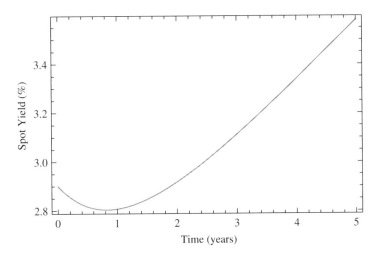

Figure 5.4 Yield curve in two-factor term structure model. The y axis is the yield in percent, and the x axis is the time in years. Model parameters are $k = 1.06$, $\mu = 0.003$, $\alpha = 0.21$, $\sigma_x = 0.009$, $\sigma_z = 0.015$, $x_0 = 0.045$, $z_0 = -0.021$, and $y_0 = 0.029$.

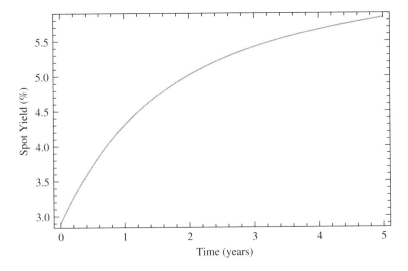

Figure 5.5 Yield curve in two-factor term structure model. The y axis is the yield in percent, and the x axis is the time in years. Model parameters are $k = 1.06$, $\mu = 0.003$, $\alpha = 0.21$, $\sigma_x = 0.009$, $\sigma_z = 0.029$, $x_0 = 0.045$, $z_0 = 0.029$, and $y_0 = 0.029$.

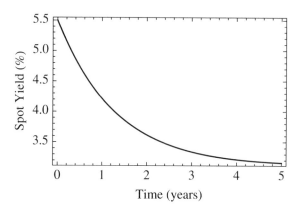

Figure 5.6   Yield curve in two-factor term structure model. The y axis is the yield in percent, and the x axis is the time in years. Model parameters are $k = 1.06$, $\mu = -0.001$, $\alpha = 0.21$, $\sigma_x = 0.009$, $\sigma_z = 0.015$, $x_0 = 0.045$, $y_0 = 0.055$, and $z_0 = -0.025$.

change the parameters of the term structure model to $k = 1.06$, $\mu = -0.001$, $\alpha = 0.21$, $\sigma_x = 0.009$, $\sigma_z = 0.015$, $x_0 = 0.045$, $y_0 = 0.055$, and $z_0 = -0.025$. The resulting yield curve is plotted in Figure 5.6. Now the (spot) yield curve $Y(T)$ is inverted (i.e., decreasing) for all the maturities shown in the plot. This is a realistic model for the yield curve only over a limited range of maturities T. Since the x parameter drift μ is negative, the spot yield becomes negative if it is evaluated at very large maturities.

A fit of this model to daily spot yields at maturities $T = 0.25$ year, 0.5 year, 1 year, 2 years, 5 years, 10 years, and 30 years, over the 5-year period from October 17, 2003, to October 17, 2008, was done.[9] The PIMCO database was used for the yield curve data. The volatilities were held fixed at $\sigma_x = 0.009$ and $\sigma_z = 0.015$. They were not fit by comparing with data. The parameters α, μ, and k were treated

---

[9]This fit was performed by Yoni Schwarzkopf.

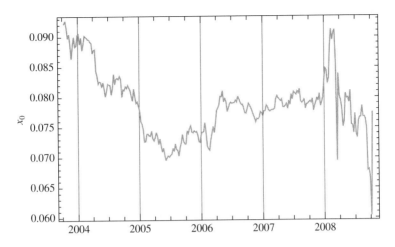

Figure 5.7 Best fit values of the parameter x_0.

as constants over this period, but they were fit to, and we found that their best fit values are $\mu = 0.0001$, $\alpha = 0.1$, and $k = 0.5$. The values of x_0, y_0, and z_0 vary daily, and we show their best fit values in Figures 5.7, 5.8, and 5.9.

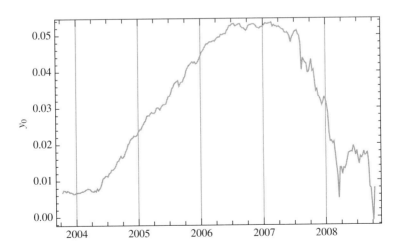

Figure 5.8 Best fit values of the parameter y_0.

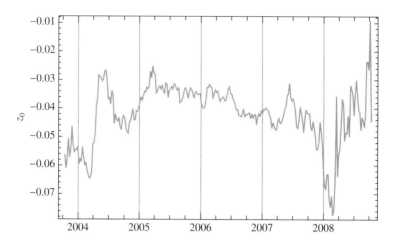

Figure 5.9 Best fit values of the parameter z_0.

5.8   Models with Explicit Time Dependence

Typically the term structure models introduced in this chapter will not precisely fit the yield curve. For option pricing, it may be desirable to have a term structure model that exactly fits the yield curve. For example, on any day the one-factor model,

$$dy(t) = \mu(t)y(t)\,dt + \sigma\,dw \qquad (5.8.100)$$

can fit the observed yield curve $Y(t)$ for some choice of function $\mu(t)$. For this choice of the function $\mu(t)$, the price of European options on zero coupon bonds will depend on the single variable σ. Options exist at different strike prices and maturities. We could also let the volatility σ depend on time $\sigma \rightarrow \sigma(t)$ and then get an exact fit, at a fixed strike price, to option prices at different maturities. These values of $\mu(t)$ and $\sigma(t)$ can then be used to price options at different strike prices. The time dependence does not necessarily prevent an analytic solution for the spot yield. Consider, for example, the one-factor Vasicek model with time-dependent coefficients,

$$dy(t) = \alpha(t)[\gamma(t) - y(t)]\,dt + \sigma(t)\,dw \qquad (5.8.101)$$

To solve for the spot yield $Y(T)$ using this model for the short rate, we change variables to $z(t)$ using

$$y(t) = \exp\left[-\int_0^t d\tau\,\alpha(\tau)\right] z(t) \qquad (5.8.102)$$

Since

$$dy(t) = -\alpha(t)y(t)\,dt + \exp\left[-\int_0^t d\tau\,\alpha(\tau)\right] dz(t) \qquad (5.8.103)$$

the variable $z(t)$ obeys a stochastic evolution without mean reversion,

$$dz(t) = \mu(t)\,dt + \sigma'(t)\,dw \qquad (5.8.104)$$

where

$$\mu(t) = \exp\left[\int_0^t d\tau\,\alpha(\tau)\right] \alpha(t)\gamma(t) \qquad (5.8.105)$$

and

$$\sigma'(t) = \exp\left[\int_0^t d\tau\,\alpha(\tau)\right] \sigma(t) \qquad (5.8.106)$$

Introducing $\bar{z}(t) = E[z(t)]$ and $\tilde{z}(t) = z(t) - \bar{z}(t)$, we have that

$$\bar{z}(t) = \int_0^t ds\,\mu(s) \qquad \tilde{z}(t) = \int_0^t ds\,\sigma'(s)\frac{dw}{ds} \qquad (5.8.107)$$

Using the relation between y and z, the yield $Y(T)$ is

$$Y(T) = \frac{1}{T} \int_0^T dt \exp\left[-\int_0^t d\tau\, \alpha(\tau)\right] \bar{z}(t)$$

$$-\frac{1}{2T} \int_0^T dt \exp\left[-\int_0^t d\tau\, \alpha(\tau)\right] \int_0^T dt' \exp\left[-\int_0^{t'} d\tau'\alpha(\tau')\right] E\left[\bar{z}(t)\bar{z}(t')\right]$$

$$(5.8.108)$$

Finally, the needed expected value is

$$E\left[\bar{z}(t)\bar{z}(t')\right] = \int_0^t ds \int_0^{t'} ds'\, \sigma'(s)\sigma'(s')\delta(s-s')$$

$$= \theta(t-t') \int_0^{t'} ds\, \sigma'(s)^2 + \theta(t'-t) \int_0^t ds\, \sigma'(s)^2$$

$$(5.8.109)$$

6

Derivatives of Bonds

6.1 Eurodollar Futures Rates and Volatilities

In this chapter, we discuss various simple derivatives of bonds, including future and forward contracts. In this section, we define some quantities that are useful for pricing futures contracts. For simplicity, we do the calculations using the one-factor Vasicek model. It is straightforward to generalize the results to more complicated multifactor models.

Consider a zero coupon Treasury bond with principal P that has maturity T in t years or equivalently maturity $t + T$ today. At the future time t its price is

$$\text{Price}_t = E_t \left[\exp \left(- \int_t^{t+T} d\tau \, y(\tau) \right) \right] P \qquad (6.1.1)$$

The spot yield in t years $Y_t(T)$ is defined by writing the price as

$$\text{Price}_t = e^{-Y_t(T)T} P \qquad (6.1.2)$$

Note that Price_t and $Y_t(T)$ are random variables. The expectation value in Equation 6.1.1 is taken at time t, so the random future value of the

Treasury short rate $y(t)$ is not averaged over.[1] It is the dependence of $Y_t(T)$ on $y(t)$ that makes it a random variable. The "eurodollar futures rate," $r_{fut}(t, T)$, is defined as the expectation value today of $Y_t(T)$,

$$r_{fut}(t, T) = E[Y_t(T)] \tag{6.1.3}$$

Since in an expectation value at time t, i.e., $E_t[\ ]$, $y(t)$ is treated as a constant, it is not difficult to show that $Y_t(T)$ is given by making the replacement $y(0) \to y(t)$, in Equation 5.2.15, which gives

$$Y_t(T) = \gamma + \left(\frac{y(t) - \gamma}{\alpha T}\right)\left(1 - e^{-\alpha T}\right)$$
$$- \frac{\sigma^2}{2\alpha^2}\left[1 + \frac{1}{2\alpha T}\left(1 - e^{-2\alpha T}\right) - \frac{2}{\alpha T}\left(1 - e^{-\alpha T}\right)\right] \tag{6.1.4}$$

Taking the expectation value gives

$$r_{fut}(t, T) = \gamma + \left(\frac{\bar{y}(t) - \gamma}{\alpha T}\right)\left(1 - e^{-\alpha T}\right)$$
$$- \frac{\sigma^2}{2\alpha^2}\left[1 + \frac{1}{2\alpha T}\left(1 - e^{-2\alpha T}\right) - \frac{2}{\alpha T}\left(1 - e^{-\alpha T}\right)\right] \tag{6.1.5}$$

Since $y(t)$ is a normal random variable, so is $Y_t(T)$, and its variance is

$$\sigma^2_{Y_t(T)} = E[\{Y_t(T) - E[Y_t(T)]\}^2] = \left(\frac{1 - e^{-\alpha T}}{\alpha T}\right)^2 \frac{\sigma^2}{2\alpha}\left(1 - e^{-2\alpha t}\right) \tag{6.1.6}$$

[1]The subscript t in E_t is used to denote that the expectation is taken at the future time t. For expectations taken today, i.e., $t = 0$, the subscript is dropped, $E_0 = E$.

6.2 Future and Forward Contracts

In Chapter 1 we discussed a forward contract on a stock. Forward contracts exist for other assets too. The buyer of a forward contract on a zero coupon bond of maturity $t + T$ receives at the settlement time t of the forward contract a zero coupon bond with principal P that matures at time $t + T$. At the settlement time t of the forward contract, the buyer of the forward contract pays P_{fwd} to the seller. In Chapter 1 we gave an arbitrage argument for the price of a forward contract on a stock. It implied that the price of a forward contract on a stock is just its price today increased by the risk-free rate of return to the time of contract settlement. The same arbitrage argument holds for a forward contract on a zero coupon Treasury bond, and so we arrive at the following formula for P_{fwd} for such a contract:

$$
P_{\text{fwd}} = E\left[\exp\left[-\int_0^{T+t} d\tau\, y(\tau)\right]\right] e^{Y(t)t} P = \frac{E\left[\exp\left[-\int_0^{T+t} d\tau\, y(\tau)\right]\right]}{E\left[\exp\left[-\int_0^{t} d\tau\, y(\tau)\right]\right]} P
$$

$$(6.2.7)$$

Futures contracts are purchased from futures exchanges and have some similarities to forward contracts. In a futures contract on an asset with price A, the holder of the contract agrees today to pay a price F_0 at some time t in the future for the delivery of the asset at that time. F_0 is today's price for the futures contract. This is just like a forward contract. However, it is different from a forward contract in a very important way: a futures contract is "marked to market" at regular time periods t_i (say daily) until the settlement time $t_n = t$. In other words, at the end of day i, the holder pays $F_i - F_{i-1}$ to the exchange, where F_i denotes the futures contract price at the end of day i. A negative payment means that the holder of the contract receives a payment from the exchange. Clearly, at the end of the last day n, the value of the futures contract must be equal to the value of the asset the holder is receiving at that time, $A(t)$. The value of the futures contract at the end of each day, F_i, is determined by the market forces. There is a clever arbitrage argument that implies that if the short Treasury rate y is a constant, independent of time, then futures and forward contracts have the same price.

Futures contracts exist for many kinds of assets, for example, stocks, bonds, and commodities. They can be used by corporations to reduce their risk from fluctuations in commodity prices. For example, an airline might buy futures contracts on oil to mitigate the risk from a potential spike up in jet fuel prices.

The risk-neutral price for a futures contract on a Treasury bond is the one that, on average, results in the holder making no daily payments. That is, $E[F_n - F_{n-1}] = 0$. After all, suppose the investor exited the futures contract after day one. No money was paid to enter the contract, and so the risk-neutral expected return on this investment $E[F_1 - F_0]$ is zero. A similar argument can be made for all $n > 1$. Writing $F_0 - A(t) = (F_0 - F_1) + (F_1 - F_2) + \cdots + [F_{n-1} - A(t)]$ and taking the expected value gives $F_0 = E[A(t)]$. Note that F_0 is not a random variable, so $F_0 = E[F_0]$.

Using this pricing argument, the price of a futures contract on a zero coupon Treasury bond that settles at time t, matures at $t + T$, and has principal P is

$$P_{\text{fut}} = F_0 = E\left[\exp\left[-\int_t^{t+T} d\tau\, y(\tau)\right]\right] P \qquad (6.2.8)$$

We can rewrite this as

$$P_{\text{fut}} = E\left[E_t\left[\exp\left[-\int_t^{t+T} d\tau\, y(\tau)\right]\right]\right] P = E\left[\exp\left[-Y_t(T)T\right]\right] P$$
$$= \exp\left[-r_{\text{fut}}(t, T)T + \frac{1}{2}\sigma_{Y_t(T)}^2 T^2\right] P \qquad (6.2.9)$$

The price of a futures contract on a zero coupon Treasury bond is not the same as that of a forward contract. Their ratio differs from unity by

$$\frac{P_{\text{fwd}}}{P_{\text{fut}}} - 1 = \frac{E\left[\exp\left[-\int_0^{t+T} d\tau\, y(\tau)\right]\right]}{E\left[\exp\left[-\int_0^{t} d\tau\, y(\tau)\right]\right] E\left[\exp\left[-\int_t^{t+T} d\tau\, y(\tau)\right]\right]} - 1$$

(6.2.10)

Recall from Chapter 2 that the covariance of two random variables a and b is $\text{cov}(a, b) = E[(a - E[a])(b - E[b])] = E[ab] - E[a]E[b]$. Thus Equation 6.2.10 can be written as

$$\frac{P_{\text{fwd}}}{P_{\text{fut}}} - 1 = \frac{\text{cov}\left\{\exp\left[-\int_0^{t} d\tau\, y(\tau)\right], \exp\left[-\int_t^{t+T} d\tau\, y(\tau)\right]\right\}}{E\left[\exp\left[-\int_0^{t} d\tau\, y(\tau)\right]\right] E\left[\exp\left[-\int_t^{t+T} d\tau\, y(\tau)\right]\right]}$$

(6.2.11)

If the volatilities are zero, then the covariance is zero and futures and forward contracts have the same price. This makes sense (and is consistent with the arbitrage argument mentioned previously), since it is the purchaser's responsibility for daily fluctuations in the price of the security that distinguishes futures and forward contracts. We can express $P_{\text{fwd}}/P_{\text{fut}}$ in terms of quantities for which we have derived explicit expressions in the one-factor Vasicek model,

$$\frac{P_{\text{fwd}}}{P_{\text{fut}}} = \exp\left[-Y(t + T)(t + T) + Y(t)t + r_{\text{fut}}(t, T)T - \sigma_{Y_t(T)}^2 T^2/2\right]$$

(6.2.12)

Using the one-factor Vasicek model with parameters $\alpha = 0.1$, $\gamma = 0.065$, and $y(0) = 1$, we plot in Figure 6.1 $P_{\text{fwd}}/P_{\text{fut}}$ as a function of the volatility σ for $t = 2$ years and $T = 5$ years.

6.3   European Options on a Zero Coupon Bond

Consider a zero coupon Treasury bond that matures at time T and has unit principal. An investor may purchase a European call option on this

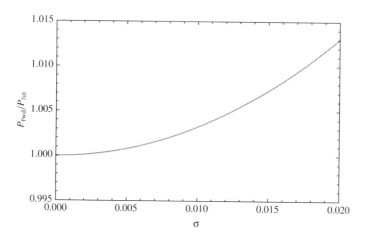

Figure 6.1 Plot of the price of a forward contract on a zero coupon Treasury bond divided by the price of a futures contract on a zero coupon Treasury bond and a function of the volatility σ in the one-factor Vasicek model.

bond at a strike price K if he feels that in the future, yields will fall far enough for the bond's price to rise above K. The price today, P, of a European call option on this zero coupon bond at strike price K that can be exercised at time t is

$$P = E\left[\exp\left[-\int_0^t d\tau\, y(\tau)\right] \max\left[\exp\left[-\int_t^T d\tau\, y(\tau)\right] - K, 0\right]\right]$$

(6.3.13)

where $E[\ ]$ is an average over all interest rate paths $y(\tau)$. We can write this as

$$P = E\left[\exp\left[-\int_0^t d\tau\, y(\tau)\right] \left\{\exp\left[-\int_t^T d\tau\, y(\tau)\right] - K\right\}\right.$$
$$\left. \theta\left[-\int_t^T d\tau\, y(\tau) - \log K\right]\right]$$

(6.3.14)

Next we use the identities

$$\theta(a - b) = \int_b^\infty dx\, \delta(x - a) \qquad (6.3.15)$$

and

$$\delta(x - a) = \int_{-\infty}^\infty \frac{db}{2\pi} e^{ib(x-a)} \qquad (6.3.16)$$

These imply that

$$P = E\left[\exp\left[-\int_0^t d\tau\, y(\tau)\right]\left\{\exp\left[-\int_t^T d\tau\, y(\tau)\right] - K\right\}\right.$$
$$\int_{\log K}^\infty dx\, \delta\left[x + \int_t^T d\tau\, y(\tau)\right]\right] = \int_{\log K}^\infty dx \int_{-\infty}^\infty \frac{db}{2\pi}$$
$$\times E\left[\exp\left[-\int_0^t d\tau\, y(\tau)\right]\left\{\exp\left[-\int_t^T d\tau\, y(\tau)\right] - K\right\}\right.$$
$$\times \exp\left\{ib\left[x + \int_t^T d\tau\, y(\tau)\right]\right\}\right] \qquad (6.3.17)$$

It is convenient to introduce the random variables $z(a, b)$, defined by

$$z(a, b) = \int_a^b d\tau\, y(\tau) \qquad (6.3.18)$$

Clearly $z(a, b) + z(b, c) = z(a, c)$. In terms of these quantities, Equation 6.3.17 becomes

$$P = \int_{\log K}^\infty dx \int_{-\infty}^\infty \frac{db}{2\pi} E\left[e^{-z(0,T)+ib[x+z(t,T)]} - Ke^{-z(0,t)+ib[x+z(t,T)]}\right]$$

$$(6.3.19)$$

Now we break the random variables $z(a, b)$ into the sum of their average part and a fluctuating part with zero average value,

$$z(a, b) = \bar{z}(a, b) + \tilde{z}(a, b) \tag{6.3.20}$$

where $\bar{z}(a, b) = E[z(a, b)]$ and $E[\tilde{z}(a, b)] = 0$. Finally, we assume that $z(a, b)$ is normal. This is true in the Vasicek term structure models discussed earlier. Then this becomes

$$P = \int_{\log K}^{\infty} dx \int_{-\infty}^{\infty} \frac{db}{2\pi} \left(\exp\left\{ -\bar{z}(0, T) + ib[x + \bar{z}(t, T)] \right.\right.$$
$$+ \frac{1}{2} E\left[[\tilde{z}(0, T) - ib\tilde{z}(t, T)]^2 \right] \right\} - K \exp\left\{ -\bar{z}(0, t) \right.$$
$$\left. \left. + ib[x + \bar{z}(t, T)] + \frac{1}{2} E\left[[\tilde{z}(0, t) - ib\tilde{z}(t, T)]^2 \right] \right\} \right) \tag{6.3.21}$$

After completing the square in the exponential, the integration over b is a gaussian integral, and so

$$P = \frac{1}{\sqrt{2\pi E[\tilde{z}(t, T)^2]}} \int_{\log K}^{\infty} dx\, e^{-Y(T)T}$$
$$\times \exp\left(-\frac{\{x + \bar{z}(t, T) - E[\tilde{z}(0, T)\tilde{z}(t, T)]\}^2}{2E[\tilde{z}(t, T)^2]} \right) - Ke^{-Y(t)t}$$
$$\times \exp\left(-\frac{\{x + \bar{z}(t, T) - E[\tilde{z}(0, t)\tilde{z}(t, T)]\}^2}{2E[\tilde{z}(t, T)^2]} \right) \tag{6.3.22}$$

Here we have used the fact that $-Y(t)t = -\bar{z}(0, t) + E[\tilde{z}(0, t)^2]/2$ for any time t. Finally, the x integration can be expressed in terms of the cumulative normal function,

$$P = e^{-Y(T)T} \Phi\left(-\frac{\log K + \bar{z}(t, T) - E[\tilde{z}(0, T)\tilde{z}(t, T)]}{\sqrt{E[\tilde{z}(t, T)^2]}} \right)$$

$$- Ke^{-Y(t)t} \Phi \left(- \frac{\log K + \bar{z}(t, T) - E[\bar{z}(0, t)\bar{z}(t, T)]}{\sqrt{E[\bar{z}(t, T)^2]}} \right) \quad (6.3.23)$$

We can evaluate the needed expectation values in any term structure model that has a normal short rate. For example, one-factor Vasicek model calculations that are very similar to those performed in Chapter 5 yield

$$\bar{z}(t, T) = \left(\frac{y(0)}{\alpha} - \frac{\gamma}{\alpha} \right) \left(e^{-\alpha t} - e^{-\alpha T} \right) + \gamma(T - t) \quad (6.3.24)$$

$$E[\bar{z}(t, T)^2] = \frac{\sigma^2}{\alpha^3} \left[T - t + \frac{1}{\alpha} \left(e^{\alpha t} + e^{-\alpha t} \right) \left(e^{-\alpha T} - e^{-\alpha t} \right) \right.$$
$$\left. - \frac{1}{2\alpha} \left(e^{-2\alpha T} - e^{-2\alpha t} \right) \right] \quad (6.3.25)$$

and

$$E[\bar{z}(0, t)\bar{z}(t, T)] = \frac{\sigma^2}{2\alpha^3} \left(e^{-\alpha t} - e^{-\alpha T} \right) \left(e^{\alpha t} + e^{-\alpha t} - 2 \right) \quad (6.3.26)$$

So far we have discussed only the price of a call option. The price of a European put option on a zero coupon bond can be related to the price of a call option by an argument similar to the relation between European call and put options on stocks:

$$P_{\text{put}} = E \left[e^{- \int_0^t d\tau\, y(\tau)} \max \left[K - e^{- \int_t^T d\tau\, y(\tau)}, 0 \right] \right]$$
$$= E \left[e^{- \int_0^t d\tau\, y(\tau)} \left(K - e^{- \int_t^T d\tau\, y(\tau)} + \max \left[e^{- \int_t^T d\tau\, y(\tau)} - K, 0 \right] \right) \right]$$
$$= Ke^{-Y(t)t} - e^{-Y(T)T} + P_{\text{call}} \quad (6.3.27)$$

6.4   Interest-Rate Swaps

In Chapter 1 we discussed coupon-paying bonds with fixed coupon payments. However, coupon-paying bonds are also issued with a coupon that varies with time depending on what the prevailing interest rates are at the time the coupon is paid. Consider a bond with principal P that pays a coupon every three months. Coupon payments are made at times t_i, $i = 1, \ldots, N$, and the coupon c_i is equal to the three-month forward return over the time period $\Delta t = [t_{i-1}, t_i]$ times the principal,

$$c_i = \left\{ \exp\left[\int_{t_{i-1}}^{t_i} d\tau\, y_L(\tau) \right] - 1 \right\} P \qquad (6.4.28)$$

Since this "floating-rate" bond is not issued by the U.S. government, its cash flows are not discounted by the Treasury rate. In this section, we use the London Interbank Offered Rate (LIBOR) to determine the floating coupon payment c_i and discount the cash flows. This is the rate that banks use to make loans to each other. The LIBOR rate includes some counterparty risk, and so it is usually larger than the Treasury rate. The corresponding short rate and yield are distinguished from the Treasury short rate and yield by the subscript L.

The present value or price of such a bond is

$$\text{Price} = E\left[\sum_{i=1}^{N} \left\{ \exp\left[\int_{t_{i-1}}^{t_i} d\tau\, y_L(\tau) \right] - 1 \right\} \exp\left[-\int_{0}^{t_i} d\tau\, y_L(\tau) \right] \right] P$$
$$+ E\left[\exp\left[-\int_{0}^{t_N} d\tau\, y_L(\tau) \right] \right] P \qquad (6.4.29)$$

where $t_0 = 0$. In Equation 6.4.29 the LIBOR short rate $y_L(\tau)$ is a random variable and the expectation $E[\ ]$ is over all possible paths for it. One could write a term structure model for the LIBOR rate $y_L(t)$, for example, the two-factor Vasicek model; however, the parameters would differ from those used to fit the Treasury yield curve $Y(T)$. The first term in Equation 6.4.29, which contains the floating coupon payments, can be rearranged:

$$\sum_{i=1}^{N} \left\{ \exp \left[\int_{t_{i-1}}^{t_i} d\tau \, y_L(\tau) \right] - 1 \right\} \exp \left[- \int_0^{t_i} d\tau \, y_L(\tau) \right]$$

$$= \sum_{i=0}^{N-1} \exp \left[- \int_0^{t_i} d\tau \, y_L(\tau) \right] - \sum_{i=1}^{N} \exp \left[- \int_0^{t_i} d\tau \, y_L(\tau) \right]$$

$$= 1 - \exp \left[- \int_0^{t_N} d\tau \, y_L(\tau) \right] \tag{6.4.30}$$

Putting this into Equation 6.4.29, we see that the price is equal to the principal, i.e., the bond trades at par.

An issuer of a floating-rate bond may wish to swap the floating payments for a fixed payment cP so that it doesn't have to risk having to make much higher coupon payments in the future if interest rates rise more than expected. Such an agreement is called an *interest-rate swap*. The value of the fixed rate c is determined so that the present value of the fixed coupon payments equal those of the floating payments. Hence this fixed-rate bond trades at par, and so

$$E \left[\sum_{i=1}^{N} \exp \left[- \int_0^{t_i} d\tau \, y_L(\tau) \right] \right] cP + E \left[\exp \left[- \int_0^{t_N} d\tau \, y_L(\tau) \right] \right] P = P$$

$$\tag{6.4.31}$$

The value of c depends on the time at which the bond matures t_N, and so we write $c = c(t_N)$. Equation 6.4.31 implies that

$$c(t_N) = \frac{1 - \exp\left[-Y_L(t_N)t_N\right]}{\sum_{i=1}^{N} \exp\left[-Y_L(t_i)t_i\right]} \tag{6.4.32}$$

The swap spread $s(t_N)$ is the difference between the fixed swap rate $c(t_N)$ and the Treasury yield of the same maturity, $s(t_N) = c(t_N) - Y(t_N)$. The bond principal is not involved in a swap agreement. Hence a swap can be made on any amount, which is usually referred to as the notional. For a swap with notional $\mathcal{N}$, the fixed coupon payments are $c\mathcal{N}$.

A European option on a swap (i.e, a swaption) gives the purchaser of the option the right to enter a swap agreement and receive the fixed-payment leg of the swap at some time t in the future at a fixed coupon $c_{\text{strike}}\mathcal{N}$. Adopting the notation $t_0 = t$, the present value (fair price) for a European swaption on a swap with unit notional is

$$
\text{Price} = E\left[\max\left[\sum_{i=1}^{N} \exp\left[-\int_0^{t_i} d\tau \, y_L(\tau)\right]\left(c_{\text{strike}}\right.\right.\right.
$$
$$
\left.\left.\left. - \left\{\exp\left[\int_{t_{i-1}}^{t_i} d\tau \, y_L(\tau)\right] - 1\right\}\right), 0\right]\right] \qquad (6.4.33)
$$

Note that the price depends on the time the option can be exercised, t_0, and also the number of payments N, i.e., the time t_N.

6.5   Interest-Rate Caps

An interest-rate cap is a derivative where the purchaser receives at the end of each period, $[t_{i-1}, t_i]$, a payment of the difference between the current floating-rate return (for that period) and the strike return c_{strike} (for the same time period) times the notional, provided the current floating-rate return for that period exceeds the strike return. Interest-rate caps are usually on the LIBOR rate. Issuers of floating-rate debt may purchase interest-rate caps to partially hedge the risk that their floating-rate coupon payments will increase substantially in the future.

The present value of an interest-rate cap on a notional $\mathcal{N}$ is

$$
\text{Price} = \sum_{i=1}^{N} E\left[\exp\left[-\int_0^{t_i} d\tau \, y_L(\tau)\right]\right.
$$
$$
\left. \times \max\left[\exp\left[\int_{t_{i-1}}^{t_i} d\tau \, y_L(\tau)\right] - 1 - c_{\text{strike}}, 0\right]\right]\mathcal{N} \qquad (6.5.34)
$$

If the short LIBOR rate y_L is normal, each term in this sum can be evaluated analytically using the same methods that were used to price a European option on a zero coupon bond.

In most cases, the exponential in the max function can be approximated by its first-order expansion, i.e., $e^x - 1 \simeq x$. With this approximation, Equation 6.5.34 simplifies to

$$\text{Price} \simeq \sum_{i=1}^{N} E \left[\exp \left[- \int_0^{t_i} d\tau \, y_L(\tau) \right] \right.$$

$$\left. \times \max \left[\int_{t_{i-1}}^{t_i} d\tau \, y_L(\tau) - c_{\text{strike}}, 0 \right] \right] \mathcal{N} \quad (6.5.35)$$

It is sometimes convenient to re-express Equation 6.5.35 in terms of an annualized strike rate of return. Suppose that in years, $\Delta t = 1/n$, then the annualized strike rate of return is $c_{\text{annual strike}} = n c_{\text{strike}}$ and

$$\text{Price} \simeq \sum_{i=1}^{N} \left(\frac{1}{n} \right) E \left[\exp \left[- \int_0^{t_i} d\tau \, y_L(\tau) \right] \right.$$

$$\left. \times \max \left[n \int_{t_{i-1}}^{t_i} d\tau \, y_L(\tau) - c_{\text{annual strike}}, 0 \right] \right] \mathcal{N} \quad (6.5.36)$$

where $n \int_{t_{i-1}}^{t_i} d\tau \, y_L(\tau)$ is approximately equal to the annualized floating rate for the time period $[t_{i-1}, t_i]$.

We can derive an analytic expression for each term in the sum of Equation 6.5.34. Recall that

$$\max \left[\exp \left[\int_{t_{i-1}}^{t_i} d\tau \, y_L(\tau) \right] - 1 - c_{\text{strike}}, 0 \right]$$

$$= \left\{ \exp \left[\int_{t_{i-1}}^{t_i} d\tau \, y_L(\tau) \right] - 1 - c_{\text{strike}} \right)$$

$$\times \theta \left[\int_{t_{i-1}}^{t_i} d\tau \, y_L(\tau) - \log \left(1 + c_{\text{strike}} \right) \right] \quad (6.5.37)$$

For a unit notional, the ith term in the sum of Equation 6.5.34 is

$$
\begin{aligned}
\text{Price}_i &= E\left[\exp\left[-\int_0^{t_i} d\tau\, y_L(\tau)\right]\max\left[\exp\left[\int_{t_{i-1}}^{t_i} d\tau\, y_L(\tau)\right]-1-c_{\text{strike}},0\right]\right]\\
&= E\left[\left\{\exp\left[-\int_0^{t_{i-1}} d\tau\, y_L(\tau)\right]-(1+c_{\text{strike}})\exp\left[-\int_0^{t_i} d\tau\, y_L(\tau)\right]\right\}\right.\\
&\quad \left.\times\, \theta\left[\int_{t_{i-1}}^{t_i} d\tau\, y_L(\tau)-\log\left(1+c_{\text{strike}}\right)\right]\right] \tag{6.5.38}
\end{aligned}
$$

Following closely the methods used for a European call option on a zero coupon bond, we find that

$$
\begin{aligned}
\text{Price}_i &= e^{-Y_L(t_{i-1})t_{i-1}}\,\Phi\left(\frac{-\log\left(1+c_{\text{strike}}\right)+\bar{z}_L(t_{i-1},t_i)-E[\tilde{z}_L(0,t_{i-1})\tilde{z}_L(t_{i-1},t_i)]}{\sqrt{E[\tilde{z}_L(t_{i-1},t_i)^2]}}\right)\\
&\quad -(1+c_{\text{strike}})e^{-Y_L(t_i)t_i}\,\times\\
&\quad \Phi\left(\frac{-\log\left(1+c_{\text{strike}}\right)+\bar{z}_L(t_{i-1},t_i)-E[\tilde{z}_L(0,t_i)\tilde{z}_L(t_{i-1},t_i)]}{\sqrt{E[\tilde{z}_L(t_{i-1},t_i)^2]}}\right) \tag{6.5.39}
\end{aligned}
$$

Here z_L is defined, as in the Treasury case, as

$$
z_L(a,b)=\int_a^b d\tau\, y_L(\tau) \tag{6.5.40}
$$

and $z_L(a,b)=\bar{z}_L(a,b)+\tilde{z}_L(a,b)$, with $E[z_L(a,b)]=\bar{z}_L(a,b)$, and $E[\tilde{z}_L(a,b)]=0$.

7

Trees

7.1 Basics

When pricing options, analytical closed-form solutions are not always available. Most practitioners use a variety of numerical techniques for pricing of both simple and exotic options. In many cases where analytical solutions are not available, lattices, trees, and Monte Carlo simulations are the only methods available to price complex securities. Broadly speaking, the simplest options are of two types: European and American. European options can be exercised only at the maturity of the option, so all we need to know is the distribution of asset prices or returns at the expiration date of the option. American options and their variants can be exercised early, so we require in addition a way to evaluate the early exercise decision. This chapter is focused on trees, which can be applied both to European and to American option pricing. Physicists are familiar with techniques such as these from lattice gauge theory, which requires the solution of field theories on lattices with some predefined boundary conditions. Evaluation using binomial trees is one of the simplest yet most useful methods by which both securities and their derivatives are priced in practice. In cases where the payoffs have early exercise or "American" features, trees are usually the only feasible methods available.

To get an understanding of the most basic trees, consider a random variable z that evolves with time. We break time into discrete steps of size Δt, and at the end of time steps $i = 1, \ldots$, the time is $t_i = i\Delta t$. At $i = 0$, the variable z takes on the initial value $z(0) = 0$. For each time step, we assume that the variable z can either increase or decrease by an amount equal to ϵ. These two choices occur with probability $1/2$. So after time step i, the variable z can take on the values $j\epsilon$, where $j = i, i - 2, \ldots, -i$ labels the state that z takes. The values of z occur at a point (i, j) in the plane, labeled by the time (i) and state (j) coordinates. Putting a point at these locations and joining the points by straight lines produces the tree appropriate for the time evolution of z. This is shown in Figure 7.1. We can think of the tree as a discrete representation of all possible paths that the random variable z can take as time evolves. The tree we are describing here is an example of a binomial recombining tree. The variable z can arrive at the point (i, j) in the tree by making n up moves and $i - n$ down moves, where $j = 2n - i$. The probability of this occurring, $p(i, j)$, is

$$p(i, j) = \left(\frac{1}{2}\right)^i \left(\frac{i!}{(i - n)!n!}\right) \tag{7.1.1}$$

This probability is properly normalized, since[1]

$$\sum_j p(i, j) = \sum_{n=0}^{i} p(i, i - 2n) = \sum_{n=0}^{i} \left(\frac{1}{2}\right)^{i-n} \left(\frac{1}{2}\right)^n \left(\frac{i!}{(i - n)!n!}\right)$$

$$= \left(\frac{1}{2} + \frac{1}{2}\right)^i = 1 \tag{7.1.2}$$

---

[1] We use the identity $(x + y)^i = \sum_{n=0}^{i} \frac{i!}{(i-n)!n!} x^{(i-n)} y^n$.

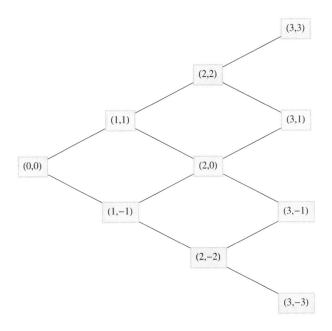

Figure 7.1 Recombining tree for the time evolution of z. The nodes are labeled by (i, j), where i is the time step and j labels the state of z.

Before we start to show the algorithms, it is important to realize that the most general branching process can get very complicated very quickly. In fact, if there are n time steps and the tree does not recombine, i.e., if the result of an up move followed by a down move is not the same as the result of a down move followed by an up move, then the number of nodes at time step n increases exponentially (depending on the branching). For example, for a nonrecombining binomial tree, the nodes grow as 2^{n-1}. On the other hand, if we can force the tree to recombine, then the number of nodes grows much more slowly; however, recombining trees are not always allowed by the stochastic dynamics. A nonrecombining binomial tree is shown in Figure 7.2.

We should also note that there is a fundamental difference between pricing options on stocks and options on bonds. Stocks can grow in

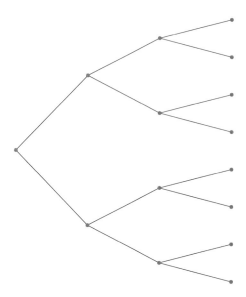

Figure 7.2   Nonrecombining binomial tree.

value without limit (or fall to zero), but bonds have a value equal to their principal at maturity. Also, the term structure at any forward time has to be consistent with the forward rates implied today and requires the modeler to perform "calibration" to the current yield curve. In this chapter, we explain some algorithms for the pricing of both stock and bond options. We describe techniques that can be applied to European and American options, using short-rate and forward-rate term structure models (known as the Heath-Jarrow-Morton class[2]), and using both recombining and nonrecombining trees. The algorithms discussed in this chapter, along with the Monte Carlo algorithms discussed in previous chapters, should give the reader a ready conceptual toolkit for using nonanalytical techniques in fixed-income finance.

_____

[2]D. Heath, R. Jarrow, and A. Morton, "A New Methodology for Contingent Claims," *Econometrica* 60, no. 1 (1992), p. 77.

We will discuss the fundamentals of tree-building algorithms and their implementation using Mathematica, with an emphasis on using recursive programming. Recursion is simply a way for a function to refer to itself. In Mathematica, the simplest way to illustrate recursion is by looking at the implementation of the Fibonacci numbers. First, note that if we define

```
f[x_]:=f[x]=rhs
```

then each evaluation of f[x] refers to all the older values of the function evaluated. For example, we can write the code to evaluate the Fibonacci numbers as

```
f[0] = f[1] = 1;
f[x_] := f[x] = f[x - 1] + f[x - 2].
```

It is illustrative to see how the "program" $f[x_] := f[x] = f[x-1] + f[x-2]$ works. The function $f[x_]$ is defined to be $f[x] = f[x-1] + f[x-2]$. When we ask for a value of the function f, the program first calculates the value of $f[x-1] + f[x-2]$, then saves the result as $f[x]$. This does away with the need to recompute the value for each $f(x)$ every time the tree is executed.

Using similar recursive definitions in trees can lead to rapid execution even if the computation is time intensive, as long as there are not too many time steps.[3] Of course, we have the option of recomputing the values at each node every time these values are needed for option pricing. However, this obscures not only the mathematical content of trees but also the financial decision process that underlies optimal option exercise. Thus the purpose of using this approach is not only to demonstrate the elegance and simplicity of the tree method but also to illuminate

---

[3] For further details on the implementation and benefits of recursive programming in Mathematica, see the Mathematica book.

the finance behind the algorithms, i.e., that it is a recursive process that underlies whether or not to exercise an option early.

To make it easy to refer to the programs and their output in this chapter, we place the Mathematica programs and the tree output in figures.

7.2   Binomial Trees and Stock Options

Consider a stock whose price S evolves as

$$\frac{dS}{S} = \mu\, dt + \sigma\, dw \qquad (7.2.3)$$

where μ is the drift and σ is the volatility. Discretizing this equation gives

$$S + \Delta S = S(1 + \mu\Delta t \pm \sigma\sqrt{\Delta t}) \qquad (7.2.4)$$

At each time step, the stock price can either go up by a factor of $(1 + \mu\Delta t + \sigma\sqrt{\Delta t})$ or go down by a factor of $(1 + \mu\Delta t - \sigma\sqrt{\Delta t})$, each with a probability of $1/2$. Note that at each time step, on average, the stock price drifts up by a factor of $(1 + \mu\Delta t)$. The possible stock prices at successive time steps form a tree with nodes (i, j), where i is the number of time steps and $j = 0, 1, 2, \ldots, i$ is the number of up moves that the stock price has made. The stock price at time $t = i\Delta t$ when the stock has had j up moves (and therefore $i - j$ down moves) is

$$S(i, j) = S_0(1 + \mu\Delta t + \sigma\sqrt{\Delta t})^j(1 + \mu\Delta t - \sigma\sqrt{\Delta t})^{i-j} \quad (7.2.5)$$

where S_0 is the original stock price. The probability of the stock price having the value $S(i, j)$ at time $t = i\Delta t$ is just the number of distinct paths through the tree from the node $(0, 0)$ to the node (i, j), times the probability of each move that was made. The number of distinct paths is the binomial coefficient, $i!/[j!(i-j)!]$, so the probability of being at node (i, j) is

$$p(i, j) = \left(\frac{1}{2}\right)^j \left(\frac{1}{2}\right)^{i-j} \frac{i!}{j!(i-j)!} = \left(\frac{1}{2}\right)^i \frac{i!}{j!(i-j)!} \qquad (7.2.6)$$

We can price a European option on a stock with maturity T on such a tree by evaluating the payoff to the purchaser of the option (assuming that μ is the risk-free rate y) at all the nodes (i, j) where $i = T/\Delta t$, taking the sum over j weighted by $p(i, j)$ (i.e., the expected value), and discounting this expected value by $\exp(-yT)$.

American option pricing requires that the holder of the option evaluate at each state in the tree whether it is optimal to hold or to exercise the option. Starting backward from the terminal date, we know that if we have not exercised the option on the final day, the payoff for a call is simply the difference between the terminal value and the strike (or its reverse for the put). A day before the last day, we have a choice to exercise, in which case we get the difference between the stock price and the strike, or not to exercise; if we do not exercise, the value of the unexercised option is the average of the discounted present value of the option in all possible states on the next day. Our decision to exercise then depends on the comparison of the unexercised option value with the payoff from the exercise. Continuing in this way, we can "roll back" through the tree all the way to today, and the value thus obtained is the correct present value of the option.

Figures 7.3 and 7.4 contain the Mathematica code for pricing a European and an American option on a stock in the manner just discussed. The code for printing a tree for an American option on a stock is presented in Figure 7.5. The American put option tree in Figure 7.6 was generated with `AmericanOptionTree[100, 1, 12, 0.25, 0.03, Max[100 - #, 0] &]`. A very similar code is used for European options.

```
EuropeanOption[s_, t_, n_, sigma_, y_,
  exercise_Function] :=
 Module[{u = (1 + y t/n + sigma Sqrt[t/n]),
   d = (1 + y t/n - sigma Sqrt[t/n])},
  Exp[-y t] (1/2)^
   n Sum[exercise[s*u^j*d^(n - j)]*Binomial[n, j],
 {j, 0, n}]]
```

Figure 7.3 Mathematica code for pricing a European option on a stock with initial price s, maturity (i.e., exercise time) t, number of time steps n, volatility sigma, and short rate y. The type of option is specified by inputting the function exercise. For example, the price of a European call option on a stock with initial price $100, exercise time 1 year, strike price $100, volatility 0.2, using 10 time steps, and assuming a short rate of 3 percent is EuropeanOption[100,1,10,0.2,0.03,Max [#-100,0]&]. The price of this call option is $9.31. To price a put option, one would input Max[100-#,0]& instead of Max[#-100,0]& as the last argument.

```
AmericanOption[s_, t_, n_, sigma_, y_,
  exercise_Function] :=
 Module[{u = (1 + y t/n + sigma Sqrt[t/n]),
   d = (1 + y t/n - sigma Sqrt[t/n]), OpRecurse},
  OpRecurse[i_, j_] :=
   OpRecurse[i, j] =
    If[i == n, exercise[s*u^j*d^(i - j)],
     Max[1/2 Exp[-y t/n] (OpRecurse[i + 1, j] +
         OpRecurse[i + 1, j + 1]),
          exercise[s*u^j*d^(i - j)]]];
  OpRecurse[0, 0]]
```

Figure 7.4 Mathematica code for pricing an American option on a stock with initial price s, maturity t, number of time steps n, volatility sigma, and short rate y. The type of option is specified by inputting the function exercise.

```
AmericanOptionTree[s_, t_, n_, sigma_, y_,
  exercise_Function] :=
 Module[{u = (1 + y t/n + sigma Sqrt[t/n]),
   d = (1 + y t/n - sigma Sqrt[t/n]), OpRecurse},
  OpRecurse[i_, j_] :=
   OpRecurse[i, j] =
    If[i == n, exercise[s*u^j*d^(i - j)],
     Max[1/2 Exp[-y t/n] (OpRecurse[i + 1, j] +
         OpRecurse[i + 1, j + 1]),
          exercise[s*u^j*d^(i - j)]]];
  Table[Table[OpRecurse[i, j], {j, 0, i,],
   {i, 0, n}]
  ]
```

Figure 7.5 Mathematica code for generating a tree of values for an American option on a stock with initial price s, maturity t, number of time steps n, volatility sigma, and short rate y. The type of option is specified by inputting the function exercise.

The function OpRecurse[i,j], defined recursively within the AmericanOption[] function, returns at each node labeled by (i, j) the greater of (1) the average of the values at the adjacent nodes ($i = 1, j + 1$) and ($i + 1, j$), discounted by the factor $\exp(-y\Delta t)$, and (2) the payoff at time $i\Delta t$ from exercising the option. The boundary condition for the recursion relation is that if $i = T/\Delta t$, where T is the time the option matures, then the value of the function is set to the payoff from exercising the option. The function AmericanOption[] returns OpRecurse[0,0]. As discussed in Chapter 3, it will never be advantageous to exercise a call option early (i.e., of the values described earlier, OpRecurse[i,j] will always return the first instead of the second). Thus the price of American and European call options is the same.

The lower the value to which the stock has fluctuated, the greater the value of the put option. This is evident in the trees of Figure 7.6. Furthermore, the difference between American and European put

```
                                    8.2
                                11.14, 5.29
                             14.75, 7.59, 3.03
                         18.99, 10.59, 4.62, 1.45
                      23.71, 14.36, 6.88, 2.38, 0.52
                   28.69, 18.84, 9.95, 3.84, 0.94, 0.11
                33.68, 23.85, 13.93, 6.03, 1.67, 0.22, 0
             38.44, 29.08, 18.74, 9.18, 2.9, 0.44, 0, 0
          42.89, 34.18, 24.12, 13.46, 4.95, 0.87, 0.01, 0, 0
        47.05, 38.95, 29.59, 18.78, 8.2, 1.72, 0.02, 0, 0, 0
      50.93, 43.4, 34.69, 24.64, 13.02, 3.43, 0.03, 0, 0, 0, 0
   54.56, 47.55, 39.45, 30.1, 19.29, 6.81, 0.06, 0, 0, 0, 0, 0
57.96, 51.44, 43.9, 35.2, 25.15, 13.54, 0.12, 0, 0, 0, 0, 0, 0
```

European put option tree.

```
                                   8.57
                               11.67, 5.51
                             15.49, 7.9, 3.14
                           20, 11.05, 4.8, 1.5
                      25.09, 15.01, 7.15, 2.47, 0.54
                   30.31, 19.75, 10.35, 3.98, 0.97, 0.11
                35.16, 25.1, 14.49, 6.26, 1.73, 0.23, 0
             39.68, 30.32, 19.51, 9.54, 3.01, 0.45, 0, 0
          43.88, 35.18, 25.12, 13.99, 5.14, 0.9, 0.01, 0, 0
        47.79, 39.69, 30.34, 19.53, 8.51, 1.79, 0.02, 0, 0, 0
      51.43, 43.89, 35.19, 25.13, 13.52, 3.55, 0.03, 0, 0, 0, 0
   54.81, 47.8, 39.7, 30.35, 19.54, 7.06, 0.06, 0, 0, 0, 0, 0
57.96, 51.44, 43.9, 35.2, 25.15, 13.54, 0.12, 0, 0, 0, 0, 0, 0
```

American put option tree.

Figure 7.6 Trees with the value (in dollars) of a European put option (top) and an American put option (bottom) on a stock with an initial stock price of $100, strike price of $100, and 1-year maturity, at time steps of 1 month. We assumed a volatility of 25 percent and a constant short rate of 3 percent. The value at $t = 0$ (i.e., the price) is on the top row, and the possible values at $t = 1$ year, after a random walk, are on the bottom row. The rightmost column corresponds to all "up" moves, and the leftmost, to all "down" moves.

options arises from the case when the stock fluctuates to a very low value, since then it pays for the investor who is long the option to exercise before maturity. That is why the numbers are greatest to the left of the tree in Figure 7.7.

```
                        0.37
                    0.52,  0.22
                0.73,  0.32,  0.12
            1.01,  0.46,  0.18,  0.05
        1.38,  0.65,  0.27,  0.09,  0.02
      1.62,  0.9,  0.39,  0.15,  0.03,  0
    1.49,  1.25,  0.56,  0.23,  0.06,  0.01,  0
   1.24,  1.24,  0.77,  0.36,  0.11,  0.02,  0,  0
  0.99,  0.99,  0.99,  0.53,  0.19,  0.03,  0,  0,  0
 0.75,  0.75,  0.75,  0.75,  0.31,  0.06,  0,  0,  0,  0
  0.5,  0.5,  0.5,  0.5,  0.5,  0.12,  0,  0,  0,  0,  0
0.25, 0.25, 0.25, 0.25, 0.25, 0.25, 0, 0, 0, 0, 0, 0
        0,  0,  0,  0,  0,  0,  0,  0,  0,  0,  0,  0,  0
```

Figure 7.7 A tree with the difference between the values (in dollars) of an American put option and a European put option on a stock at each month in a random walk, with an initial stock price of $100, strike price of $100, and maturity of 1 year. We assumed a volatility of 25 percent and a constant short rate of 3 percent. The value at $t = 0$ (i.e., the difference between the prices) is on the top row, and the possible values at $t = 1$ year, after a random walk, are on the bottom row. The rightmost column corresponds to all "up" moves and the leftmost to all "down" moves.

Using the programs presented in this section, we constructed the plots of the price of American and European put options as a function of volatility and strike price; they are presented in Figures 7.8 and 7.9. In these plots, the value of the stock today is $100 and the option matures in 1 year. The American option is always more expensive, since the purchaser has the added freedom to choose when to exercise it.

7.3   The Black-Derman-Toy Model for Interest Rates

When constructing trees for interest rates, we are faced with an additional complication: since there are yields for different maturities, it is important to make sure that the rates implied by the tree for bonds of

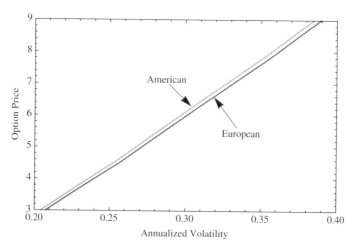

Figure 7.8 Price of European and American put options in dollars as a function of stock volatility σ. The present value of the stock is $100, the strike price is $90, and the risk-free rate is $y = 3$ percent. The option maturity is 1 year, and the time step used for the computation is $\Delta t = 0.01$ year.

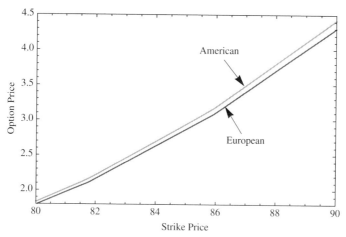

Figure 7.9 Price of European and American put options in dollars as a function of strike price in dollars. The present value of the stock is $100. An annualized volatility $\sigma = 25$ percent and risk-free rate $y = 3$ percent were used. The option maturity is 1 year, and the time step used for the computation is $\Delta t = 0.01$ year.

every maturity at each node are consistent with those implied by the current yield curve. This requires, in practice, solving for the parameters of the interest-rate stochastic process so that the observed yield curve is recovered from the tree. This process of calibration is central to term structure modeling that is used to price options on bonds. When there are other market observables, such as the term structure of volatility, then some other parameters in the process can also be calibrated. More complex term structure models simply allow more degrees of freedom to be incorporated and calibrated to markets. Description of the most complex models is beyond the scope of this book, and there are numerous excellent references available. However, we will describe in detail (along with Mathematica code) the calibration of the workhorse Black-Derman-Toy[4] interest-rate model, which, despite its numerous shortcomings, is still used in practice.

The Black-Derman-Toy or BDT model is determined by the following evolution of short rates:

$$\mathrm{dlog}\,[y(t)] = \left[\theta(t) + \frac{\sigma'(t)}{\sigma(t)}\log\,[y(t)]\right]dt + \sigma(t)\,dw \quad (7.3.7)$$

where $\theta(t)$ and $\sigma(t)$ are functions of time chosen to match the initial term structure of spot rates and spot rate volatilities of the yield curve. The quantity $\sigma'(t)$ represents the derivative of the volatility.

At first glance, the time evolution in Equation 7.3.7 seems rather peculiar because of the mean reversion term proportional to σ'/σ. However, we will soon understand why it is there. To solve this evolution

---

[4]F. Black, E. Derman, and W. Toy, "A One-Factor Model of Interest Rates and Its Application to Treasury Bond Options," *Financial Analysts Journal* (January–February 1990), p. 24.

equation, we write

$$\log y(t) = \exp\left(\int_0^t d\tau \frac{\sigma'(t)}{\sigma(t)}\right) \xi(t) = \frac{\sigma(t)}{\sigma(0)}\xi(t) \qquad (7.3.8)$$

Then

$$d\log[y(t)] = \sigma'(t)/\sigma(t)\log[y(t)]\,dt + [\sigma(t)/\sigma(0)]\,d\xi(t) \quad (7.3.9)$$

and so

$$d\xi = \frac{\theta(t)\sigma(0)}{\sigma(t)}\,dt + \sigma(0)\,dw \qquad (7.3.10)$$

Hence,

$$\xi(t) = G(t) + \sigma(0)w(t) \qquad (7.3.11)$$

where $G(t)$ is a function of time that depends on $\theta(t)$ and $\sigma(t)$. Finally, using the relation between ξ and y, we arrive at

$$y(t) = F(t)e^{\sigma(t)w(t)} \qquad (7.3.12)$$

The factor of σ'/σ in Equation 7.3.7 was inserted so that the exponential in Equation 7.3.12 is simply proportional to $\sigma(t)$ instead of having a more complicated dependence; if the value of $y(t)$ depended not just on the value of $w(t)$ but also on its previous values, then the evolution could not be implemented on a recombining tree. Here $F(t) = \exp[G(t)\sigma(t)/\sigma(0)]$.

Since short-rate changes are lognormally distributed, this model does not allow for negative short rates. But because the short rates are lognormal, this model is not analytically tractable, and we have to resort to numerical methods to obtain the prices of bond options and other derivatives such as swaps and swaptions. To illustrate how this is done in practice, we discretize the short rate in Equation 7.3.12. On the tree, the random variable $y(t) \rightarrow y_{i,j}$, where i labels the number of time steps, $i, \ldots, N$, and j the state of y, $j = -i, -i + 2, \ldots, i - 2, i$. At each time step there are thus $i + 1$ states. The pair (i, j) represents the state j at time step i. At each node, the tree requires that we determine the short rate $y_{i,j}$ such that the string of short rates, put together, gives the current yield curve. We assume that the short rate at each time step can go up or down by the same probability of $1/2$. Then we can write

$$y_{i,j} = F_i e^{\sigma_i j \sqrt{\Delta t}} \tag{7.3.13}$$

where F_i is the value of $F(t)$ at the time labeled by i (i.e., after time step i) and σ_i is the value of $\sigma(t)$ at the time labeled by i.

We can use recursion to calculate the values $y_{i,j}$ given the yield curve and yield curve volatility in the following way. We define $f_{i,j}$ to be the price of a zero coupon bond at time $i = 0$ that has the value 1 at node (i, j). Then the price of a unit principal zero coupon bond maturing at time $(i + 1)\Delta t$ is

$$P_{i+1} = \sum_{j=-i}^{i} f_{i,j} d_{i,j} \tag{7.3.14}$$

where $d_{i,j}$ is the one-period discount factor

$$d_{i,j} = e^{-y_{i,j} \Delta t} \tag{7.3.15}$$

Expanding this, we can see that

$$i = 0 \quad P_1 = f_{0,0} d_{0,0} = d_{0,0} \tag{7.3.16}$$

$$i = 1 \quad P_2 = f_{1,-1} d_{1,-1} + f_{1,1} d_{1,1}$$

$$i = 2 \quad P_3 = f_{2,-2} d_{2,-2} + f_{2,0} d_{2,0} + f_{2,2} d_{2,2}$$

and so on. Further, for all nodes except for the $j = \pm i$ nodes, we can update the values of $f_{i,j}$ from the values in the previous time step $i - 1$ using

$$f_{i,j} = \frac{1}{2}(f_{i-1,j-1}d_{i-1,j-1} + f_{i-1,j+1}d_{i-1,j+1}) \qquad (7.3.17)$$

For the boundary nodes, we use the relationships

$$f_{i,i} = \frac{1}{2}f_{i-1,i-1}d_{i-1,i-1} \qquad (7.3.18)$$

$$f_{i,-i} = \frac{1}{2}f_{i-1,-i+1}d_{i-1,-i+1} \qquad (7.3.19)$$

Now, to obtain the $f_{i,j}$, at each step we equate the bond price obtained from the short-rate equation to the bond price from spot rates Y_i, i.e.,

$$P_{i+1} = \sum_{j=-i}^{i} f_{i,j}d_{i,j} = e^{-Y_{i+1}(i+1)\Delta t} \qquad (7.3.20)$$

For computational speed, it is sometimes more efficient to use the linearized version of the last equation:

$$P_{i+1} = \sum_{j=-i}^{j=i} f_{i,j}\frac{1}{1 + F_i e^{\sigma j\sqrt{\Delta t}}\Delta t} = \frac{1}{(1 + Y_{i+1}\Delta t)^{i+1}} \qquad (7.3.21)$$

So, to review, we build the tree recursively using the following steps:

1. We initialize at the first step, where $F_0 = y_{0,0}$, $f_{0,0} = 1$, and $d_{0,0} = e^{-y_{0,0}\Delta t}$.
2. For $i > 0$, we first determine at time step $i - 1$ the values for F_{i-1}, $f_{i-1,j}$, $y_{i-1,j}$, and $d_{i-1,j}$.

3. We use Equations 7.3.17 and 7.3.18 to determine the $f_{i,j}$. Then we use Equation 7.3.20 to solve for F_i from the observed yield.
4. Once the F_i are known, then we can calculate the rates $y_{i,j}$ and compute the discount factors $d_{i,j}$ using Equations 7.3.13 and 7.3.15.

We will now go through, by hand, a simple tree with constant volatility that has two time steps. For this example, we use time steps of one year and take the one-year and two-year spot yields to be $Y_1 = 0.40$ percent and $Y_2 = 0.80$ percent, respectively. Finally we assume a constant short-rate volatility (lognormal) of 20 percent.[5] Then, $y_{0,0} = 0.0040$ and $d_{0,0} = e^{-0.0040} = 0.996$. Also, $f_{1,1} = f_{1,-1} = \frac{1}{2} f_{0,0} d_{0,0} = 0.5 \times 0.996 = 0.498$. Now, since the two-year yield is 0.80, we can use the linearized equation, Equation 7.3.21, to obtain the right-hand side $P_2 = 1/[1 + (0.0080)]^2 = 0.984$. Thus,

$$P_2 = \sum_{j=-1}^{1} f_{1,j} \frac{1}{1 + F_1 e^{\sigma j \sqrt{t}}} \qquad (7.3.22)$$

and the value of P_2 gives

$$0.984 = (0.498) \frac{1}{1 + F_1 e^{0.20}} + (0.498) \frac{1}{1 + F_1 e^{-0.20}} \qquad (7.3.23)$$

Solving numerically for F_1, we obtain $F_1 = 0.0118$. Thus, at node $(1, 1)$, we get $y_{1,1} = (0.0118) \times e^{0.20} = 0.0144 = 1.44$ percent, and the discount factor $d_{1,1} = 0.986$. Similarly, at the down node $(1, -1)$, we get $y_{1,-1} = (0.0118) \times e^{-0.20} = 0.964$ percent, and the discount factor $d_{1,-1} = 0.990$. Finally we can move to the nodes at time step 2. Here, $f_{2,2} = 0.5 f_{1,1} d_{1,1} = 0.5(0.498)(0.986) = 0.245$. Also, $f_{2,-2} = 0.5 f_{1,-1} d_{1,-1} = 0.5(0.498)(0.990) = 0.247$. Finally,

---

[5] We use continuous compounding throughout.

```
rates[yields_List, sigma_List, deltaT_] :=
  Module[{fF, f, d, y, n = Length[yields] -
    1, i, j, price},
  y[i_, j_] := fF[i] Exp[sigma[[i]]
    j Sqrt[deltaT]];
  d[i_, j_] := 1/(1 + y[i, j] deltaT);
  price[i_] := Sum[f[i - 1, j] d[i - 1, j],
    {j, -i + 1, i - 1, 2}];
  (* definitions *)
  f[0, 0] = 1;
  fF[0] = yields[[1]];
  y[0, 0] = fF[0];
  (* initialize *)
  For[i = 1, i <= n, i++,
   f[i, j_] :=
    f[i, j] =
     If[Abs[j] == i, 1/2 f[i - 1, j - Sign[j]]
       d[i - 1, j - Sign[j]],
       1/2 (f[i - 1, j - 1] d[i - 1, j - 1] +
         f[i - 1, j + 1] d[i - 1, j + 1])
       ];
   fF[i] =
    fF[i] /.
     FindRoot[
      price[i + 1] == 1/(1 + yields[[i + 1]]
        deltaT)^(i + 1), {fF[i],
        yields[[i + 1]]}];
   ];
  Table[Table[y[i, j], {j, -i, i, 2}], {i, 0, n}]
  ]
```

Figure 7.10 Mathematica function that generates an array (i.e., a tree) of normalized short rates given a list of yields, volatilities, and the time step. The $(i + 1, k + 1)$ entry of the array is: rates[Y, σ, ΔT][[$i + 1, k + 1$]] = $y_{i,j}$ where $j = k - 2i$. Here, Y is a list of yields and σ a list of volatilities at times $i\Delta T$ for $i = 1, 2, \ldots$, and ΔT is the time step.

```
                        0.035
                    0.037, 0.046
                0.035, 0.043, 0.054
            0.032, 0.039, 0.048, 0.06
        0.028, 0.035, 0.043, 0.053, 0.066
     0.025, 0.031, 0.039, 0.048, 0.059, 0.073
  0.024, 0.029, 0.036, 0.045, 0.055, 0.068, 0.084
0.021, 0.026, 0.032, 0.04, 0.05, 0.061, 0.076, 0.094
0.018, 0.023, 0.028, 0.035, 0.043, 0.053, 0.066, 0.081, 0.101
```

Figure 7.11 Tree of short rates normalized to the yield curve shown in Figure 7.12. The volatility was assumed to be $\sigma(t) = 0.15$. The time steps are $\Delta t = 1/2$ year. The top row is the rate at $t = 0$, and the bottom row contains rates at $t = 4$ years.

using Equation 7.3.17, $f_{2,0} = 0.5 f_{1,1} d_{1,1} + 0.5 f_{1,-1} d_{1,-1} = 0.245 + 0.247 = 0.492$.

The code in Figure 7.10 (on page 230) generates a tree of interest rates by implementing the algorithm just described. A rate tree generated from this program is shown in Figure 7.11 using the input yield in Figure 7.12, volatility $\sigma(t) = 0.15$, and time step $\Delta t = 0.5$ year.

It is useful to test the convergence of the discrete algorithm as Δt gets smaller. Since we input the yield curve, we know the exact price of a zero coupon bond, and we can compare it with the result of a numerical calculation of that price calculated by rolling back through the tree to compound the discount factors. In Figure 7.13 we show the calculated bond price minus the exact value (computed using the input yield and volatility mentioned earlier) in dollars for a zero coupon bond with maturity $T = 4$ years and principal $100 as a function of the size of the time step Δt in years. So, for example, $\Delta t = 0.025$ year corresponds to a tree with $160 = 4/0.025$ time steps in it. We see that the difference is decreasing, indicating the convergence of the algorithm. With 160 time steps, the difference in price is less than one cent.

To price an option on a bond using a normalized rate tree such as the one in Figure 7.11, all we need to do is to evaluate at each node the

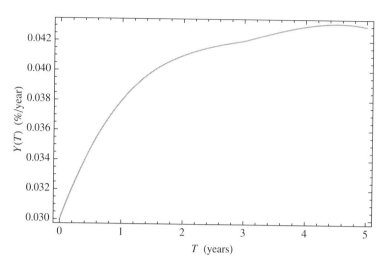

Figure 7.12 Yield curve generated by interpolating from the yearly values, $Y(0) = 0.03$, $Y(1) = 0.038$, $Y(2) = 0.041$, $Y(3) = 0.042$, $Y(4) = 0.043$, and $Y(5) = 0.043$ using the `Interpolation[]` function in Mathematica.

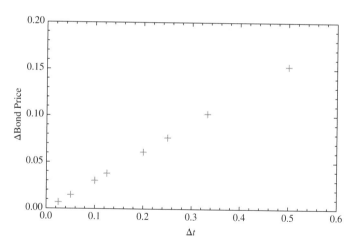

Figure 7.13 Price of a \$100 zero coupon bond with maturity 4 years on BDT trees with time steps Δt, minus the exact price, \$100 $\exp[-4Y(4)] = $ \$84.198, calculated from the input yield. The trees were normalized to the yield curve in Figure 7.12, with $\sigma = 0.15$.

value of exercising the option (remembering that the value at that node is simply the difference between the bond price and some predetermined strike price) or holding the option. This requires rolling back through the tree and obtaining the present value of the decision from each node.

7.4   A Heath-Jarrow-Morton Model on a Recursive Tree

In this section we discuss the implementation of a member of the popular Heath-Jarrow-Morton class of models on a recursive tree. These models are different from the term structure models that we have considered so far. Instead of using the short rate, the driving variables in these models are the forward rates observed at any time for the full yield curve; the model describes the evolution of all the forwards simultaneously. The forward rate $f(t_a, t_b)$ is the continuous discounting rate at time t_b as seen from time t_a. Hence, the time t_a must be less than or equal to t_b. Treating the forwards $f(t, \tau)$ at times $t > 0$ as random variables, at time t the price of a zero coupon riskless bond that matures at time T, $P(t, T)$, is related to the forward rates by

$$P(t, T) = E\left[\exp\left[-\int_t^T d\tau\, f(t, \tau)\right]\right] \qquad (7.4.24)$$

The familiar short rate $y(t)$ is the discounting rate at time t as seen from time t, and so $y(t) = f(t, t)$.

Now we discretize time and take the time steps to be Δt. A fairly general form for the stochastic evolution of an instantaneous forward rate $f(t_a, t_b)$ as the time at which we observe it, t_a, is

$$f(t_a + \Delta t, t_b) = f(t_a, t_b) + \mu(t_a, t_b)\Delta t + \sigma(t_a, t_b)X(t_a)\sqrt{\Delta t} \quad (7.4.25)$$

where $X(t_a)$ are independent {i.e., $E[X(t)X(t')] = 0$ for t not equal to t'} binomial random variables that take values ± 1 (each with probability 1/2), $\mu(t_a, t_b)$ is a drift for the forward rates, and $\sigma(t_a, t_b)$ is a volatility for the forward rates. It is possible to consider more general forms of the evolution where the drift and volatility also depend on $f(t_a, t_b)$. In the limit that $\Delta t \to 0$, this model gives forwards $f(t_a, t_b)$ that are normal variables. Hence, bond and option prices can be studied analytically using methods similar to those that were developed in the previous two chapters. However, this model provides a nice example of a nonrecombining tree, and hence we briefly study it here.

The price of a zero coupon Treasury bond with maturity T at time t is

$$P(t, T) = E[P(t, T)] = E\left[\exp\left[-f(t, t)\Delta t - f(t, t + \Delta t)\Delta t - \cdots\right.\right.$$
$$\left.\left. - f(t, T - \Delta t)\Delta t\right]\right] = E\left[\exp\left[-\sum_{i=n}^{N-1} f(t, i\Delta t)\Delta t\right]\right]$$

$$(7.4.26)$$

where the natural number n is the number of time steps to the time of observation, $n = t/\Delta t$, and N is the number of time steps to maturity, $N = T/\Delta t$. At time $t = 0$, the initial values for the forwards $f(0, i\Delta t)$ can be determined from the observed Treasury yield curve,

$$e^{-Y(T)T} = \exp\left[-\sum_{i=0}^{N-1} f(0, i\Delta t)\Delta t\right] \qquad (7.4.27)$$

On average, $P(t, T)$ grows with t at the risk-free rate $y(t) = f(t, t)$, and hence

$$E\left[\frac{P(t + \Delta t, T)}{P(t, T)} e^{-f(t,t)\Delta t}\right] = 1 \qquad (7.4.28)$$

Equation 7.4.28 provides a consistency recursion relation that determines the drifts in terms of the volatilities. Using Equation 7.4.26, this becomes

$$E\left[\exp\left[-\sum_{i=n+1}^{N-1} f(t+\Delta t, i\Delta t)\Delta t + \sum_{i=n}^{N-1} f(t, i\Delta t)\Delta t - f(t, t)\Delta t\right]\right]$$

$$= E\left[\exp\left\{-\sum_{i=n+1}^{N-1} [f(t+\Delta t, i\Delta t) - f(t, i\Delta t)]\Delta t\right\}\right] = 1$$

$$(7.4.29)$$

Using Equation 7.4.25, this implies

$$E\left[\exp\left\{-\sum_{i=n+1}^{N-1} \left[\mu(t, i\Delta t)\Delta t + \sigma(t, i\Delta t)X(t)\sqrt{\Delta t}\right]\Delta t\right\}\right] = 1$$

$$(7.4.30)$$

which yields the following recursive relation for the drifts in terms of the volatilities:

$$\sum_{i=n+1}^{N-1} \mu(t, i\Delta t) = \left(\frac{1}{\Delta t}\right)^2 \log\left\{E\left[\exp\left[-\sum_{i=n+1}^{N-1} \sigma(t, i\Delta t)X(t)\sqrt{\Delta t}\Delta t\right]\right]\right\}$$

$$(7.4.31)$$

At $N = n + 2$, this implies that

$$\mu[t, (n+1)\Delta t] = \left(\frac{1}{\Delta t}\right)^2 \log\left(E\left[\exp\left\{-\sigma[t, (n+1)\Delta t]X(t)\sqrt{\Delta t}\Delta t\right\}\right]\right)$$

$$(7.4.32)$$

Recall that $t = n\Delta t$, so for any $n = 1, 2, \ldots$ we have the values $\mu[n\Delta t, (n + 1)\Delta t]$ expressed in terms of the volatilities $\sigma[n\Delta t, (n + 1)\Delta t]$. Moving to $N = n + 3$ then determines all the $\mu[n\Delta t, (n + 2)\Delta t]$ in terms of the volatilities, and so on.

It is instructive to take the limit as $\Delta t \to 0$ of Equation 7.4.31. Multiplying this equation by Δt and taking this limit gives

$$\int_t^T ds\, \mu(t, s) = \frac{1}{\Delta t}\log\left\{E\left[\exp\left[-\int_t^T ds\, \sigma(t, s)X(t)\sqrt{\Delta t}\right]\right]\right\}$$

$$= \frac{1}{2}\left[\int_t^T ds\, \sigma(t, s)\right]^2 \tag{7.4.33}$$

Differentiating with respect to t, we arrive at an expression for the drift in terms of the volatility,

$$\mu(t, s) = \sigma(t, s)\int_t^T d\tau\, \sigma(t, \tau) \tag{7.4.34}$$

Now we implement the HJM model on a tree to price an interest-rate cap, which is simply a string of call options on forward interest rates. Recall from Chapter 6 that the price of an interest-rate cap for an annualized strike rate, c_{strike}, with \$100 notional is

$$\text{Price} \simeq \$100\Delta t \sum_{i=1}^N E\left[\exp\left[-\int_0^{t_i} d\tau\, y(\tau)\right]\right.$$

$$\left. \times \max\left[\frac{\int_{t_{i-1}}^{t_i} d\tau\, y(\tau)}{\Delta t} - c_{\text{strike}}, 0\right]\right] \tag{7.4.35}$$

where $\Delta t = t_i - t_{i-1}$ is the time between payments in units of 1 year.
   The forward rates are

$$f_{i-1,i} \equiv f[(i-1)\Delta t, i\Delta t] \simeq \frac{\int_{t_{i-1}}^{t_i} d\tau\, y(\tau)}{\Delta t} \tag{7.4.36}$$

where $\Delta t = t_i - t_{i-1}$. So in terms of the forward rates,

$$\text{Price} \simeq \$100\Delta t \sum_{i=1}^N E\left[\exp\left(-\sum_{j=1}^i f_{j-1,j}\Delta t\right)\max\left[f_{i-1,i} - c_{\text{strike}}, 0\right]\right]$$

$$\tag{7.4.37}$$

Consider the function p defined by

$$p(n) = \sum_{i=n+1}^{N} \exp\left(-\sum_{j=n+1}^{i} f_{j-1,j}\Delta t\right) \max\left[f_{i-1,i} - c_{\text{strike}}, 0\right]$$

(7.4.38)

It is clear that the value of the option at time $n\Delta t$ is given by $\Delta t\, E[p(n)]$ and, in particular, Price $= \$100\Delta t E[p(0)]$. The function p can be defined recursively:

$$p(n) = \exp\left(-f_{n,n+1}\Delta t\right) \max\left[f\left[n\Delta t, (n+1)\Delta t\right] - c_{\text{strike}}, 0\right]$$
$$+ \exp\left(-f_{n,n+1}\Delta t\right) p(n+1)$$

(7.4.39)

and it has the nice property that at each step n in the recursion, the function depends on only one short rate, $f_{n,n+1}$, in addition to the dependence on $p(n+1)$. The boundary condition for the recursive function is

$$p(N-1) = \exp\left(-f_{N-1,N}\Delta t\right) \max\left[f_{N-1,N} - c_{\text{strike}}, 0\right]$$ (7.4.40)

We can use the HJM model to find the short rates $f_{n,n+1}$, given a set of "initial" short rates $f_{0,i}$ and volatilities $\sigma(j\Delta t, i\Delta t)$. Here we will assume that the volatilities do not depend on the observation time, i.e., $\sigma(t_a, t_b) = \sigma(t_b)$. The function HJMPrice[] defined in Figure 7.14 prices an interest-rate cap assuming HJM evolution of short rates given a list of initial short rates $f_{0,i}$ and volatilities $\sigma(i\Delta t) \equiv \sigma_i$ for $i = 1, 2, \ldots, N$. (The function is described in more detail in the appendix to this chapter.) The Price function defined within HJMPrice[] is essentially the recursive function p described earlier. But in addition to taking the argument n, it also takes a list of short rates $f_{n,n+k}$ and volatilities σ_{n+k} with list index $k = 1, 2, \ldots, N - n$. The tree generated within HJMPrice is nonrecombining because the short-rate drift depends on time.

```
HJMPrice[f0_, sig0_, deltat_, xrate_] :=
 Module[{n, Price}, n = Length[f0];
  Price[timestep_, f_, sig_] :=
   Price[timestep, f, sig] =
    Module[{i, m, j, mu, fu, fd, sigma, result},
     If[timestep == n - 1,
      result = Exp[-f[[1]] deltat] Max[0, (f[[1]] - xrate)]];
     If[timestep < n - 1, m = Length[f] - 1;
      fu = Take[f, -m];
      (*initialize the array of forward rates from the end*)
      fd = Take[f, -m];
      sigma = Take[sig, -m];
      (*initialize the array of volatilities from the end*)
      mu = Table[0, {k, m}];
      For[j = 1, j <= m, j++,
       If[j == 1,
        mu[[j]] =
          Log[0.5*(Exp[-sigma[[j]]*deltat*Sqrt[deltat]] +
               Exp[sigma[[j]]*deltat*Sqrt[deltat]])]/deltat^2;];
       (*evolve drifts*)
       If[j > 1,
        mu[[j]] =
          Log[0.5*(Exp[-Sum[sigma[[k]],
               {k, j}]*deltat*Sqrt[deltat]] + Exp[Sum[sigma[[k]],
                {k, j}]*deltat*Sqrt[deltat]])]/
            deltat^2 - Sum[mu[[k]], {k, j - 1}];];];
      fu = fu + mu*deltat + sigma*Sqrt[deltat];
      (*determine up forward rate using stochastic process*)
      fd = fd + mu*deltat - sigma*Sqrt[deltat];
      (*determine down forward rate using stochastic process*)
      result =
       Exp[-f[[1]] deltat] Max[0, (f[[1]] - xrate)] +
        Exp[-f[[1]]*deltat]*0.5*(Price[timestep + 1, fu, sigma]+
           Price[timestep + 1, fd, sigma]);
      (*average prices from the two possible outcomes*)];
     Return[result];];
  Return[100 deltat Price[0, f0, sig0]];]
```

Figure 7.14 Mathematica function that prices an interest-rate cap with
$100 notional using HJM evolution given lists of initial short rates and
volatilities, f0 and sig0; the time step, deltat, in units of 1 year; and
the annualized strike rate, xrate.

Entering

```
HJMPrice[{0.033,0.036,0.037,0.038,0.038},
 {.02, .02, .02, .02, .02},1,0.038]
```

gives the cap price of $4.207. Here, the first argument is a list that
contains forward rates observed at time zero for 1, 2, 3, 4, and 5 years.
The second argument is a list of corresponding volatilities (all equal to
0.02 in this example). The third argument is the time step of one year,
and the last argument is the annualized strike rate of 0.038. Since we
entered forward rates for five years and a time step of one year, the cap
is on one-year forward rates and expires in five years.

The simple implementations we have discussed in this chapter
are hardly sufficient for full-scale practical computations. Most trad-
ing desks spend a lot of time thinking about issues such as calibration
to the market, the accuracy of the assumed processes, and details that
are specific to the option contracts. However, the methods that we have
described here are still the backbone of the numerical algorithms that
do all the hard work.

7.5   Appendix: Discussion of HJM Code

Here[6] we discuss, in detail, the HJMPrice function defined in Figure 7.14.

The Price function defined within HJMPrice[] is essentially
the recursive function p defined in Equation 7.4.39. But in addition
to taking the argument n, it also takes a list of short rates $f_{n,n+k}$ and
volatilities σ_{n+k} with list index $k = 1, 2, \ldots, N - n$. At each step n
in the recursion, the drifts, $\mu_{n,n+1+k'} \equiv \mu[n\Delta t, (n + 1 + k')\Delta t]$, and
possible short rates, $f^{\text{up}}_{n+1,n+1+k'}$ and $f^{\text{down}}_{n+1,n+1+k'}$, for $k' = 1, \ldots, N -$

---

[6]This section was written by Moira Gresham.

$n - 1$ are calculated. These new short rates become inputs to $p(n + 1)$ in the recursive definition.

More specifically, the recursive function `Price[n, f, σ]` executes the following process:

- If $n = N - 1$, then set `result` equal to $\exp(-f[[1]]\Delta t)$ $\max[f[[1]] - c_{\text{strike}}, 0]$. Here, $f[[1]]$ denotes the first element in the list f.[7] The recursive relation will be set up so that for $n = N - 1$, f is the one-dimensional list, $f = \{f_{n,n+1}\}$. This is the boundary condition for the recursive function.
- If $n < N - 1$, then execute the following subprocess:
  1. Set m equal to the length of the list, f, minus 1. The recursion will be set up so that the kth element of f will be $f_{n,n-1+k}$, where $k = 1, 2, \ldots, N - n + 1$. So $m = N - n$.
  2. Initialize the lists f^{up} and f^{down} by setting them equal to the last m elements of f, i.e., set the kth element of f^{up} and f^{down} to $f_{n,n+k}$.
  3. Initialize the list σ' as the last m elements of the input list σ. The recursion will be set up so that the input list σ will be σ_{n-1+k}. Therefore, $\sigma'[[k]] = \sigma_{n+k}$.
  4. Build the list of drifts, μ, by (a) setting its first element equal to (see Equation 7.4.32)

$$\mu[[1]] = \mu_{n,n+1} = \left(\frac{1}{\Delta t}\right)^2 \log \left\{\frac{1}{2}[\exp(-\sigma'[[1]]\Delta t\sqrt{\Delta t})\right.$$
$$\left. + \exp(\sigma'[[1]]\Delta t\sqrt{\Delta t})]\right\} \qquad (7.5.41)$$

and (b) successively calculating its other elements via (see Equation 7.4.31)

---

[7] Similarly, $f[[k]]$ denotes the kth element of the list f.

$$\mu[[k]]=\mu_{n,n+k}=\left(\frac{1}{\Delta t}\right)^{2}\log\left\{\frac{1}{2}\left[\exp\left(-\sum_{j=1}^{k}\sigma'[[j]]\Delta t\sqrt{\Delta t}\right)\right.\right.$$

$$\left.\left.+\exp\left(\sum_{j=1}^{k}\sigma'[[j]]\Delta t\sqrt{\Delta t}\right)\right]\right\}-\sum_{j=1}^{k-1}\mu[[j]]$$

$$(7.5.42)$$

5. Set the lists f^{up} and f^{down} equal to

$$f^{\text{up}} = f^{\text{up}} + \mu\Delta t + \sigma'\sqrt{\Delta t} \qquad (7.5.43)$$

and

$$f^{\text{down}} = f^{\text{down}} + \mu\Delta t - \sigma'\sqrt{\Delta t} \qquad (7.5.44)$$

Thus now, $f^{\text{up(down)}}[[k]] = f^{\text{up(down)}}_{n+1,n+k}$

6. Set `result` equal to

$$\exp\left(-f[[1]]\Delta t\right)\max\left[f[[1]] - c_{\text{strike}}\right]$$

$$+\exp\left(-f[[1]]\Delta t\right)\frac{1}{2}(\text{Price}[n+1, f^{\text{up}}, \sigma']$$

$$+\text{Price}[n+1, f^{\text{down}}, \sigma']) \qquad (7.5.45)$$

Here, $f[[1]] = f_{n,n+1}$. Note that the list of forward rates input into `Price` at one time step higher, $n+1$, is indeed a list of rates at an observation time of one time step higher. Furthermore, the prices from the two possible outcomes of the stochastic process that determines the forward rates are averaged at each time step. As in the trees discussed in previous sections, this is how the expectation value is effectively taken. But unlike the previous trees, since f^{up} and f^{down} are evolved forward in time with different drifts, $\mu(n)$, at each time step, this tree is nonrecombining: the price at a node at time step $n - 2$ after evolving back from a node at time step n with $f^{\text{up}}(n)$ and then $f^{\text{down}}(n - 1)$ is not the same as the price after evolving back from a node at time step n with $f^{\text{down}}(n)$ and then $f^{\text{up}}(n - 1)$.

- Return result.

The function HJMPrice$[f_0, \sigma_0, \Delta t, c_{\text{strike}}]$ returns $100 \ \Delta t$ Price$[0, f_0, \sigma_0]$. The lists f_0 and σ_0 should be

$$f_0[[k]] = f_{0,k} \qquad \text{and} \qquad \sigma[[k]] = \sigma_k \qquad (7.5.46)$$

where $k = 1, 2, \ldots, N$.

Index

Page citations followed by *f* indicate a figure, and those followed by *t* indicate a table.